PRE-COURSE ASSESSMENT

This self-assessment will help you and your instructor see how you perceive your college success skills as you begin this course. Be honest and take your time. There are no wrong answers, and this is not a test! For each question, rate yourself according to the following scale:

1	**2**	**3**	**4**	**5**
Definitely Like Me	Somewhat Like Me	Not Sure	Somewhat Unlike Me	Not At All Like Me

Please circle the number which best represents your answer:

1. I believe this course will help me build skills for college success.   1   2   3   4   5

2. I know how to find the people and resources that can help me make the transition to college.   1   2   3   4   5

3. I understand how habits can affect my ability to succeed.   1   2   3   4   5

4. I am aware of my learning styles and preferences.   1   2   3   4   5

5. I make choices in school and out based on how I learn.   1   2   3   4   5

6. I am effective at planning and managing my schedule.   1   2   3   4   5

7. I manage my finances actively and budget well.   1   2   3   4   5

8. I know exactly what goals I want to achieve in college.   1   2   3   4   5

9. I am effective at managing stress.   1   2   3   4   5

10. I take steps to keep my mind and body as healthy as possible.   1   2   3   4   5

11. I am comfortable with students who are different than me.   1   2   3   4   5

12. I work well in groups and teams.   1   2   3   4   5

13. I ask questions and think critically about what I hear and read.   1   2   3   4   5

14. I solve problems effectively.   1   2   3   4   5

15. I have strong memory and recall abilities.   1   2   3   4   5

16. I feel prepared to handle the reading in my college courses.   1   2   3   4   5

17. I use particular techniques to read textbooks in different academic areas.   1   2   3   4   5

18. I take comprehensive and clear notes.   1   2   3   4   5

19. I have excellent test-taking skills for college courses.   1   2   3   4   5

20. I manage text anxiety well.   1   2   3   4   5

21. I know how to work with a group on a presentation.   1   2   3   4   5

22. I am confident that I will succeed in college.   1   2   3   4   5

POST-COURSE ASSESSMENT

This self-assessment will help you and your instructor see how you developed skills during this course. Please be honest, take your time, and answer each question in terms of your experience in this course. For each question, rate yourself according to the following scale:

1 Definitely Like Me	**2** Somewhat Like Me	**3** Not Sure	**4** Somewhat Unlike Me	**5** Not At All Like Me

Please circle the number which best represents your answer:

1. This course helped me build skills for college success.	1	2	3	4	5
2. I know how to find the people and resources that can help me complete a successful transition to college.	1	2	3	4	5
3. I understand how habits can affect my ability to succeed.	1	2	3	4	5
4. I am aware of my learning styles and preferences.	1	2	3	4	5
5. I make choices in school and out based on how I learn.	1	2	3	4	5
6. I am effective at planning and managing my schedule.	1	2	3	4	5
7. I manage my finances actively and budget well.	1	2	3	4	5
8. I know exactly what goals I want to achieve in college.	1	2	3	4	5
9. I am effective at managing stress.	1	2	3	4	5
10. I take steps to keep my mind and body as healthy as possible.	1	2	3	4	5
11. I am comfortable with students who are different than me.	1	2	3	4	5
12. I work well in groups and teams.	1	2	3	4	5
13. I ask questions and think critically about what I hear and read.	1	2	3	4	5
14. I solve problems effectively.	1	2	3	4	5
15. I have strong memory and recall abilities.	1	2	3	4	5
16. I feel prepared to handle the reading in my college courses.	1	2	3	4	5
17. I use particular techniques to read textbooks in different academic areas.	1	2	3	4	5
18. I take comprehensive and clear notes.	1	2	3	4	5
19. I have excellent test-taking skills for college courses.	1	2	3	4	5
20. I manage text anxiety well.	1	2	3	4	5
21. I know how to work with a group on a presentation.	1	2	3	4	5
22. I am confident that I will succeed in college.	1	2	3	4	5

Study for Quiz	Study for Quiz	Study for Quiz	Study for Quiz	Study for Quiz	Study for Quiz	Study for Quiz
Study for Quiz	Study for Quiz	Study for Quiz	Study for Quiz	Study for Quiz	Study for Quiz	Study for Quiz
Review This	Review This	Review This	Review This	Review This	Review This	Review This
Review This	Review This	Review This	Review This	Review This	Review This	Review This
ASK for HELP	ASK for HELP	ASK for HELP	ASK for HELP	ASK for HELP	ASK for HELP	ASK for HELP
ASK for HELP	ASK for HELP	ASK for HELP	ASK for HELP	ASK for HELP	ASK for HELP	ASK for HELP
Important	Important	Important	Important	Important	Important	Important
Important	Important	Important	Important	Important	Important	Important
Study for Quiz	Study for Quiz	ASK for HELP	ASK for HELP	Review This	Review This	Important

Bridges to Excellence

A PEARSON LEARNING SOLUTIONS PUBLICATION FOR U100:
THRESHOLD LEARNING COMMUNITY FOR INDIANA UNIVERSITY SOUTH BEND

Excerpts taken from:

Cornerstone: Creating Success Through Positive Change, Sixth Edition
by Robert M. Sherfield and Patricia G. Moody

Keys to Effective Learning: Study Skills and Habits for Success, Sixth Edition
by Carol Carter, Joyce Bishop, and Sarah Lyman Kravits

Learning Solutions

New York   Boston   San Francisco
London   Toronto   Sydney   Tokyo   Singapore   Madrid
Mexico City   Munich   Paris   Cape Town   Hong Kong   Montreal

Pearson Learning Solutions, 501 Boylston Street, Suite 900, Boston, MA 02116
A Pearson Education Company
www.pearsoned.com

Printed in the United States of America

1 2 3 4 5 6 7 8 9 10 XXXX 15 14 13 12 11 10

0002000010270582916

NM/AM

ISBN 10: 0-558-81836-6
ISBN 13: 978-0-558-81836-4

BRIEF CONTENTS

ABOUT YOUR AUTHORS

Robert M. Sherfield, Ph.D.

Robert Sherfield has been teaching public speaking, theatre, and student success and working with first-year orientation programs for over 25 years. Currently, he is a professor at the College of Southern Nevada, teaching student success, professional communication, public speaking, and drama.

An award-winning educator, Robb was named **Educator of the Year** at the College of Southern Nevada. He twice received the **Distinguished Teacher of the Year Award** from the University of South Carolina Union, and has received numerous other awards and nominations for outstanding classroom instruction and advisement.

Robb's extensive work with student success programs includes experience with the design and implementation of these programs—including one program that was presented at the International Conference on the First-Year Experience in Newcastle upon Tyne, England. He has conducted faculty development keynotes and workshops at over 350 institutions of higher education across the United States. He has spoken in 46 states and several foreign countries.

In addition to his co-authorship of *Cornerstone, Opening Doors to Career Success* (Prentice Hall, 2009), he has authored or co-authored *Solving the Professional Development Puzzle: 101 Solutions for Career and Life Planning* (Prentice Hall, 2009), *Cornerstone: Discovering Your Potential, Learning Actively, and Living Well* (Prentice Hall, 2008), *Roadways to Success* (Prentice Hall, 2001), the trade book *365 Things I Learned in College* (Allyn & Bacon, 1996), *Capstone: Succeeding Beyond College* (Prentice Hall, 2001), *Case Studies for the First Year: An Odyssey into Critical Thinking and Problem Solving* (Prentice Hall, 2004), *The Everything® Self-Esteem Book* (Adams Media, 2004), and *Cornerstone: Building On Your Best for Career Success* (Prentice Hall, 2006)

Robb's interest in student success began with his own first year in college. Low SAT scores and a dismal high school ranking denied him entrance into college. With the help of a success program, Robb was granted entrance into college, and went on to earn five college degrees, including a doctorate. He has always been interested in the social, academic, and cultural development of students and sees this book as his way to help students enter the world of work and establishing lasting, rewarding careers. Visit www.robertsherfield.com.

Patricia G. Moody, Ph.D.

Patricia G. Moody is Dean Emerita of the College of Hospitality, Retail and Sport Management at the University of South Carolina, where she served on the faculty and in administration for over 30 years. An award-winning educator, Pat was honored as **Distinguished Educator of the Year** at her college and as **Collegiate Teacher of the Year** by the National Business Education Association. She was also a top-five finalist for the **Amoco Teaching Award** at the University of South Carolina. She received the prestigious **John Robert Gregg Award**, the highest honor in her field of over 100,000 educators.

Pat has co-authored many texts and simulations including: *Solving the Professional Development Puzzle: 101 Solutions for Career and Life Planning, Cornerstone: Discovering Your Potential, Learning Actively, and Living Well, 365 Things I Learned in College, Capstone: Succeeding Beyond College, Case Studies for the First Year: An Odyssey into Critical Thinking and Problem Solving*, and *Cornerstone: Opening Doors to Career Success*.

A nationally known motivational speaker, consultant, and author, Pat has spoken in most states, has been invited to speak in several foreign countries, and frequently keynotes national and regional conventions. She has presented her signature, motivational keynote address, *"Fly Like an Eagle"* to tens of thousands of people, from Olympic athletes to corporate executives to high school students.

As the Dean of her college, Dr. Moody led international trips to build relationships and establish joint research projects in hospitality. Under her direction, faculty members in her college began a landmark study of Chinese Tourists. Pat now travels the country delivering workshops, keynotes, and presentations on topics such as Managing Change, Working in the New Global Community, The Future of the Future, Student Motivation, and Emotional Intelligence. She also serves as a personal coach for business executives.

Carol Carter

was a C student in high school. During her senior year, she got a wake up call when her brother told her that she had intelligence, but she wouldn't go far in life unless she believed in herself enough to work hard. She began college knowing she was "behind the 8-ball." What she lacked in experience, she made up for with elbow grease and persistence. She maximized her strength as an interpersonal and intrapersonal learning. The work paid off. She graduated college with honors and a desire to help other students.

Carol is committed to helping students turn on their brains, get motivated, and discover their abilities. As President of LifeBound, she teaches study, interpersonal, and career skills to middle and high school students in order to help them become competitive in today's global world. She trains and certifies coaches in academic coaching skills, and focuses on at-risk students with her volunteer teaching at the federal prison and her LifeBound work in the Denver housing projects. "All students are at-risk for something whether it is academic, emotional, social, or economic," says Carol. "If we are allowed to accept our flaws, we can overcome our limitations and be the best for ourselves and others."

Carol also speaks on educational topics nationally and internationally, and is pictured here with some students at the Aziza Schoolhouse in Phnom Penh, Cambodia. Her first book, *Majoring in the Rest of Your Life,* launched her writing career and opened the door to her work on the *Keys to Success* series.

Joyce Bishop

has taught college students for more than twenty-two years. After struggling with a learning disability as a student, she focused on her visual and logical-mathematical learning abilities and went on to earn a PhD in psychology. Right now, she is in her dream job as Staff Development Coordinator at Golden West College while still teaching three classes. She enjoys training other faculty in effective teaching and learning strategies and also in how to teach online. For five years Joyce was voted "favorite teacher," she was Teacher of the Year of 1995 and 2000, and in 2008 received the Hayward Award, a State Teaching Award.

Joyce co-founded a program 19 years ago for poor young women from abusive backgrounds. Since that time, the Pathways to Independence non-profit foundation has sent 255 young women to colleges and 195 have graduated into gainful employment. While the young women have come from backgrounds as diverse as prison, extreme poverty, abuse, or psychological disorders, Joyce has been their champion. This photo is of Joyce with one of the Pathways graduates, Valerie, who obtained her degree in nursing and is now working at a major university hospital as a pediatric nurse. "It is so inspiring to see what these young women do with their lives," says Joyce, "once they know that they can do anything."

Sarah Kravits

lives the strategies for success she writes about. As an author and mother of three children aged 10, 8, and 4, she faces the challenges of time management, goal achievement, and fulfilling responsibilities (not to mention eating right and getting enough sleep). In her writing and research, she works to keep up with technology and the growth of knowledge. In her relationships with work colleagues all over the country, she strives for integrity, effective communication, productive teamwork, and, most of all, flexibility. Creativity also plays a dominant role. Along with her husband, an actor and musician, she promotes creative ideas and actions in the home as well as during her writing hours at the computer.

Unlike Carol and Joyce, Sarah thrived in school from and early age based on her strength in verbal-linguistic and logical-mathematical learning. A few years after graduating from the University of Virginia as a Jefferson Scholar, she worked as program director for LifeSkills, Inc., a nonprofit organization that aims to further the career and personal development of high school students. This work led her into co-authoring her first student success text and the realization she was driven to empower students to reach their goals. "Lifelong learning is the essential success skill," says Sarah. "Learning gives you a chance to go beyond just thinking about your dreams so that you can make them happen."

BEGIN

THE GOAL OF CORNERSTONE AND OUR COMMITMENT TO YOU

Talent alone won't make you a success. Neither will being in the right place at the right time, unless you are ready. The most important question is: 'Are you ready?'

—Johnny Carson

If you look at the figure printed here you will see the Chinese symbol (verb) for "*to change*." It is made up of two symbols—the first means *to transform* or to be flexible. The second means *to do* or *to deliver*. In its purest form, the symbol means to *deliver transformation*. That is what *Cornerstone* is all about, helping you deliver or bring about transformation, positive change if you will, to your life. It is about helping you discover ways to change your thoughts, change your performance, and change your life.

Our goal in writing *Cornerstone* is to help you discover your academic, social, and personal strengths so that you can build on them and to provide **concrete and useful tools** that will help you make the changes that might be necessary for your success. We believe that in helping you identify and transform areas that have challenged you in the past, you can *discover your true potential, learn more actively, and have the career you want and deserve*.

Cornerstone: Creating Success through Positive Change is devoted to three specific areas where positive change can help you become the individual you would like to be. The book is divided into three parts:

Changing Your Thoughts
Changing Your Performance
Changing Your Life

PART ONE, Changing Your Thoughts, addresses a broad spectrum of topics that begins with a focus on change as it relates to becoming a college student in a different culture and setting than you may have known before. In this section, you will be introduced to tools of self-management as they relate to college life. You will be exposed to a variety of new terms, ideas, and thoughts—all of which begin your journey of change. You will learn to enhance your communication skills, improve your self-concept, and manage conflict, all valuable tools on the road to change. You will become more adept at critical thinking and problem solving as you study this section. When you have completed this section, you should notice a difference in the way you approach tasks and think about subjects, challenges, and people.

PART TWO, Changing Your Performance, focuses on you and how you physically and mentally manage yourself. You will begin this part of the journey to change by learning to manage your time and control the inherent stress that accompanies being a college student. You will realize that you have a dominant intelligence, learning style, and personality type and how to use them to your advantage. Even though you have been reading for some time, you will be shown strategies to improve both your speed and comprehension since reading is a major part of college studies. You will be shown several note-taking systems designed to improve your ability to record what your professors are teaching. Finally, you will be taught strategies for empowering your memory, learning to study more effectively, and taking tests with confidence. When you complete this section, you should be able to perform most tasks more effectively and confidently.

PART THREE, Changing Your Life, is a culmination of the journey you have embarked on as a first-year student. This section is designed to round out your total personal profile and springboard you to success as you move into a different realm. Many college students do well on the topics covered in the first two sections and fall short when they arrive to this point. To be the complete successful college student, you need to address all these areas because they are significant to the changes you need to embrace. You will learn to manage your money and your debts wisely. So many college students are burdened with astronomical college debts when they graduate; our desire is for you to have accumulated as little debt as possible at the same time you are taking advantage of all that college has to offer. You will study the important emerging topic of information literacy and improve your writing and speaking skills. On this important journey to change, you will be shown how to immerse yourself in many categories of diversity while you learn to celebrate all kinds of people. You will be taught to be responsible for your own wellness and how to exercise personal responsibility. Finally, you will be introduced to techniques for planning your professional career in the face of dramatic global changes. When you finish this section, you should be prepared to move through the next few years of college and beyond with confidence and optimism.

We know that your **time is valuable** and that you are pulled in countless directions with work, family, school, previous obligations, and many other tasks. For this reason, we have tried to provide only the most concrete, useful strategies and ideas to help you succeed in this class and beyond.

We have spent over 55 years collectively gathering the information, advice, suggestions, and activities on the following pages. This advice and these activities have come from trial and error, colleagues, former students, instructors across the United States, and solid research. We hope that you will enjoy them, learn from them, and most of all, use them to change your life and move closer to your dreams.

Let the journey to positive change begin!

Robb *Pat*

Robb and Pat

SQ3R

What Is It and Why Do I Need to Know It?

You may be asking, "*What does SQ3R mean and what could it possibly have to do with me, my text, this course, and my success?*" The answer: *SQ3R* (**S = Scan, Q = Question, 3 R = Read, Recite, Review**) is one of the most successful and widely used learning and study tools ever introduced.

This simple, yet highly effective mnemonic (memory trick) asks that *before you actually read the chapter*, you look over the contents, check out the figures and photos, look at section headings, and review any graphs or charts. This is called **scanning**. Step two, **question**, asks that you jot down questions that you think you will need to answer about the chapter's content in order to master the material. These questions might come from charts or figures, but most commonly, they come from the chapter's section headings. Examine the example below of a section heading from: *Criminal Justice, A Brief Introduction*, 6th Edition by Frank Schmalleger (Prentice Hall, 2006).

(1) *What are the categories of crime?*
(2) *Why do they matter?*
(3) *What is crime typology?* or
(4) *When are categories of crime most often used?*

reported data.[64] Crimes that result from an anomalous event, but which are excluded from reported data, highlight the arbitrary nature of the data-collection process itself.

Special Categories of Crime

crime typology

A classification of crimes along a particular dimension, such as legal categories, offender motivation, victim behavior, or the characteristics of individual offenders.

A **crime typology** is a classification scheme that is useful in the study and description of criminal behavior. All crime typologies have an underlying logic, and the system of classification that derives from any particular typology may be based on legal criteria, offender motivation, victim behavior, the characteristics of individual offenders, or the like. Criminologists Terance D. Miethe and Richard C. McCorkle note that crime typologies "are designed primarily to simplify social reality by identifying homogeneous groups of crime behaviors that are different from other clusters of crime behaviors."[65] Hence one common but simple typology contains only two categories of crime: violent and property. In fact, many crime typologies contain overlapping or nonexclusive categories—just as violent crimes may involve property offenses, and property offenses may lead to violent crimes. Thus no one typology is likely to capture all of the nuances of criminal offending.

After writing these questions from the section heading, you will read this section and then answer those questions. This technique gives you more focus and purpose for your reading. Each chapter in *Cornerstone* begins with this technique through a feature called **Scan & Question**.

We included this feature in *Cornerstone* to help you become a more active reader with greater comprehension skills in all of your other classes.

BLOOM'S TAXONOMY

What Are All of Those Little Triangles Throughout My Book?

Another feature that you will notice in your text is small triangles throughout followed by questions pertaining to the content. These triangles help you recognize which of the six levels of learning is being used from Bloom's Taxonomy. A quick reference chart of Bloom's Taxonomy (Revised) is on the inside front cover of this text and on page xi.

Bloom's Taxonomy (also called Levels of Thinking and Learning) is simply a way of explaining the stages at which we all acquire information. These levels, explained in detail on the next page, progress from simple learning and thinking (levels 1, 2, 3) to more complex learning and thinking (levels 4, 5, 6). In addition to having questions from Bloom's Taxonomy throughout your text, each chapter will end with an exercise called *Knowledge in Bloom*. This chapter-end activity is included to help you process and apply the information from the chapter.

So, Why Use Bloom in the *Cornerstone* Text?

Bloom's Taxonomy is important to us all because it helps us determine the level at which we understand important information. For example, it is important to be able to answer questions at Level 1 such as:

> ▶ *Abraham Lincoln was the _____ President of the United States.*

or

> ▶ *Abraham Lincoln's wife's name was _____ Lincoln.*

However, it is also important to be able to answer questions at levels 5 and 6 such as:

> ▶ *Based on your knowledge of the Civil War era, predict what would have happened to the United States without the Emancipation Proclamation. Justify your answer.*

or

> ▶ *Summarize the main events that led to President Lincoln's assassination.*

As you can clearly see, there is a great difference between these levels of learning. The higher the level, the more information and knowledge you need to be able to understand and respond to the question or problem.

The chapter-end activity, **Knowledge in Bloom,** will help you process and demonstrate your knowledge at different levels. This is important because you will have professors who **teach and test** at levels 1, 2, and 3 and those who **teach and test** at levels 4, 5, and 6. Learning to process and demonstrate your knowledge at every level can assist you in:

- doing well in other classes by providing a foundation for effective studying/learning,
- learning to solve problems more thoroughly,
- predicting exam questions,
- learning how to critically evaluate and assess ideas and issues,
- learning to thoroughly and objectively research topics for papers and presentations, and
- testing your own reading comprehension.

Examine the following chart for Bloom's Taxonomy (Levels of Thinking and Learning).

BLOOM'S TAXONOMY (Revised)
Examining the Levels of Thinking and Learning

LEVELS OF *THINKING AND LEARNING.*	WHAT **SKILLS** YOU SHOULD HAVE AT THIS LEVEL.	**EXAMPLES** OF *QUESTIONS* OR *ACTIVITIES* YOU MIGHT ANTICIPATE OR *PRODUCTS* YOU MAY HAVE TO GENERATE
1—REMEMBERING This level is based on simple recall of information. This type of knowledge usually comes from being told or from basic reading. It is the "lowest" or most simple type of learning.	write, list, label, name, state, define, describe, identify, recognize, recall, draw, select, locate, recite, quote, order, state, reproduce, match, tell, and the five standards, who, what, when, where, and how	What is . . . , When did . . . , Why did . . . , Who were . . . , Describe the . . . , Which of the following . . . , Define the . . . , Name the . . . , Identify who . . . , Describe what happened after . . . **SAMPLE:** What are the six levels of learning in Bloom's Taxonomy?
2—UNDERSTANDING This level determines your grasp or comprehension level of the information presented. It asks, "Do you understand the meaning?" and "Can you explain the ideas or concepts?"	summarize, describe, interpret, contrast, predict, associate, distinguish, estimate, differentiate, discuss, extend, convert, explain, generalize, give examples, rewrite, restate, classify, translate, paraphrase, illustrate, visualize, retell	How would you contrast . . . , Explain why the . . . , Summarize the main . . . , What facts show . . . , Predict the outcome of . . . , Restate the story in your own words . . . , prepare a flow chart to illustrate . . . **SAMPLE:** Explain why Bloom's Taxonomy is being used in *Cornerstone* and describe its importance.
3—APPLYING This level asks you to "use" the information you have by solving, showing, or applying that information in "real-world" or workplace situations. Can you use the information in a new way?	apply, demonstrate, discover, modify, operate, predict, solve, draw, dramatize, model, sketch, paint, produce, prepare, make, calculate, record, compute, manipulate, modify, use, employ	How could you use . . . , How could you solve . . . , What approach would you take . . . , Write an essay to explain why . . . , Prepare a timeline of . . . , Predict what would happen if . . . **SAMPLE:** Prepare a plan to show how you could use Bloom's Taxonomy to get a better grade in your history class?
4—ANALYZING This level asks you to "take apart" the information for clarification, classification, and prioritizing. It also asks you to recognize what is "not" said, i.e., . . . hidden meanings and unstated assumptions. This level requires that you distinguish between facts and inferences.	break down, distinguish, infer, arrange, prioritize, order, divide, categorize, appraise, test, examine, separate, deduce, choose, compare/contrast, detect, group, sequence, scrutinize, connect, outlines, research, point out	How is ___ related to ___?, What conclusions can be drawn . . . , What is the relationship between . . . , Categorize the main . . . , Based on X, why is Y . . . , What were the motives behind . . . , What was the turning point in . . . , Write a survey to find out if . . . **SAMPLE:** What assumptions can be made about the rest of the term if your history teacher's first two exams included 20 questions, all from level six?
5—EVALUATING This level of thinking and learning asks you to make personal judgments about the value of issues, ideas, policies, and evidence based on your complete understanding of the information AND based on stated judging criteria. Basically, it asks that you justify a decision, idea, or belief that you have formulated.	decide, rank, test, measure, recommend, defend, conclude, appraise, assess, judge, predict, rate, select, critique, justify, estimate, validate, measure, discriminate, probe, award, rank, reject, grade, convince, weigh, support	Defend your position about . . . , How would you have handled "X"? Why? Debate the issue of . . . , Prepare a paper or speech to present your ideas of . . . , What is your opinion of . . . , How would you rate . . . , What judgment could you make . . . , Justify your opinion of . . . , Based on your research, convince the reader of your paper or speech that . . . , What criteria would you use to assess the . . . **SAMPLE:** Assess how effective Bloom's Taxonomy was when used to study for your history exam. Recommend two ways to improve the use of Bloom's for the next test.
6—CREATING This level asks you to integrate your previous knowledge with your new knowledge and come up with new ideas, plans, and solutions. It also asks you to be able to predict outcomes based on what you have learned. This level asks you to be innovative and creative.	compose, combine, compile, create, design, generate, construct, revise, write, rewrite, tell, role play, formulate, invent, develop, modify, arrange, rearrange, prepare, assemble, set-up, forecast, imagine, act, improvise, propose, substitute, integrate, incorporate	Design a plan to . . . , Write a speech or paper that . . . , Create a marketing plan that . . . , Devise a way to . . . , Compose a mnemonic that . . . , Generate a list of questions that . . . , Propose a solution to . . . , Revise the story of . . . **SAMPLE:** Write two possible test questions from each level of Bloom's Taxonomy from Chapter 1 of *Cornerstone*.

STICKERS FOR SUCCESS

What Are Those Colorful Stickers in the Back of My Book?

In the back of this text, you will find a sheet of peel off stickers to help you "tag" pages and content that (1) you need to study for a quiz, (2) review for mastery, (3) seek help with, or (4) mark as important. We have also included a row of blank stickers for your personal use (5). We encourage you to use them to help you locate information easily. The tabs include:

Study for Quiz   Use to tag information that your instructor tells you will be on the test.

Review This   Use to identify key terms, definitions, or difficult material that you need to revisit.

ASK for HELP   Use to remind you to ask questions about the content you may not understand.

Important   Use to tag important information.

Create your own tab to mark important quotes, charts, or other material you would like to reference quickly.

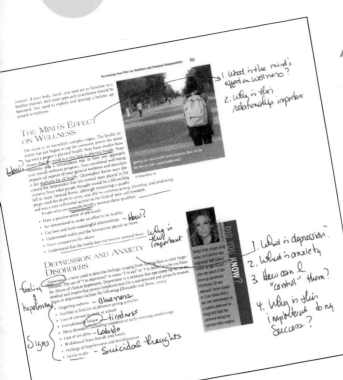

A WORD ABOUT *READING* AND *USING CORNERSTONE*

We encourage you to read this text (and every text) with great care so that you can learn from the ideas presented within its pages. We also encourage you to USE this book –

- write in the margins,
- circle important terms,
- highlight key phrases,
- jot down word definitions in the margins,
- dog-ear the pages, and
- write questions that you have in the white spaces provided.

By treating this book like your "foundation to success," you will begin to see remarkable progress in your study practices, reading comprehension, and learning skills. Review the example from another *Cornerstone* text.

UNIT 1

LEARN ABOUT YOURSELF AS A COLLEGE STUDENT

CHAPTER 1
CHANGES

ADJUSTING TO
THE CULTURE
OF COLLEGE,
NURTURING
CHANGE,
AND SETTING
YOUR GOALS

"The greatest reward of an education is to be able to face the world with an open mind, a caring heart, and a willing soul."

—R. M. Sherfield

WHY READ THIS CHAPTER?

What's in it for me?

WHY read this stuff on positive change? WHY will a chapter on change and goal setting help me in college, at work, with my friends, and beyond? WHY spend my time reading something that I'm not sure will help me at all? WHY is it important to understand the "Culture of College"?

Why? Because this chapter, indeed this whole book and course in which you are enrolled, is about helping you become the best college student, thinker, citizen, leader, and lifelong learner that you can possibly be. The information in this chapter is included to help you understand some of the basic truths about college life and academic survival. Quite simply, this chapter was written to help you learn how to adjust to college life, discover your potential, build on your strengths, and bring about positive change in your life through self-analysis, reflection, and goal setting. By reading this chapter and working through the activities, you will begin to see how important change is to your life, your growth, and your future, and more importantly, how to bring about that positive change.

By carefully reading this chapter and taking the information provided seriously, you will be able to:

1. Understand the relationship between your education and the new world economy.
2. Identify and apply the Ten Essential Cornerstones for Success in a Changing World.
3. Understand the basic truths about how college can help you beyond the classroom.
4. Understand the differences among high school, college, and career.
5. Understand why change is important and how to bring about change through goal setting.

CHAPTER 1 / CHANGE

"When it comes to the future, there are three kinds of people: those who let it happen, those who make it happen, and those who wonder what happened."

—John Richardson, Jr.

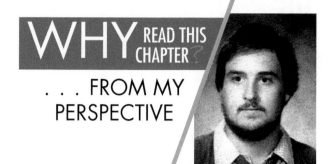

WHY READ THIS CHAPTER?

. . . FROM MY PERSPECTIVE

NAME: Mark
INSTITUTION: Spartanburg Methodist College, Spartanburg, SC
MAJOR: Associate of Arts—Theatre and Speech
AGE: 18

Change has been a major part of my life, and learning how to transform myself was a very important tool that helped me succeed in my first year of college. A major change in my life was learning how to overcome years of self-defeating behaviors, a horrible academic background, a negative attitude, and terrible study skills. I quickly learned that my success depended on my becoming an open-minded person who knew how to set goals, work to achieve those goals, develop self-motivation skills, and study effectively. These were not easy steps for me after 12 years of failure and disappointment.

I am the son of textile workers. Both of my parents worked in a cotton mill for over 30 years. My hometown is in the rural south about 35 miles from the nearest metropolitan area. I attended a small high school and was never a good student. Because of my poor performance through the years, working full time, and family commitments, I decided to attend a community college and then transfer to a four-year college.

I barely finished high school with a D– average and my SAT scores and class rank were so bad that I was denied entrance to a community college. The college granted me provisional acceptance with the stipulation that I enroll in, and successfully complete, a summer preparatory program. I graduated high school on a Friday night and began my college studies the very next Monday morning enrolled in the prep program. I never realized what lay ahead. I never realized how my life was about to change forever. I never realized at that point how much I would have to change.

My first class that semester was English. Professor Brannon walked in, handed out the syllabus, called the roll, and began to lecture. Lord Byron was the topic for the day. The class ended and after an hour's break, I headed across campus for history. Professor Wilkerson entered with a dust storm behind her. She went over the syllabus, and before we had a chance to blink, she was involved in the first lecture. "The cradle of civilization," she began, "was Mesopotamia."

We all scurried to find notebooks and pens to begin taking notes. I could not believe I was already behind on the first day. "Who teaches on the first day?" I thought.

One minute before class ended, she closed her book, looked directly at us, and said, "You are in history now. You elected to take this class and you will follow my rules. You are not to be late, you are to come to this class prepared, and you are to do your homework assignments. If you do what I ask you to do, read what I've assigned to you, and do your homework activities, you will learn more about Western civilization than you ever thought possible. If you don't keep up with me, you won't know if you are in Egypt, Mesopotamia, or pure Hell! Now get out!"

On the 30-mile trip home, my mind was filled with new thoughts . . . *Lord Byron, Mesopotamia, professors who talked too fast, tuition, parking, and the size of the library*. I knew that something was different, *something had changed in me*. I couldn't put my finger on it. It would be years before I realized that the change had not been my classes, not my schedule, not the people, not the professors—but me; *I had changed*. In one day, I had tasted something intoxicating, something that was addictive. *I had tasted a new world*.

I had to go to work that afternoon at the mill, and even my job and my coworkers had changed. I had always known that I did not want to spend the rest of my life in the factory, but this day the feeling was stronger. My job was not enough, my family was not enough, the farm on which I had been raised was not enough anymore. *There was a new light in me, and I knew that because of that one day in college, I would never be the same.* It was like tasting Godiva chocolate for the first time—Hershey's kisses were no longer enough. It was like seeing the ocean for the first time and knowing that the millpond would never be the same. *I couldn't go back. What I'd known before was simply no longer enough.*

My name is Robert **Mark** Sherfield, and 34 years later, as I coauthor your *Cornerstone* text, I am still addicted to that new world. College changed my life, and I am still changing—with every day I live, every new book I read, every new class I teach, every new person I meet, and every new place to which I travel, I am changing. I wish the same for you.

SCAN & QUESTION

In the preface of this book (page ix), you read about the **SQ3R Study Method**. Right now, take a few moments, **scan this chapter**, and on page 27, write **five of your own questions** that you think will be important to your mastery of this material. In addition to the two questions below, you will find five questions from your authors. Use one of your **"On The Test"** stickers to flag this page for easy reference.

EXAMPLES:

▶ **What are the six basic truths about the culture of college?** (from page 11)

▶ **Why must goals be measurable?** (from page 21)

THE TIMES . . . THEY ARE A-CHANGIN'

What Is the Relationship Between Your Education and the New World Economy?

Composer, singer, and activist Bob Dylan once wrote, *"The times, they are a-changin'."* Truer words have never been spoken—especially for anyone living at this moment. This is not your daddy's economy. It is not your mama's workplace, and it certainly is not your grandfather's job market. To glide over this simple truth *could be the most costly decision of your life.*

"New world economy," you might say, *"who cares about a world economy?"*

"China? Who cares about the fluctuating but growing economy in China, Russia, Dubai, or India? I live in Kansas and I'm worried about America's future."

"An iPhone? A Blackberry? A podcast? Twittering? I can't even afford my bus ticket this month," you may be thinking.

While you may not be alone in thinking, *"This does not matter to me,"* you would be very wrong and exceptionally foolish to think that today's world affairs do not concern **you**, your **education**, and your **future**. Yes, it may be true that you are simply trying to get a degree in medical assisting to work in a small doctor's office in Spokane, Washington—or to obtain a degree in criminal justice to work at the local police department in Union, South Carolina—or to earn a degree in education so that you can teach first grade in Stockton, California. However, no certificate, no degree, no job, and certainly no person will be exempt from the changes and challenges of "the new world economy."

"So, where does this leave ME?" you might be asking. It leaves you in an exciting, vulnerable, challenging, scary, and wonderful place. We did NOT include this information to scare you or to turn you off, but rather to give you a jolt, to open your eyes to the world in which you live and the workforce for which you are preparing. We included it to encourage you to use *every tool* available, *every resource* possible, *every connection* imaginable, and *every ethical, moral, and legal means* possible to prepare yourself for this ever-changing world in which you live today. The present and the future may not be as rosy as you had hoped, but the future is here, and it is yours. However, you must know this: If you make strategic changes in your life now, you can have a much brighter future. No workplace will be immune from the changes facing our world today, and your very survival depends on your being prepared and knowing how to quickly adapt to and change in a variety of situations.

In his book *The 2010 Meltdown* (2005), Edward Gordon writes, *"Simply stated, today in America, there are just too many people trained for the wrong jobs. Many jobs have become unnecessary, technically obsolete . . . or worse yet, the job/career aspirations of too many current and future workers are at serious odds with the changing needs of the U.S. labor market"* (p. 17).

However, all is not lost to you or your future. People who are well-skilled, possess superb oral and written communication skills, know how to solve problems, have the capacity to change, and can work well with others will *be in high demand* for many years to come.

What Employers Are Saying

According to the report *College Learning for the New Global Century* (2008), "Employers want college graduates to acquire versatile knowledge and skills. Fully sixty-three percent of employers believe that too many recent college graduates do not have the skills they need to succeed in the global economy and a majority of employers believe that only half or fewer recent graduates have the skills or knowledge needed to advance or to be promoted in their companies." Skills listed as vitally important to employers include:

computer literacy	attention to detail
accuracy	tact
self-confidence	character
humor	the ability to learn new skills quickly

Whether we like it or not, a massive transformation is going on all around us in this country, as well as all over the world. Thriving in the coming years is going to be more difficult than in the past and will require certain new and different abilities and attitudes for us to be successful. You will need to learn and acquire the skills that will make you competitive, give you an edge, and help you master a life filled with changes and challenges. Many of these skills are outlined in the **Ten Essential Cornerstones for Success in a Changing World** (Figure 1.1). These skills will be needed for your success, personal independence, and growth in the new millennium. Study them carefully, as you will see them throughout the text and be asked to reflect upon each one.

Why is it important to learn as much as possible about technology?

By learning to develop these enduring skills, you will be able to carry them with you on your first job, your 10th job, and well into your future. By learning how to change and reinvent yourself with the times and demands of the world, you will position yourself to become—AND remain—competitive.

FIGURE

1.1   *Ten Essential Cornerstones for Success in a Changing World*

PASSION—The ability to show the world a person who is passionate about his or her mission and who has aligned his or her goals with his or her education, talents, experiences, and skills. A person who cares not only about his or her own success, but also about the world and his or her surroundings—a person who possesses *Civic Literacy* and sees himself or herself as "a citizen of the world."

MOTIVATION—The ability to find the *inner strength and personal drive* to get up each day and face the world with an "I can, I will" attitude. The ability to develop a strong personal value and belief system that motivates you when the going gets tough. The ability to know who you are and to never let anyone steal your identity or erode your personal ethics.

KNOWLEDGE—The ability to become *highly skilled in a profession* or craft that will enable you to make a good living for yourself and your family in a rapidly changing workplace and to use lifelong learning to maintain your marketable skill sets. The ability to master important academic information beyond that of your major field in areas such as math, science, psychology, history, technology, economics, and communication and to practically apply that information in an evolving and highly technical work environment.

RESOURCEFULNESS—The ability to apply *information literacy*—to know WHERE to find information and the resources that will help you be successful in your academic studies and your chosen profession, and HOW to evaluate that information to determine if it is useful and accurate. The ability to look for and to seek new opportunities, options, and outcomes. The ability to imagine, integrate, and implement new ways of solving old problems.

CREATIVITY—The ability to use *creativity and innovation* in solving problems, which will enable you to anticipate new and emerging issues and to communicate and use what you know and what you have learned and discovered to answer critical questions and solve complex and demanding problems.

ADAPTABILITY—The ability to make good choices based on future opportunities and a changing workplace and to constantly *reinvent yourself* as change brings about necessity and opportunity. The ability to work effectively in a climate of changing priorities and uncertainty.

OPEN-MINDEDNESS—The ability to *accept and appreciate a highly diverse workplace* and the inherent differences and cultures that will be commonplace. The ability to listen to others with whom you disagree or with whom you may have little in common and to learn from them and their experiences. The ability to learn a new language, even if your mastery is only at a primitive, broken, conversational level. The ability to conduct yourself in a respectable and professional manner.

COMMUNICATION—The ability to develop and maintain healthy, *supportive personal and professional relationships* and to build a solid network of well-connected professionals who can help you and who YOU can help in return.

ACCOUNTABILITY—The ability to *accept responsibility and be accountable* for all aspects of your future including your psychological well-being, your spiritual well-being, your relationships, your health, your finances, and your overall survival skills. Basically, you must develop a plan for the future that states, "If this fails, I'll do this," or "If this job is phased out, I'll do this," or "If this resource is gone, I'll use this," or "If this person won't help me, this one will."

VISION—The ability to guide your career path in a new global economy and to understand and take advantage of the inherent impact of worldwide competition—even if you live in a small town and work for a small "mom and pop" company. The ability to *"see" what is coming* and prepare for the changes, adapt to circumstances, and grow with grace and style.

THE M & M THEORY

What Have Your Money and Your Mama Got to Do with It?

What is the M & M Theory? It is quite simple really. We all pay attention to and try to protect the things that matter most to us. Your "**m**oney and your **m**ama" are symbolic of what you care about. Most people care deeply about what happens to their families, their income, their friends, their careers, and the environment, and most people do care and are concerned about world events and what is happening around them.

However, in the hustle and bustle of finding day care, studying for classes, working a full-time job, cleaning the house, helping the kids with homework, and trying to prepare a meal from time to time, we may lose sight of some of the most important things in our lives. Try to keep this thought in mind: *Your EDUCATION is important, too.* In fact, it is of paramount importance to your future on many levels—culturally, socially, intellectually, and in preparing you for the future. Your education is a part of the M & M Theory because it involves your money—the future financial health of you and your family.

According to one of the leading research sources in higher education, *The Chronicle of Higher Education* (August 29, 2008, p. 18), first-year students have a variety of thoughts regarding a college education and money. Of the 272,000 students who responded to the survey, 74% said that *"being very well-off financially"* was an essential or very important objective; 66% responded that *"the chief benefit of a college education is that it increases one's earning power."* Another interesting finding was that 79% of those responding to the survey stated that they believed that *"through hard work, everybody can succeed in American society."*

How can your friends, classmates and peers help you achieve your goals?

According to the U.S. Census Bureau in their annual report *Education and Training Pay* (2007), people with college degrees can earn considerably more than those who do not have a degree. For a complete look at the earning power of U.S. citizens age 25 and older, look at the Education, Pay, and Unemployment chart in Figure 1.2.

By focusing on money in this section, we do not mean to suggest that the only reason to attend college is to make more money. As a matter of fact, we feel that it is a secondary reason. Many people *without college degrees* earn huge salaries each year. However, as the data in Figure 1.2 suggests, those with college degrees traditionally **earn MORE** money and **experience LESS**

FIGURE 1.2 *Education, Pay, and Unemployment Statistics of Full-Time Workers, 25 and Over*

Unemployment Rate	Degree	Mean Earnings
1.35%	Professional Degree	$122,480
1.40%	Doctorate Degree	$108,563
1.85%	Master's Degree	$80,407
2.20%	Bachelor's Degree	$66,133
3.15%	Associate Degree	$47,196
3.85%	Some College, No Degree	$44,488
4.35%	High School Graduate	$37,424
7.40%	Less than High School Graduate	$28,539

Source: Department of the Census, Department of Labor, 2007.

unemployment. Basically, college should make the road to financial security easier, but college should also be a place where you learn to make decisions about your values, your character, and your future. College can also be a place where you make decisions about the changes that need to occur in your life so that you can effectively manage and prosper in an ever-changing world.

COLLEGE AND YOU

Why Is It the Partnership of a Lifetime?

What can college do for you? The list will certainly vary depending on whom you ask, but basically, college can help you develop in the areas listed below. As you read through the list, place a checkmark beside the statements that most accurately reflect which skills you hope to gain from attending college. If there are other skills that you desire to achieve from your college experience, write them at the end of the list.

_____ Grow more self-sufficient and self-confident
_____ Establish and strengthen your personal identity
_____ Understand more about the global world in which you live
_____ Become a more involved citizen in social and political issues
_____ Become more open-minded
_____ Learn to manage your emotions and reactions more effectively
_____ Understand the value of thinking, analyzing, and problem solving
_____ Expand and use your ethical and moral thinking and reasoning skills
_____ Develop commanding computer and information literacy skills
_____ Manage your personal resources such as time and money

How can your college classes help you grow, change, and prosper?

_____ Become more proficient in written, oral, nonverbal, and technical communication
_____ Grow more understanding and accepting of different cultures
_____ Become a lifelong learner
_____ Become more financially independent
_____ Enter a career field that you enjoy

_____ _____

_____ _____

Which skill is THE most important to you? _____

Discuss how you think this skill will help you in your college classes, in your profession, and in your personal life. _____

_____

BLOOM LEVEL 2 QUESTION

The Chronicle of Higher Education's annual report mentioned earlier on first-year students does not list _"I want to change"_ as one of the reasons for attending college. However, you are going to experience changes in your attitudes, your values, your actions, and your intellectual character. You are going to notice changes in old relationships and even in the relationships with your family members. Many of the changes will be positive and rewarding. Sure, there will be a few changes that test your nature and temperament, but that is why this chapter is included in this book—to help you understand how to navigate difficult changes and create positive changes in your life by goal setting, planning, hard work, and persistence.

THE CULTURE OF COLLEGE

What Are the Basic Truths about College Success?

> "Forget mistakes. Forget failures. Forget everything except what you're going to do now . . . and do it."
>
> —Will Durant

In your lifetime, you will experience many things that influence and alter your views, goals, and livelihood. These may include travel, relationships, and personal victories or setbacks. However, few experiences will have a greater influence than your college experience. College can mean hopes realized, dreams fulfilled, and the breaking down of social and economic walls. To get the most from your college experience and to lay a path to success, it will be important for you to look at your expectations and the vast differences among high school, jobs you may have held, and the culture of college. This section will introduce you to some of the changes you can expect and give you a brief introduction into the "culture of college."

Basic Truth #1

SUCCESS IS ABOUT CHOICES, SACRIFICES, AND CHANGE

Life is a series of choices. Hard choices. Easy choices. Right choices. Wrong choices. Nevertheless, the quality of *your life* is determined by the *choices you make* and your willingness to evaluate your life and determine if changes are in order. You will have many important and hard choices in the near future such as deciding whether to devote your time to studying or partying; whether to ask for help in classes that challenge you or give up and drop out; whether to get involved in campus life or "go it alone"; and/or whether to make the sacrifices needed for your future success or take the easy road. Those choices will determine the quality of your future. Some of the choices that you make will force you to step beyond your comfort zone—to move to places that may frighten you or make you uncomfortable. That's OK. That's good. In fact, that's very good.

So what is a *Comfort Zone?* It sounds cozy, doesn't it? Warm and fuzzy. However, do not let the term fool you. A comfort zone is not necessarily a happy and comfortable place. It is simply a place where you are familiar with your surroundings and don't have to work too hard. It is where you feel confident of your abilities, but it is also a place where your growth stops. *It can be a prison and staying there is a cop-out.* Successful people who have won personal and professional victories know that moving beyond one's comfort zone helps in nurturing change, reaching one's potential, and creating opportunities for positive growth.

What sacrifices do you think you'll need to make in your personal life to be academically successful?

Basic Truth #2

HIGHER EDUCATION IS A TWO-WAY STREET

Perhaps the first thing that you will notice about higher education is that you have to **give** in order to **receive**. Not only do you have expectations of your institution and instructors, but your institution and instructors have expectations—great expectations—of you. To be successful, you will need to accept substantially more responsibility for your education than you may have in the past. By attending your college of choice, you have agreed to become a part of its community, values, and policies. You now have the responsibility to stand by its code of academic and moral conduct, and you also have the responsibility to give your very best to every class and organization in which you are involved. And, you have a responsibility to YOURSELF to approach this new world with an

THINKING *for* CHANGE: An Activity for Critical Reflection

After the first week of classes, Devon was very disheartened about the difficulty of the classes for which he was registered. He had not thought that he was going to have so much reading or homework, and he never thought the instructors would be so demanding. He had never been strong at math, but he was just floored at how difficult his beginning math course had become. He failed his first test. He passed his first essay in English, but only with a grade of C. He seriously considered dropping out. It was just too much. It was more than he had expected.

Devon knew, however, that he had to succeed. He looked at his current financial situation, his dead-end job, and his desire to work in the health profession. Dropping out would never get him there. Dropping out would never make him a better, more prepared person. Dropping out would never afford him the opportunity to provide a better life for his family. However, Devon felt that he was just too far behind to catch up. He was at a loss as to what to do.

Pretend that Devon is enrolled at your institution. In your own words, what would you suggest that Devon do at this point? List at least two things that he could do to ensure his success and that would help him change his mind about dropping out. Think about what services are offered and what people might be of assistance to him.

1. _____

   _____

2. _____

   _____

open mind, curiosity and enthusiasm. In return, your institution will be responsible for helping you reach your fullest potential and live the life you desire.

So, what are your thoughts at the moment? Respond to the following questions honestly and personally.

1. Thus far, I think my most rewarding class is _____ taught by Mr./Mrs./Ms./Dr. _____

2. I believe this because _____

   _____

   _____

3. To date, I've learned that he or she expects me to _____

   _____

4. To meet this expectation, how will my academic habits have to change?

   _____

   _____

BLOOM LEVEL 3 QUESTION

Basic Truth #3

YOU'RE IN CHARGE HERE—IT'S ALL ABOUT SELF-MOTIVATION AND SELF-RESPONSIBILITY

ONE person and ONLY one person has the power to determine your thoughts and the direction of your future. It is YOU! You will decide the direction of your future. You are NOT a victim and you will not be treated as a victim at this institution. You will not be allowed to use "Victim Excuses" or employ the "Victim Mentality." This is all about you and your desire to change your life. Higher education is not about others doing the work, but rather about you finding internal motivation and

FIGURE 1.3   *Victim and Winner Chart*

The VICTIM	The WINNER
The victim blames others for his or her problems.	The winner accepts responsibility for what happens in his or her life.
The victim procrastinates and makes excuses for not doing a good job.	The winner thinks ahead and plans for success.
The victim sees adversity as a permanent obstacle.	The winner sees adversity as a way to get stronger.
The victim constantly complains and has a negative mentality about most things.	The winner has an optimistic attitude and is pleasant to be with most of the time.
The victim does just enough to get by and is happy with poor grades and mediocre accomplishments.	The winner works hard to raise his or her level of achievement and constantly seeks to improve.
The victim lets life happen without trying to make things happen.	The winner has a plan and sets goals and works every day to make positive things happen.
The victim is always late and often absent and always has an excuse.	The winner is on time, prepared, and rarely ever negligent regarding his or her responsibilities.
The victim hangs out with negative people who are troublemakers and party animals and have low ambition and a poor work ethic.	The winner surrounds himself or herself with people who are working hard to make something of themselves and who are encouraging and motivating.

accepting responsibility for your actions, your decisions, your choices, and yourself. It is not about making excuses and blaming others. *You are in charge here.* This is YOUR education, and no one else will be responsible for acquiring the knowledge and skills you will need to survive and thrive. No one else will be able to "give you" personal motivation.

Regardless of your circumstances, that **late paper** for English is not your husband's fault. That **missed lab report** is not your child's problem. Your **tardiness** is not your mother's mistake. That **unread chapter** is not your partner's liability. Likewise, that **98 you scored** on your Drug Calculation Test is yours. That **A you got** on your paper about the criminal justice system is yours. That **B+ you got** on your first math test is yours. This is about YOU! Your life. Your future. Your attitude is going to greatly affect your possibility of success.

Consider the preceding chart (Figure 1.3) describing the differences between a "Victim" and a "Winner."

1. Name one person available to you (personally or professionally) who can offer you support, encourage you, and to whom you can turn when things get tough. _____

   _____

2. Why do you respect and/or admire this person enough to ask him or her for help? _____

   _____

3. Generate a list of three questions you would like to ask this person about his or her life, how he or she "made it," and how he or she overcame adversity.

   1. _____

   2. _____

   3. _____

BLOOM LEVEL 6 QUESTION

Basic Truth #4

SELF-MANAGEMENT WILL BE YOUR KEY TO SUCCESS

A major change coming your way involves the workload for your courses and the choices YOU will need to make regarding your schedule and time. You may be assigned a significant amount of reading as homework; in fact, the amount of reading that college classes demand is usually a shock to many students. Although you may have only two or three classes in one day, the basic guideline is that for every hour spent in class, a minimum of 2–3 hours should be spent in review and preparation for the next class.

QUICK MATH: If you are taking five classes and are in class for 15 hours per week, you need to spend 30 hours studying; this makes a 45-hour week—5 hours more than a normal workweek for most people! "Not I," you may say, and you may be right. It all depends on how wisely you use your time, how difficult the work is, and how strong your academic background is. We will discuss time management and study techniques later in this text.

Basic Truth #5

THIS IS NOT HIGH SCHOOL

It sounds so simple, but this is perhaps the most universal and important truth discussed here: College is very different from high school OR the world of work and perhaps one of the most different places you'll ever encounter. The expectations for four different areas are outlined on the following chart (Figure 1.4). Review each area carefully and consider your past experiences as you study the differences.

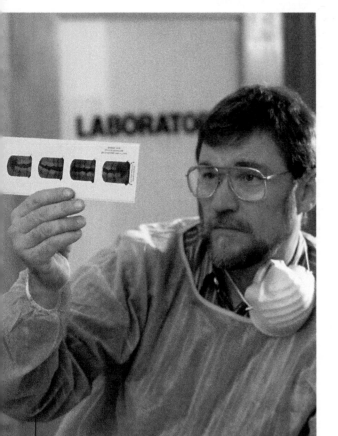

What is the most surprising thing you have learned about your institution's curriculum thus far?

Basic Truth #6

ELIMINATING THE "THIS ISN'T HARVARD SYNDROME" WILL BE ESSENTIAL TO YOUR SUCCESS

Some students enter college with little or no perception of how much work is involved or how much effort it is going to take to be successful. They do not think that the local community college or state university they are attending could possibly be *"that difficult."* Many even perceive their college or university to be less rigorous than it actually is. *"It's only Maple State University,"* or *"It's just Trion Technical College,"* some might reason. They do not think that the college they are attending has the academic standards of a Harvard, a Yale, or a Stanford University. The truth is that your college education is what *YOU make of it.* When you graduate and you are interviewing for a job, the name of your institution may hold some weight, but your skills, your passion, your experiences, your knowledge, and your thinking abilities will be the paramount "tipping point."

True, you may not be at Harvard or Yale, but the rigor of your programs, the amount of reading required, the level of math skills needed, and the degree to which critical thinking, communication, and information literacy skills will be required may surprise you. We thus think that it is important for you to dispel the *"This Isn't Harvard Syndrome"* as quickly as possible so that you can prepare yourself for the coursework and requirements ahead and make the most of your college experience.

You've probably already attended a few of your classes and received syllabi from those classes as you read this. Examine the syllabi of two of your current classes. What surprises you the most about what is going to be required of you this semester? Enter your response in the chart on page 17. By embracing these truths about college life, learning, self-motivation, and education in general, you will have taken some very important steps toward your success.

FIGURE 1.4 *A Guide to Understanding Expectations*

	HIGH SCHOOL	COLLEGE	WORK
PUNCTUALITY AND ATTENDANCE	**Expectations:** • State law requires a certain number of days you must attend • The hours in the day are managed for you • There may be some leeway in project dates Penalties: • You may get detention • You may not graduate • You may be considered a truant • Your grades may suffer	**Expectations:** • Attendance and participation in class are strictly enforced by many professors • Most professors will not give you an extension on due dates • You decide your own schedule and plan your own day Penalties: • You may not be admitted to class if you are late • You may fail the assignment if it is late • Repeated tardiness is some times counted as an absence • Most professors do not take late assignments	**Expectations:** • You are expected to be at work and on time on a daily basis Penalties: • Your salary and promotions may depend on your daily attendance and punctuality • You will most likely be fired for abusing either
TEAMWORK AND PARTICIPATION	**Expectations:** • Most teamwork is assigned and carried out in class • You may be able to choose teams with your friends • Your grade may reflect your participation Penalties: • If you don't participate, you may get a poor grade • You may jeopardize the grade of the entire team	**Expectations:** • Many professors require teamwork and cooperative learning teams or learning communities • Your grade will depend on your participation • Your grade may depend on your entire team's performance • You will probably have to work on the project outside of class Penalties: • Lack of participation and cooperation will probably cost you a good grade • Your team members will likely report you to the professor if you do not participate and their grades suffer as a result	**Expectations:** • You will be expected to participate fully in any assigned task • You will be expected to rely on coworkers to help solve problems and increase profits • You will be required to attend and participate in meetings and sharing sessions • You will be required to participate in formal teams and possess the ability to work with a diverse workforce Penalties: • You will be "tagged" as a non-team player • Your lack of participation and teamwork will cost you raises and promotions • You will most likely be terminated

(continued)

1.4   *A Guide to Understanding Expectations (continued)*

	HIGH SCHOOL	COLLEGE	WORK
PERSONAL RESPONSIBILITY AND ATTITUDE	**Expectations:** • Teachers may coach you and try to motivate you • You are required by law to be in high school regardless of your attitude or responsibility level Penalties: • You may be reprimanded for certain attitudes • If your attitude prevents you from participating you may fail the class	**Expectations:** • You are responsible for your own learning • Professors will assist you, but there is little "hand holding" or personal coaching for motivation • College did not choose you, you chose it and you will be expected to hold this attitude toward your work Penalties: • You may fail the class if your attitude and motivation prevent you from participating	**Expectations:** • You are hired to do certain tasks and the company or institution fully expects this of you • You are expected to be positive and self-motivated • You are expected to model good behavior and uphold the company's work standards Penalties: • You will be passed over for promotions and raises • You may be reprimanded • You may be terminated
ETHICS AND CREDIBILITY	**Expectations:** • You are expected to turn in your own work • You are expected to avoid plagiarism • You are expected to write your own papers • Poor ethical decisions in high school may result in detention or suspension Penalties: • You may get detention or suspension • You will probably fail the project	**Expectations:** • You are expected to turn in your own work • You are expected to avoid plagiarism • You are expected to write your own papers • You are expected to conduct research and complete projects based on college and societal standards Penalties: • Poor ethical decisions may land you in front of a student ethics committee or a faculty ethics committee or result in expulsion from the college • You will fail the project • You will fail the class • You may face deportation if your visa is dependent on your student status	**Expectations:** • You will be required to carry out your job in accordance with company policies, laws, and moral standards • You will be expected to use adult vision and standards Penalties: • Poor ethical decisions may cause you to be severely reprimanded, terminated, or in some cases could even result in a prison sentence

Activity

CLASS	SURPRISING REQUIREMENT	YOUR PLAN FOR SUCCESS
#1		
#2		

CREATING SUCCESS THROUGH POSITIVE CHANGE

How Can You Bring Change to Your Daily Life?

Why is change so important to you and your future? Quite simply, change that you direct creates opportunities for you to grow and prosper in ways you may have never imagined. It allows you to become and remain competitive. It allows you to actively live in a world that is fluid and unpredictable. There are several things you need to know about creating success in your life through positive change. Consider the following ideas:

How can surrounding yourself with positive, upbeat, optimistic people help you with personal change?

1. **Change is a skill.**   Change is a LEARNED SKILL that any willing person can engage in. Period. Public speaking is a skill. Learning how to drive a car is a skill, and just like those activities, change is a skill, too. You'll need to familiarize yourself with the tools and skills discussed below to bring positive change to your life.

2. **Change takes time.**   Change does not happen immediately at the snap of your fingers. If you've ever taken piano, guitar, or drum lessons, you know it takes time to learn how to play an instrument because it is a skill—just like change. You did not learn to play overnight just as you won't learn everything about math or history or nursing in one semester. Often, change is a slow, systematic series of events that eventually lead you to your desired end.

3. **Change requires an "attitude adjustment."**   As corny or hokey as the following example may sound, a recent contestant on *America's Got Talent* was being interviewed about her chances of success on the show. Queen Emily was an African-American single mother working full time. She had given up her dream of being a professional singer years earlier to raise her children. She stated that before her audition, she stood and looked in the mirror crying. Her only thought was, *"My time has passed; this is never going to happen for me. Never!"* Then she looked herself in the eyes and said, *"Why NOT me? I'm talented. I'm good at performing, and I KNOW I can sing.* **WHY NOT ME?"** Her attitude adjustment was the key to her being able to change her life. She auditioned for the show, surpassed thousands of contestants, and was invited to Los Angeles as one of five finalists. She now performs in a major show in Las Vegas, Nevada.

"The key to change . . . is to let go of fear."
—Rosanne Cash

From Ordinary to Extraordinary

REAL PEOPLE | REAL LIVES | REAL CHANGE

BILL CLAYTON
ACE Certified Personal Trainer / Post-Rehabilitation Specialist
Owner/Operator, Clayton Personal Fitness – Las Vegas, NV

"I was..." Those are powerful words. For example, *I was* the manager of the gardening department of a major retail chain. *I was* an employee in a shop that prints and mails inserts and flyers. *I was* a rock band drummer for several bands. *I was* a crystal meth addict. Yes . . . *I was!*

It seems strange to write that now, but the term, "I was...." is impossible to erase. My friends and clients often ask me how I managed to go from the life of a meth addict to a personal trainer. The journey was a strange one and often difficult.

I began playing the drums when I was six years old and by the time I was eight, I had my first "garage band." Writing and playing music were my only passions. They were my life. After high school, I worked many odd jobs, but my love of performing never waned.

In my 20's, I had a band that steadily played gigs and I was living the life of a rocker. We traveled. We sang. We partied. We traveled some more and we partied some more . . . and more. Before I really realized what was happening with me, I had become addicted to meth. It was my life. I hung around people who used with me and they became my family. I met Kathy, the woman I would eventually marry, while performing with my band. She and I hit it off even though she knew of my addiction. One evening after we were married, Kathy and I were talking and she mentioned that she would like to have children one day. I wanted children, too. At that moment, the strangest thing came to my mind. I thought, "If she gets pregnant, I'll stop doing meth." How could I be so messed up that I would work to abolish my addiction for a child not yet born, BUT I would not consider trying to stop *just for ME*? That was my wake-up call. I knew I had to change my life. I was 29 years old.

I was one of the lucky ones. I was able to stop "cold turkey" on my own. I know that others are not so lucky. I began to look at my life and tried to determine what I wanted to do. I had to seriously evaluate every aspect of who and what I was. I knew that I had to set goals to get my life back on track.

I had been in a life-threatening motorcycle accident years earlier and remembered the great care I received from my physical therapist. So, I began to look at PT programs and that is when I found the Personal Trainer Program at our local college. Something about this was very attractive to me. Again, I was lucky. I happened to find my passion and my life's vocation without much struggle.

Today, after working through my addiction, surviving a divorce, and mourning the death of my mom, I can say without a doubt that I am one of the luckiest people on earth. Because I was willing to change and stay committed to finding a better life, I own my own gym, hold certifications from every major fitness and rehabilitation organization in America, and count each day as a true gift.

EXTRAORDINARY REFLECTION

Read the following statement and respond to it in your online journal or class notebook.

Mr. Clayton mentions that he was one of the "lucky ones." What role do you think luck plays in one's success? Is there a difference among luck, readiness, and action? If so, what is it?

> *My friends and clients often ask me how I managed to go from the life of a meth addict to a personal trainer.*

4. **Change demands action.**   While circumstances and desire may drive the need for change in your life, don't lose sight of the fact that ultimately, change is an action. It is something you must do—mentally, physically, spiritually, and intellectually. Just as Queen Emily in the previous example knew, without action by her, her life was not going to change.

5. **Change is about working toward something, not running away from something.**   If you want true, lasting, meaningful change in your life, you have to think about it as working toward good, positive, useful things, not as running away from bad, negative, unpleasant things. "Working toward" is *positive and internal*. "Running away from" is *negative and external*. Try to work **toward a goal** and not **run from a problem**.

6. **Change is about letting go and holding on.**   As with any new endeavor, you will have to decide what is working in your life and what is not. By doing so, you can decide what you need to hold onto and what you finally need to let go of. You will want to hold onto the positive strengths and talents you have while letting go of the negative, destructive attitudes that you may have held in the past.

ELIMINATING ROADBLOCKS TO YOUR SUCCESS

What Should You Do if Your Fears and Self-Talk Try to Derail Your Efforts to Change?

Try as you might, sometimes harmful emotions, fear of the unknown, and that nagging little voice inside your head (negative self-talk) can cause you problems. Negative self-talk usually appears when you are afraid, uneasy, hurt, angry, depressed, or lonely. By the time you read this, you may have experienced these feelings. When you experience change, your body, mind, and soul typically go through a process of physical and emotional change as well. Learning to recognize these symptoms of change in order to control them can help you control the stress that can accompany change.

LISTEN TO YOURSELF FOR A FEW DAYS. Are you more of an optimist or a pessimist? Do you hear yourself whining, complaining, griping, and finding fault with everything and everybody around you? Do you blame others for things that are wrong in your life? Do you blame your bad grades on your professors? Do you feel that someone else is responsible for your unhappiness? If these thoughts or comments are in your head, you are suffering from the *"I CAN'T Syndrome"* (**I**rritated, **C**ontaminated, **A**ngry, **N**egative **T**houghts). This pessimistic condition can negatively influence every aspect of your life, from your self-esteem to your motivation level to your academic performance, your relationships, and your career success.

If you want to eliminate *I CAN'T* from your life, consider the following tips:

☑ Think about the many positive aspects of your life and show gratitude for them.
☑ Work every day to find the good in people, places, and things.
☑ Eliminate negative thoughts that enter your mind before you begin your day.
☑ Discover what is holding you back and what you need to push yourself forward.
☑ Visualize your success—visualize yourself actually being who and what you want to be.
☑ Locate and observe positive, optimistic people and things in your life.

DID YOU KNOW

ABRAHAM LINCOLN was born on February 12, 1809, in Hardin, Kentucky, to two uneducated farmers. They lived in a one-room log cabin. His mother died when he was 10 years old, just a few years after his father had moved the family to Illinois.

He was raised in great poverty and had only 18 months of formal schooling. He studied very hard on his own and learned to read, write, and do mathematical problems. He went on to become a lawyer. One of his law partners once said of him, *"His ambition was a great engine that knew no rest."*

He lost the love of his life when he was 26, suffered a nervous breakdown at age 27, failed in business twice, lost eight elections, and suffered the death of three children all BEFORE he became our president and changed the course of our nation. On Good Friday, April 14, 1865, Lincoln was assassinated at Ford's Theatre in Washington, D.C., by John Wilkes Booth. (Adapted from whitehouse.gov)

"You gain strength, experience, and confidence by every experience where you stop to look fear in the face. You must do the thing you think you cannot."
—Eleanor Roosevelt

Tips for Personal Success

Consider the following tips for adjusting to the many changes in the days to come:

► Approach change with an open mind.

► Don't be afraid to ask people in your class or your professor questions about things that are confusing or unclear.

► If you are not technologically savvy, find out what other resources are available to you.

Now it is your turn. Create a list of at least three more tips that you would offer a fellow classmate to assist him or her in bringing about positive change in his or her life.

1. _____

2. _____

3. _____

☑ Make a list of who helps you, supports you, and helps you feel positive—then make a point to be around them more often.

☑ Take responsibility for your own actions and their consequences.

☑ Force yourself to find five positive things a day for which to be thankful.

You've seen the differences between an optimist and a pessimist. They are both everywhere—at work, at school, and maybe in your own family. Think of the optimist for a moment. You've probably sat next to him or her in one of your classes or seen him or her at work—the person who always seems to be happy, motivated, bubbling with personality, organized, and ready for whatever comes his or her way. Optimists greet people as they enter the room, respond in class, volunteer for projects, and have a presence about them that is positive and lively. You may even look at an optimist out of the corner of your eye and wonder, "What is he on?"

Positive, upbeat, and motivated people are easy to spot. You can see their attitude in the way they walk, the way they carry themselves, the way they approach people, and the way they treat others.

Be wary, however, of *"the others,"* the ones you need to avoid. Whiners. Degraders. Attackers. Manipulators. Pessimists. Backstabbers. Abusers. Cowards. Two-faced racists, sexists, ageists, and people who are homophobic or ethnocentric. These people carry around an aura so negative that it can almost be seen as a dark cloud above them. They degrade others because they do not like themselves. They find fault with everything because their own lives are a mess. They do nothing and then attack you for being motivated and trying to improve your life. We call them ***contaminated people***. Contaminated people are unhappy with who they are. To make themselves feel better, they try to tear down people who are the opposite of what they are. They belittle positive actions and try to make others' lives as miserable as their own.

Sure, everyone has bad days and bad stretches in his or her life. ***This is not the person*** we are talking about here. With contaminated people, being negative and trying to bring you down is epidemic in their lives. It is the way they operate all the time. It is constant. Having a bad day and complaining is normal for some people at various times, but contaminated people see life (and you) as negative and bad on an hourly and daily basis.

BUILDING A NEW YOU

How Can You Change Your Life Through Goal Setting?

Positive change can be brought about in several ways, but the most effective way is through goal setting and having a "change plan." Think about what you really want or need to change in your life. More importantly, think about why you want "this thing" and what it is going to mean to your life. By thinking about what you want, what needs to change, and where you want to be, goals become easier to achieve.

Characteristics of Attainable Goals

The following characteristics will help you in your quest to bring about change through effective goal setting. Goals should be:

► **Reasonable**   Your goal should be a challenge for you, but also within reason based on your abilities.

▶ **Believable**   To achieve a goal, you must really believe it is within your capacity to achieve it.

▶ **Measurable**   Your goal needs to be concrete and measurable in some way. Avoid such terms as "earn a lot" or "lose some weight."

▶ **Adaptable**   Your goals may need to be adapted to changing circumstances in your life.

▶ **Controllable**   Your goals should be within your own control; they should not depend on the whims and opinions of anyone else.

▶ **Desirable**   To attain a difficult goal, you must want it very badly. You should never work toward something just because *someone else* wants it.

ESSENTIAL CORNERSTONE

Vision:
How can having a clear vision of your future and what you want help you become a more optimistic person?

Social Networking Moment:
Share your response to this Essential Cornerstone with peers in your social network. Choose two responses from your peers and respond to their postings.

How to Write Your Goals to Bring about Positive Change

"I will pass my next math test with a B or better" is an example of a short-term goal. *"I will purchase my first home in 7 to 10 years"* is probably a long-term goal. During college, more of your goals may be short term than long term, but you can certainly begin setting both. Goals can be lofty and soaring, but great goals can also be as simple as *"I will spend two hours at the park with my children tomorrow afternoon."*

Well-written, exciting, and effective goals include:

▶ a goal statement with a target date,

▶ action steps,

▶ a narrative statement,

▶ an "I deserve it" statement, and

▶ a personal signature.

The **goal statement** should be specific and measurable; that is, it should entail some tangible evidence of the goal's achievement and have a **target date** and a timeline for accomplishing your goal. Your goal statement MUST also use an action verb. An example of a goal statement with an action verb and target date is: *"I will lose 10 pounds in six weeks"* or *"I am going to join a campus club by the fifth week of this term."* These are much more powerful statements than: "I am thinking about joining a club" or "I wanna have a new car."

After you write the goal statement, you'll need to create **specific action steps** that explain exactly what you are going to do to reach your goal. There is no certain number of steps; it all depends on your goal and your personal commitment. An example of action steps for weight loss might be: (1) I WILL join the campus health center, (2) I WILL meet with a personal trainer on campus, (3) I WILL set an appointment with a nutrition counselor in the health center, (4) I WILL . . .

What exactly is it going to take to achieve your biggest, most important goals?

The next step is to write a **narrative statement** about what your goal accomplishment will mean to you and how your life will change after you reach this goal. For example, if your goal is to lose 30 pounds, paint a "verbal picture" of how your life is going to look once this goal has been reached. Your verbal picture may include statements such as: "I'll be able to wear nicer clothes." "I'll feel better." "I'll be able to ride my bicycle again." "My self-esteem will be stronger." If your goals don't offer you significant rewards, you are not likely to stick to your plan.

Next, write two reasons why you deserve this goal. This is called your **"I Deserve It Statement."** It may seem simple, but this is a complex issue. Many people do not follow through on their goals because deep down, they don't feel they deserve them. The narrative statement helps you understand how your life will look once the goal is met, but your "I deserve it statement" asks you to consider *why* you deserve this goal.

Finally, **sign your goal statement**. This is an imperative step in that your signature shows that you are making a personal commitment to see this goal to fruition. This is your name. Use it with pride. Use the goal sheet on page 23 to build your goals.

CHANGING IDEAS TO *Reality*

REFLECTIONS ON
CHANGE AND GOAL
SETTING

The transition from one place to another is seldom easy, even when the change is one you want. Entering college has given you the opportunity to assume new roles, develop new friendships, meet new people, work under different circumstances, and perhaps adjust your lifestyle. It is an opportunity to improve who you are at this moment or to build an entirely new person. College helps you do this. Going to college gives you the opportunity to reflect on your strengths and consider areas where you might need to change. These changes form the very essence of the college experience; they create wonderful new experiences and help you discover who you really are and what you have to offer the world.

As you reflect upon this chapter, keep the following pointers in mind:

▶ Evaluate your reason(s) for attending college and what it means to your life.
▶ Use goal setting to help you direct changes in your life.
▶ Don't just let change happen; get involved in your own life and learning.
▶ Focus on the positive by eliminating your negative self-talk.
▶ Keep your sense of humor.
▶ Be courageous by facing your fears, before they derail you.

"A possibility was born the day you were born,
and it will live as long as you live."
—R. Burak

My Personal Goal

To help you get started, use this goal-setting sheet as a template for this and future goals.

Name _____

Goal Statement (with action verb and target date) _____

_____

_____

Action Steps (concrete things you plan to do to reach your goal)

1. _____

2. _____

3. _____

4. _____

5. _____

Narrative Statement (how your life will look when you reach your goal) _____

_____

_____

_____

_____

_____

_____

I deserve this goal because:

1. _____

_____

2. _____

_____

I hereby make this commitment to myself.

_____   _____
My Signature   Date

KNOWLEDGE *in* BLOOM

Bringing Positive Change to Your Life

Each chapter-end assessment is based on *Bloom's Taxonomy of Learning*. See the inside front cover for a quick review.

UTILIZES LEVELS 1–6 OF THE TAXONOMY

EXPLANATION: After reading and reflecting thus far, you may have identified several changes that you need to make in your academic or personal life. Also, changes may have been thrust upon you by choices you or those around you have made. The following model provides a method for bringing positive changes into your life and/or reshaping the changes over which you had little control.

PROCESS: Based on Bloom's Taxonomy, the **Change Implementation Model** asks you to consider questions and recommends actions at each level of learning. The chart moves from less difficult questions (Levels 1, 2, 3) to more challenging questions (Levels 4, 5, 6). To begin the change process in your life, follow the steps in this chapter-end activity.

Step 1: Review the steps of the **Change Implementation Model** based on **Bloom's Taxonomy**.

LEVEL 1—REMEMBER	*Describe* one behavior, belief, or action that you need to change in your life. Also, *list* the possible obstacles that you might encounter.
LEVEL 2—UNDERSTAND	*Explain* why this change needs to occur in order for you to be successful. Also, *give two examples* of the options available to you at college, at home, or in the community for making the desired change.
LEVEL 3—APPLY	*Using* the information from Levels 1 and 2, *show* your plan (action steps) to overcome the obstacles listed above.
LEVEL 4—ANALYZE	*Compare* your current action steps to the steps you have previously taken to overcome obstacles and enact change. What conclusions can be drawn from this comparison?
LEVEL 5—EVALUATE	Pretend that someone very close to you asks what you are doing with this plan and why. Write a detailed paragraph *justifying* what you are doing, why you need to do it, and how it is going to positively affect your life.
LEVEL 6—CREATE	Based on the information you have gathered above from investigation and reflection, *design your plan* to bring about this change in your life. Consider using the goal-setting format illustrated in this chapter to create a plan and action steps that are truly unique to you.

Step 2: After studying the change model above, read the following fictional scenario in which you encounter difficulty in Accounting 101.

You enter your Accounting 101 class eager to take the first course in your major field. You are shocked to find that the professor begins lecturing on the first day. Not only is the material difficult to understand, so is the professor, whose first language is not English.

For homework, the professor assigns two chapters to read per class, but the lectures are not based on material found in the textbook. You try to study as you had in high school but now you feel overwhelmed and isolated. The material is much harder.

After three weeks and a failed first test, you notice that the students who passed the test have formed study groups, something that you once thought only the brightest students did.

Using the **Change Implementation Model,** you decide to make positive changes in your study habits. As an example, plans for change are shown in Step 3.

Step 3: Review this EXAMPLE and determine how you might use the **Change Implementation Model** to enact changes to save your grade in Accounting 101.

LEVEL 1—REMEMBERING

Identify one behavior, belief, or action that you need to change in your life. Also, *list* the possible obstacles that you might encounter.

If I could, I would change my study habits in accounting and become stronger in my math skills.

Obstacles: fear of change, shyness, pride, and time constraints

LEVEL 2—UNDERSTANDING

Explain why this change needs to occur in order for you to be successful. Also, *give two examples* of the options available to you at your college, home, or in the community for making the desired change.

Why change is needed: Weak math skills are causing me to fail accounting.

Campus: tutoring center and math lab

Professor's office hours

Community: Aunt works in accounting office

LEVEL 3—APPLYING

Using the information from Levels 1 and 2, *show* your plan (action steps) to overcome the obstacles listed above.

Step 1—I will join a study group.

Step 2—I will make an appointment for tutoring in the math lab.

Step 3—I will talk to my advisor about services available.

Step 4—I will plan at least five hours per week to study for my accounting class.

Step 5—I will seek help from my aunt who is an accountant.

LEVEL 4—ANALYZING

Compare your current action steps to the steps you have previously taken to overcome obstacles and enact change. What conclusions can be drawn from this comparison?

Past: I took notes in class, looked them over before a test.

New: Join study group, go to tutoring center and math lab

New: Talk with advisor

New: Meet with my aunt for advice and assistance

Conclusion: In taking personal responsibility for my education, taking calculated risks to bring about change, and asking for help, I'm more likely to pass accounting.

LEVEL 5—EVALUATING

Pretend that someone very close to you asks what you are doing with this plan and why. Write a detailed paragraph justifying what you are doing, why you need to do it, and how it is going to positively affect your life.

I am working so hard to pass accounting because I want this degree and I want the knowledge of how to run my own business. If I don't change my habits, I will not pass accounting and I will not have this degree. Without this degree, I will most likely have to work in low-paying jobs for the rest of my life. By asking for help, spending more time studying, and spending more time around people who have some of the same interests, I can develop the skills to graduate, start my own business, and help my family out financially.

LEVEL 6—CREATING

Based on the information you have gathered above from investigation and reflection, *design your plan* to bring about this change in your life. Consider using the goal-setting format illustrated in this chapter to create a plan and action steps that are truly unique to you.

Goal: I WILL get involved with a study group, schedule a tutor, and spend at least five hours per week studying for accounting. I will do this by the *end of this week*.

Action Steps:

Step 1—I will join a study group/get an accounting tutor.

Step 2—I will talk to my advisor about services available.

Step 3—I will study five hours per week for accounting class.

Step 4—I will work w/ my boss to design a plan for more study time.

Step 5—I will meet with my aunt once a week to get her help.

Narrative Statement: Basically, by getting involved and not trying to do this alone, I will begin to enjoy college more and do better in my classes.

I DESERVE this goal because I have the courage to ask for help and the intelligence to put my pride aside and seek assistance. I deserve to learn this material so that I can successfully run my own business.

Step 4: After studying the **Change Implementation** example, focus on a few things that you might want to change about your own academic life such as study habits, motivation level, financial or time management, or your attitude. Now, choose **one** of the major changes you wish to incorporate into your life from the list. Using the Change Implementation Model, devise a strategy to effect this change.

LEVEL 1—REMEMBERING

Identify one behavior, belief, or action that you need to change in your life. Also, *list* the possible obstacles that you might encounter.

LEVEL 2—UNDERSTANDING

Explain why this change needs to occur in order for you to be successful. Also, *give two examples* of the options available to you at college, at home, or in the community for making the desired change.

LEVEL 3—APPLYING

Using the information from Levels 1 and 2, *show* your plan (action steps) to overcome the obstacles listed above.

LEVEL 4—ANALYZING

Compare your current action steps to the steps you have previously taken to overcome obstacles and enact change. What conclusions can be drawn from this comparison?

LEVEL 5—EVALUATING

Pretend that someone very close to you asks what you are doing with this plan and why. Write a detailed paragraph justifying what you are doing, why you need to do it, and how it is going to positively affect your life.

LEVEL 6—CREATING

Based on the information you have gathered above from investigation and reflection, *design your plan* to bring about this change in your life. Consider using the goal-setting format illustrated in this chapter to create a plan and action steps that are truly unique to you.

SQ3R *Mastery* STUDY SHEET

EXAMPLE QUESTION *(from page 11)* What are the six basic truths about the culture of college?		**ANSWER:**
EXAMPLE QUESTION *(from page 21)* Why must goals be measurable?		**ANSWER:**
AUTHOR QUESTION *(from page 11)* Why is it important to know and understand the basic "truths" about college success?		**ANSWER:**
AUTHOR QUESTION *(from page 14)* What is the "This Isn't Harvard" syndrome?		**ANSWER:**
AUTHOR QUESTION *(from page 17)* Why does change take time?		**ANSWER:**
AUTHOR QUESTION *(from page 22)* Explain the "I can't" syndrome (from page 19).		**ANSWER:**
AUTHOR QUESTION *(from page 21)* What is a narrative statement?		**ANSWER:**
YOUR QUESTION *(from page ____)*		**ANSWER:**
YOUR QUESTION *(from page ____)*		**ANSWER:**
YOUR QUESTION *(from page ____)*		**ANSWER:**
YOUR QUESTION *(from page ____)*		**ANSWER:**
YOUR QUESTION *(from page ____)*		**ANSWER:**

Finally, after answering these questions, recite this chapter's major points in your mind. Consider the following general questions to help you master this material.

▶ What was it about?
▶ What does it mean?
▶ What was the most important thing I learned? Why?
▶ What were the key points to remember?

Campus/Community Success Centers

CAMPUS/COMMUNITY SERVICE	HOW IT CAN HELP YOU	PHONE NUMBER AND LOCATION
Academic Advisement Center	Assists in choosing classes for each semester and offers career assessments and advice on careers.	
Computer Lab	Offers students the use of e-mail, Internet services, and other online applications, usually free of charge.	
Writing Center	Offers assistance with your writing skills. They will not rewrite your paper for you, but they can give you advice on how to strengthen your project.	
Math Center	Offers help with math problems, one-on-one or group tutoring, and study sessions.	
Tutoring or Mastery Learning Center	Offers assistance in almost any subject matter. Many colleges offer this service free of charge (or for a very nominal fee).	
Language Lab	Offers assistance with international languages or sign language.	
Library	Your college library can be the hub of your learning experience from printed materials to Internet usage to computer-assisted tutorials. Your library and librarians are vital to helping you succeed in your classes and to become information literate.	
Veteran Affairs	Offers assistance to veterans, especially with government paperwork and financial aid.	

(continued)

Campus/Community Success Centers (continued)

CAMPUS/COMMUNITY SERVICE	HOW IT CAN HELP YOU	PHONE NUMBER AND LOCATION
Health Services	Some campuses offer student services for physical and mental health, complete with a nurse or physician's assistant.	
International Student Services	Assists international students with admissions, housing, cultural adjustment, and language barriers.	
Minority Student Services	Offers services and programming for minority students on campus.	
Financial Aid Office	Assists students with federal, state, and local paperwork to apply for financial aid and scholarships. They are especially helpful in assisting with your FAFSA form each year.	
Student Activities	Offers a wide variety of programming in social and cultural activities.	
Disabled Student Services	If you have a documented disability, colleges and universities across the United States are required by law to offer you "reasonable accommodations" to ensure your success (Americans with Disabilities Act, Sec. 504). Some of these accommodations include: Handicapped parking, Special testing centers, Extended time on tests and timed projects, Textbook translations and conversions, Interpreters, Note-taking services, TTY/TDD services.	

CHAPTER 2
RELATE

CELEBRATING
PEOPLE,
CULTURES,
AND DIVERSITY

"We must learn to live together as brothers or perish together as fools."

—Martin Luther King, Jr.

WHY READ THIS CHAPTER?

what's in it for me?

Why? Because when we think of change, there are few places where many people need more work than in the area of diversity awareness and appreciation. A truly educated person knows how to listen to others, learn from others, and grow from others' experiences and cultures. This chapter will provide a chance for you to rethink and evaluate some of your long-held beliefs and challenges you to open yourself and your thinking up to new possibilities regarding diversity—indeed, to learn to celebrate differences and to relate to all kinds of people. Few things will do more to make you an educated, sophisticated, and competitive person than expanding your thinking about diversity and being able to build lasting and rewarding relationships with people from many walks of life.

By carefully reading this chapter and taking the information provided seriously, you will be able to:

1. Understand the concept of globalization and its impact on personal and work relationships.
2. Define and discuss ethnocentrism and xenocentrism.
3. Identify and understand the dimensions of diversity.
4. Understand the power of having an open mind.
5. Understand how the dimensions of diversity can bring people together.

WHY is it important to study diversity? WHY does it matter whether I get along with people from cultures and backgrounds that are different from mine? WHY will learning to celebrate diversity help me be able to get along with other people? WHY does my personal community need to include people who are not just like me?

CHAPTER 2 / RELATE

"I feel my heart break to see a nation ripped apart by its own greatest strength ... its diversity."

—Melissa Etheridge

. . . FROM MY PERSPECTIVE

NAME: Patricia Renew
INSTITUTION: Houston Community College, Houston, TX
MAJOR: Business Technology
AGE: 49

As an older African-American student with four grown children, I am not the typical college student. I am, however, representative of a very diverse personal culture. I grew up in the South Carolina low country and am a descendant of the Gullah people. I am actually a Gullah Priestess with responsibilities for teaching young women about caring for families. As a high school student, I was privileged to attend an all-black Catholic high school where I graduated as Salutatorian. This environment was the beginning of my learning to embrace diversity and to grow from it.

I moved to Houston, where all my children live; this move opened up a new world of different kinds of diversity that I had not previously experienced. I encourage all college students to embrace diversity of all kinds because it is a big part of your college education. Everyone in my high school was basically very much alike, but in college I have met people from many different nationalities, religions, and races. On one team, we had students from five different nationalities. I learned as much from them about their cultures, their dress, their religions, and their dating and marital customs as I did from the project itself.

I recommend that you build solid relationships with fellow students, professors, and even college administrators. If you have a problem paying your tuition, for example, a college administrator will know how to advise you and walk you through requesting an extension or applying for financial aid.

The college environment is very different from high school. In college you will meet people who are there from all over the world. I have friends who are from Pakistan, Nigeria, Taiwan, Guatemala, and India. They have been a great part of my education, and I feel fortunate to have known them.

I also embrace diversity at work and have learned to be open to being friends with older and younger workers. They all have something to teach me that makes me a better person and a better employee.

As a person with a very diverse background myself, I know I have a lot I can teach, and I know I can learn so much from others. I highly recommend that college students open up their hearts and minds to all kinds of people because you will be blessed by the experiences and the knowledge.

SCAN & QUESTION

In the preface of this book (page ix), you read about the **SQ3R Study Method**. Right now, take a few moments, **scan this chapter**, and on page 47, write **five questions** that you think will be important to your mastery of this material. In addition to the two questions below, you will find five questions from your authors. Use one of your "**On The Test**" stickers to flag this page for easy reference.

EXAMPLES:

▶ **Define personal community and how it relates to diversity.** (from page 40)

▶ **Define the difference between age and generational diversity.** (from pages 40–41)

LEARNING TO THINK GLOBALLY WHILE MAKING LOCAL APPLICATIONS

Is It Really a Small World After All?

> "I am not a citizen of Athens or Greece but of the world."
> —Socrates

"Think Globally, Act Locally" was a phrase that emerged from an international conference on environmental issues in the early '70s. In the world where we live and work today, that phrase encompasses so much more than just the environment. Today we are connected by technology and economics, as well as social networks. Because we are so mobile and interconnected, what happens in another part of the world can have immediate implications for our part of the world. For example, war in a Middle Eastern country can interrupt oil supplies and thus impact our economy. As we have seen, a melt-down in U.S. financial markets can severely impact world markets because other countries' citizens own a significant portion of U.S. stocks and bonds.

Because of technology, primarily the Internet, we are now connected with people all over the world. "Internet users are roughly 35 percent English and 65 percent Non-English with Chinese at 14 percent. Google's Index now stands at over 8 billion pages. Today we have over a billion internet users and that number is growing rapidly" (21 Facts About the Internet, 2008). Consider the following statistics in Figure 2.1.

Technology has opened the doors to the world and brought with it amazing opportunities. But it has also brought a new set of problems and concerns as it exposes our differences to a

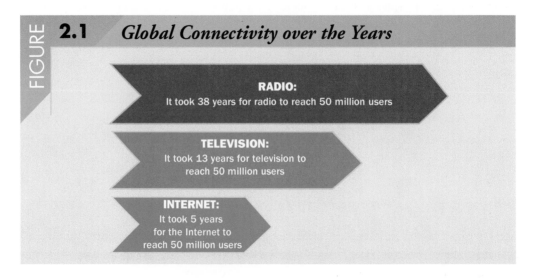

FIGURE 2.1 *Global Connectivity over the Years*

RADIO:
It took 38 years for radio to reach 50 million users

TELEVISION:
It took 13 years for television to reach 50 million users

INTERNET:
It took 5 years for the Internet to reach 50 million users

greater degree than in the past and pits us against each other as competitors for jobs, business ventures, and tourists. So we all have work to do to become good global citizens in this brave new world where we live and work. As a citizen and an employee, you will need new skills and knowledge to function at your best capacity. Some of the ideas to consider as you begin to *think globally and act locally* are:

▶ To act with compassion and understanding for people who are different from you.

▶ To develop a good understanding of the different cultures, beliefs, and issues embraced by people from locations all over the world that may be vastly different from yours.

▶ To travel internationally and experience firsthand people from other parts of the world.

▶ To examine multiple viewpoints and philosophies and make decisions that are respectful of many types of differences.

▶ To listen carefully, think differently, and solve problems that emerge in the workplace and in communities because of cultural differences.

▶ To study and grasp historical perspectives in order to understand reasons for the tensions between and among different cultures.

How has living in a global world affected your career path? Has it affected your current job?

Take a Virtual Global Field Trip

You may be thinking to yourself at the moment, *"Have these people gone crazy? Travel internationally? Associate with different cultures?* I don't have the time or money to leave my own backyard." That's OK. As a matter of fact, because we are all so connected through technology, you can travel to many places with the tips of your fingers. You can sit at your computer and learn a great deal about a country and its people without ever leaving your home. Sure, it would be nice to actually travel to China or Australia—and you will one day, if you so desire—but until that time, you can use the Internet to travel virtually.

In the spaces in Figure 2.2, take a virtual trip somewhere in the world. Think about a place you've always wanted to travel. Africa? India? Finland? Scotland? Saudi Arabia? You decide! Consider each question on the left and respond on the right. You might even consider asking your children, spouse, or friends to help you with this exercise. There is nothing that says you have to travel alone. If you have a child, this could be an excellent opportunity to introduce him or her to different parts of the world, the study of geography, and the opportunity to learn about other cultures. This is also an excellent opportunity to learn HOW to learn about other cultures, places, and peoples. Begin this assignment with an open mind and see where it takes you and what you learn. You may surprise yourself.

ESSENTIAL CORNERSTONE

Resourcefulness:
How can researching and learning more about a culture, subculture, or religion help you in the workplace?

Social Networking Moment:
Share your response to this Essential Cornerstone with peers in your social network. Choose two responses from your peers and respond to their postings.

ANYTHING YOU CAN DO, I CAN DO BETTER!

What Are Ethnocentrism and Xenocentrism?

Many people truly believe that they are not prejudiced against any group and that they have no stereotypes in their thought processes about certain groups of people. If we dig deep enough, however,

FIGURE **2.2** *My Virtual Global Fieldtrip*

QUESTION	RESPONSE
The place I've chosen to "travel" is . . .	
Why do you want to travel here?	
What is the population?	
What is the primary language spoken?	
What is the literacy rate of its people?	
What is their primary form of energy?	
What is the primary religion practiced?	
Who are their neighbors (other countries)?	
What is one cultural trait you learned about this country that surprised you?	
What is the normal temperature of this country during the summer and winter?	
What is this country's primary industry?	
What is this country's most treasured site?	
What is the country's health system like?	
How many of this country's citizens are college graduates?	

> "We don't see things as THEY are, we see things as WE are."
> —Anaïs Nin

Have you ever made a snap judgment about something unfamiliar to you?

we would find that most of us have some kind of prejudice and that we all discriminate in some ways. Because most of us have lived in rather homogeneous neighborhoods and have primarily hung out with people like us, we may tend to be *ethnocentric*, believing that our particular ethnic background is superior and tending to stay with our own kind. If you remember, the idea of striving to be *"nonethnocentric"* was discussed in Chapter 9, "Think," as an important aspect of becoming a critical thinker.

Ethnocentrism suggests that we tend to fear people from other ethnic backgrounds or we lump them together and view them **as a group** rather than **as individuals**. We don't think that their culture, religion, or race could possibly be as important or worthwhile as our own. Think about the ramifications to your *own* life if you were judged by "your group" of people instead of as an individual—if everyone judged you *as a woman* and not as Suzanne; if everyone judged you *as a Northerner* and not as Joe; if everyone judged you *as a Pentecostal* and not as Raymond; if everyone judged you *as a lesbian* and not as Sandra.

Think about the negative terms many people use to describe a few practices from other cultures:

"People in England drive on the WRONG side of the road."
"The Islamic language is written and read BACK-WARD."
"Europeans use the WRONG KIND of money."
"Africans dress FUNNY."
"Asians eat WEIRD things."

Ask yourself this: "Is it really wrong?" "Is it really backward?" "Is it really weird?" Or are these customs simply *different* from your own?

Xenocentrism is the opposite of ethnocentrism in that one believes that other cultures are superior to

2.3 *Getting a Grasp on Ethnocentrism*

Read each statement *very carefully* and then, based on YOUR personal feelings, experiences, and upbringing, circle the number on the scale that best reflects your opinion as to whether this behavior or action is *"good or bad."*

STATEMENT	BAD		NEUTRAL		GOOD
1. Looking at someone when you talk to them.	1	2	3	4	5
2. Eating any type of food with your bare hand.	1	2	3	4	5
3. Having a pierced eyebrow.	1	2	3	4	5
4. Smelling someone as a greeting.	1	2	3	4	5
5. Eating someone's cremated ashes as a tribute to him or her.	1	2	3	4	5
6. Being late for an appointment.	1	2	3	4	5
7. Participating in an arranged marriage.	1	2	3	4	5
8. Believing in more than one god.	1	2	3	4	5
9. Eating cows.	1	2	3	4	5
10. Eating pigs.	1	2	3	4	5
11. Eating dogs.	1	2	3	4	5
12. Eating horses.	1	2	3	4	5
13. Having sex before marriage.	1	2	3	4	5
14. Chewing food with your mouth open (smacking your food).	1	2	3	4	5
15. Believing that money is a good thing.	1	2	3	4	5
16. Requiring that women cover all body parts except their eyes.	1	2	3	4	5
17. Staring at someone.	1	2	3	4	5
18. Moving away or out of your parent's home.	1	2	3	4	5
19. Shaking hands with your right hand.	1	2	3	4	5
20. Taking a bath every day.	1	2	3	4	5
21. Duty and country should always come first.	1	2	3	4	5
22. Calling a person by their first name.	1	2	3	4	5
23. Everyone should have a chance to be educated.	1	2	3	4	5
24. Nose rings are ok.	1	2	3	4	5
25. Tattoos are ok on any part of the body.	1	2	3	4	5
26. Using profanity to express one's self.	1	2	3	4	5
27. Having more than one wife at a time.	1	2	3	4	5
28. Having "barn yard" animals live in your home.	1	2	3	4	5
29. Believing that all citizens have a right to know "the truth" about what its government does.	1	2	3	4	5
30. Showing no emotions to others.	1	2	3	4	5
31. Having healthy self-esteem.	1	2	3	4	5
32. Believing in fate.	1	2	3	4	5
33. Believing that the arrangement of furniture in your home can help determine your health and happiness.	1	2	3	4	5
34. Always finish what you start regardless of the cost or consequences.	1	2	3	4	5
35. Hard work is more important than fun.	1	2	3	4	5
36. Honesty is always the best policy.	1	2	3	4	5
37. Participating in a nomadic lifestyle.	1	2	3	4	5
38. Mercy or honor killing.	1	2	3	4	5
39. Marrying children under the age of 16.	1	2	3	4	5
40. Lying to protect someone's feelings.	1	2	3	4	5

one's own culture and that one's own culture has very little of value to offer. Some people use xenocentrism as an "overcorrection" for their ethnocentrism. This can be just as dangerous as ethnocentrism because once again, we cut ourselves off from learning from everyone and everything we encounter. All people, places, cultures, religions, races, genders, and orientations have something to offer. This does not mean that we have to accept and embrace every notion, but being an educated citizen does mean learning to listen, evaluate, analyze, and then make our decisions.

Take a few moments to complete Figure 2.3 on the previous page. As you consider each statement, respond as honestly as possible.

Analysis:

Now that you have circled a response for each statement, work with a group of students in your class or online to determine how your answers are different from or similar to theirs. This can be of significance when your responses vary by at least two numbers on the scale. (Example: If you responded with a 5 on #30 and your partner(s) responded with a 1, this is a major difference.) After you have discussed your responses with each other, write a brief statement about what conclusions can be drawn from this experience.

BLOOM LEVEL 4
QUESTION

_____

_____

_____

_____

LIVING AND LEARNING IN THE BRAVE NEW WORLD

What Are the Dimensions of Diversity?

Among the kinds of diversity you might encounter are race, religion, gender, age, ethnic group, nationality, cultural, sexual orientation, social class, geographic region, and physical challenges. It is important for you to become open and accepting of individuals in all categories of diversity. The most significant thing you can do is to think of people who are different from you as individuals, not as groups. Some people need to make bigger changes in their overall belief systems than others; it all depends on what kind of background they come from and what experiences they have had. An explanation of some major types of diversity follows.

Racial Diversity

What have you learned about a culture other than your own since beginning your studies?

Racism is a prejudicial feeling that exists when an individual has a negative attitude about any race or ethnic group. Racism can be institutionalized in actions such as racial profiling or refusing to hire certain races except for menial manual labor. It can also mean that certain races are charged higher interest rates when borrowing money or have to pay more for an automobile than another race. Racist language usually implies that one group of people or an individual is inferior in some way to others. In many cases, races that are discriminated against have been relegated to inferior positions in society due to economic and political oppression.

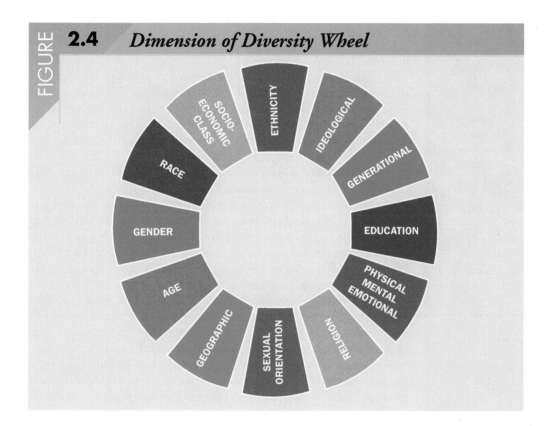

FIGURE 2.4 *Dimension of Diversity Wheel*

Religious Diversity

Many types of religions are practiced in this country and around the world. Ranging from orthodox practices that have been in place for hundreds of years to newly formed "cults," people who practice each of these forms of worship are sensitive to unkind remarks about their beliefs. There are actually three major beliefs people have about other religions: *exclusivism*, *inclusivism*, and *pluralism*. Those who believe in exclusivism think that other faiths are in grave error and often view them as opponents. Those who practice inclusivism believe that other faiths have some truth in them, but are only partly developed. Finally, those who believe in pluralism think that all faiths are legitimate and valid—when viewed from within their particular cultures.

The biggest problem, quite simply, is that people tend to believe their religion is the only right one and is superior to all others. Such a position can also be dangerous, as wars frequently break out over religious differences. The terrible events that took place in the United States on September 11, 2001, when the World Trade Center and Pentagon were attacked, were perpetrated by individuals who no doubt believed they were martyring themselves in the name of their religion. You live in a country where you are free to worship as you choose. We must all expand our worldviews to the point that we can allow others the same choice without judging them in a negative manner and without engaging in hate crimes against others because of their beliefs.

Tips for Personal Success

Consider the following tips for dealing with cultural diversity as you meet new and different kinds of people:

▶ Keep an open mind and don't make assumptions about people.

▶ Don't let your prejudices from the past interfere with your being an open-minded person.

▶ Make a point every day of talking to people who have different backgrounds from you.

Now it is your turn. Name three more tips that you would give a fellow classmate who is trying to enlarge his or her personal community of friends.

1. _____

2. _____

3. _____

Gender Diversity

Since the '60s and the Women's Rights Movement, women in this country have made steady gains toward being treated as equals to men, although there are still biases to be found among some institutions and, certainly, among some individuals. The fact that Hillary Clinton was a strong contender for the 2008 Democratic Party presidential nomination and that Sarah Palin was named the Republican vice presidential candidate highlights the fact that women have made significant gains. There is still a large number of **men and women**, however, who will make the statement, "I just can't vote for a woman for president."

"Cross-cultural research indicates that gender roles are among the first that individuals learn and that all societies treat males differently from females. . . . What is considered natural behavior for each gender is based more on cultural belief than on biological necessity" (Slavin, 2009). Just a few years ago, boys were expected to grow up and be masculine and to pursue certain types of careers while girls were expected to be *feminine* and perhaps pursue roles as homemakers, nurses, or teachers. Many of the women who ventured out and did become involved in the business or academic world ran up against the "glass ceiling." Today men and women are attending college in record numbers, with more women actually in attendance than men. Although dramatic progress has been made to improve gender bias, there is still some confusion regarding "women's roles" as well as stigma attached to certain careers for men such as nursing.

What are your personal feelings about diverse groups of people succeeding in areas where there were previous limitations?

Age Diversity

In your college classes, you are likely to find people ranging in age from 16 to 90. In fact, a large percentage of college students today are nontraditional students (24 and older), as many adults continue their educations and return to college to study in entirely new fields. Large numbers of older people return to college to take classes simply for enjoyment after they retire. You might very well find an older person on one of your teams. Certainly, when you enter the workforce, you will immediately be thrust into a community with people of all ages.

Older people are very much like you underneath their skin, which naturally looks older than that of typical 18-year-olds. They want to be treated with respect; they want to laugh and have fun; they want to see the latest movies; they are likely to enjoy sporting events; and they want to be included in discussions. The college years provide you a great opportunity to start learning to relate well to older people. You might find that some of the most helpful and valuable people in your classes are much older than you; certainly, there will be people of all ages when you enter the workplace. The fastest-growing group of people in this country consists of those age 85 and older.

Ethnic Diversity

The word *ethnic* is derived from the Greek word *ethnos,* meaning "nation," and some people refer to ethnic groups simply by the country from which they originated. Scholars don't always agree on exactly what constitutes an ethnic group. Some consider an ethnic group to be a social group that is typically distinguished by race, religion, or national origin. These groups may be identified by distinguishing features and physical characteristics. But in some cases, they can be identified by their religion or language when physical differences do not exist. Ethnicity might simply mean national origin to others. According to Feagin and Feagin (2008), an ethnic group is "a group socially distinguished or set apart, by others or by itself, primarily on the basis of cultural or national-origin characteristics."

Sexual Orientation

According to the American Psychological Association, sexual orientation "refers to an enduring pattern of emotional, romantic, and/or sexual attractions to men, women, or both sexes. Sexual orientation also refers to a person's sense of identity based on those attractions, related behaviors, and a membership in a community of others who share those attractions. . . . There is no consensus among scientists about the exact reasons that an individual develops a heterosexual, bisexual, gay, or lesbian orientation. Some think that both nature and nurture play complex roles" (2008). The conclusion, however, is that most people experience little or no sense of choice about their sexual orientation. "Most scientific thinking holds that one's sexuality is genetically determined rather than being a matter of choice" (DeVito, 2008).

Regardless of one's sexual orientation, a person needs to have a positive self-image and good mental health regarding his or her sexuality. It is a great misconception to assume that people of different sexual orientations have different goals and values than any other group. "Research shows that the factors that influence relationship satisfaction, commitment, and stability are remarkably similar for both same-sex cohabiting couples and heterosexual married couples" (American Psychological Association, 2008). So the truth is that there are very intelligent, engaging, attractive people of all sexual orientations—people who can become good friends and colleagues if you are open to expanding your views.

> ### ESSENTIAL CORNERSTONE
>
> **Adaptability:**
> How can learning about different types of diversity help you become more adaptable in a changing workplace?
>
> **Social Networking Moment:**
> Share your response to this Essential Cornerstone with peers in your social network. Choose two responses from your peers and respond to their postings.

Social Class Diversity

Socioeconomic status or social class can be defined using the parameters of a person's income, education level, type of work he or she does, and family heritage. Someone may have social status because his grandfather was a U.S. senator, but he may still not have great wealth. In this country when class is discussed, this terminology is generally used: upper class (wealthy), middle class (people who have jobs requiring considerable education or who own businesses that afford them a certain level of income), and lower class (people who are unemployed or hold very low-level jobs that do not provide them with a good standard of living).

If you follow our advice and consider people as individuals rather than as part of a class, you will probably meet some really great people from all classes. Wealth and status certainly provide opportunities and advantages not enjoyed by everyone, but you can find outstanding people in all classes to include in your personal community.

> What do you think a person who is older than you can teach you about "the world?"

Generational Diversity

While you may have heard of many different types of diversity, you are less likely to have been informed about generational diversity. More than likely, you know that different generations have been labeled with names such as the "Traditionals," the "Boomers, "Generation X," and the current generation, which is referred to as the "Millennials." For the first time, four distinctly different generations, each with its own loyalties, priorities, and expectations, are working side by side in the workplace (Glenn, 2007). Naturally, with such a wide range of ages, there are conflicts over how work should be completed, what constitutes company loyalty, how many hours one should work after closing time, and how best to communicate.

You may very well work with an older person from the "Traditional" generation, who is very focused on a team approach and less focused on the individual. In the same group, you will have a "Boomer," who believes strongly in visibility or face time at the office and equates that as time spent working. Your team might include a member of "Generation X," who believes that his time is as important as money and that it doesn't matter if he works overtime as long as he does the job and does it well. Members of your own generation—if you are a traditional-age, first-year student—might be focused on technology and finding a job that makes them happy.

Geographic Region Diversity

As strange as it may seem, there are some who are prejudiced against people from certain geographic regions in this country. It is true that there are people in all parts of our country who have ideas that are very different from those of the masses; however, we should not label an entire section of the country based on the actions of a few from that part of the country. In the case of geographic regions, as in all cases, one should determine the characteristics of an individual beyond her or his belonging to the group of those who live in a certain part of the country. You might find that a friend from California could open up all kinds of new ideas and thinking for you, or that a friend from the South could show you beautiful beaches and golf courses, or that a friend from New York could introduce you to Broadway or Central Park. As you expand your personal community of friends, make a special effort to get to know people from other regions of the country and learn to consider their unique characteristics rather than focus on where they come from.

What is the biggest ideological difference you have had with someone on campus?

"Everything we shut our eyes to, everything we run away from, everything we deny, denigrate or despise, serves to defeat us in the end. What seems nasty, painful, and evil, can become a source of beauty, joy, and strength, if faced with an open mind."
—Henry Miller

Physical, Mental, and Emotional Diversity

You will encounter a number of students who deal with physical, mental, and emotional challenges. They could be visually impaired or deaf or confined to a wheelchair. Quite a few college students suffer from depression and others battle bipolar disorders. Research shows that 49.2% of all students experience some kind of learning disability such as dyslexia. We tend to assume, for instance, that students who are labeled legally blind cannot see, when, in fact, 80% can read large- or regular-print books. They may have a problem in only one eye. Truthfully, these students are just like everyone else except that they have a physical problem that makes life a little more difficult. They have feelings just like the rest of us; they want to be included in social life and activities; and they don't want to be treated as disabled, different, and unable to participate. You might consider getting to know a physically, mentally, or emotionally challenged person and bringing this person into your social network.

Ideological Diversity

The fact that we all have different opinions and ideas that are rooted in our family backgrounds, socioeconomic status, religious beliefs, cultural experiences, political beliefs, educational levels, and travel experiences creates great diversity and can cause difficulties among individuals and groups of people. "Individuals tend to come to more extreme views if they deliberate a given issue with like-minded people" (Kallock, 2008). In other words, internal diversity among individuals tends to be squelched by the forces of group polarization. People tend to remain moderate when expressing their beliefs, until they are confident that they are among others who agree with them, and then they tend to become more extreme in their beliefs. These personal beliefs create diversity in thoughts, reasoning, ideas, and creativity. Political beliefs, for example, can be quite polarizing among individuals and groups. As an educated, enlightened individual, you will need to practice patience and understanding of other people's viewpoints and why they believe them even when you are diametrically opposed to those beliefs.

SEEING THE WORLD WITH CLEAR EYES

Why Is Having an Open Mind So Powerful?

As you seek to develop an open mind and become an educated citizen, you need to be aware of the terms **discrimination** and **prejudice**. If you discriminate against someone, you negatively judge that person on the basis of the group or class to which he or she belongs, rather than according to merit. For example, you might discriminate against a person who is highly qualified for a job, because he is of a certain race or religion, and ignore his qualifications. Prejudice, on the other hand, is an unreasonable opinion or feeling formed beforehand or without knowledge, thought, or reason; it is a preconceived opinion of a hostile nature regarding a racial, religious, or national group (Webster's College Dictionary, 1995).

If you discriminate against someone, it is because you are prejudiced against him or her due to preconceived ideas that are based on insufficient knowledge, irrational feelings, or inaccurate stereotypes. As you can see, prejudice is usually not based on reason or knowledge but on opinions most likely shaped by someone who influenced you or by a region of the country where you grew up. Finally, prejudice is not an illegal act, whereas discrimination in many cases is an illegal act. Discrimination is illegal in employment, housing, loans, and many other areas outlined in the Civil Rights Act of 1964.

To experience other people and to receive the benefits of knowing someone, you need to enter all relationships with an open mind. If you have a derogatory mind-set toward a race, an ethnic group, a sexual orientation, or a religion, for example, you have internal barriers that can keep you from getting to know who a person really is.

Distinguish between prejudice and discrimination by giving examples of each in the space below:

_____

_____

_____

_____

DID YOU KNOW

DITH PRAN was born in 1942 in Cambodia. He learned English and French and worked for the U.S. government as a translator, he also had jobs with a British film crew and as a hotel receptionist. In 1975, after meeting a *New York Times* reporter, he taught himself how to take photographs.

After U.S. forces left Cambodia, he stayed behind to cover the fall of Phnom Penh to the communist Khmer Rouge. Having stayed behind, he was forced to remain while foreign reporters were allowed to leave. From this point, Dith witnessed many atrocities and had to hide the fact that he was educated or knew some Americans. He pretended to be a taxicab driver.

Cambodians were forced to work in labor camps and Dith was not immune from this. He endured four years of starvation and torture before Vietnam overthrew the Khmer Rouge and he escaped the camp. He coined the term "The Killing Fields" because of the number of dead bodies he encountered during his escape. He later learned that his three brothers and 50 other members of his family had been killed during the genocide.

Dith escaped to Thailand in 1979, fearing for his life because of his association with Americans and his knowledge of what had happened in Cambodia. He moved to the United States in 1980. In 1984, the movie *The Killing Fields,* detailing the horrors and triumphs of his life, was released. He died of pancreatic cancer in 2008.

BLOOM LEVEL 4 QUESTION

CHANGING IDEAS TO *Reality*

As a college student, you have an opportunity to make many new changes as you build a personal community of friends. You can have relationships with people from all over the world, people who espouse and embrace many ideas that are different from what you had been exposed to in the past. You can learn almost as much from this diverse population of students and peers as you learn from the lessons in the classroom. If you will open up your heart and mind to all of the possibilities, you will leave college a much more enlightened and interesting person than you were when you arrived. Perhaps this opportunity to experience such a great variety of people, ideas, and cultures is the most important aspect of a college education.

College will provide you an opportunity to expand your horizons and to change in many different ways. Here you will have classes with people from all over the world and from many regions of this country. Some of your fellow students will not only speak and dress differently; they will also most likely have different religions, beliefs, customs, values, and experiences. Instead of closing out those people who are different from you, embrace new and different cultures. While you don't have to be just like these new people, you are certain to learn to appreciate and benefit from the relationships.

Remember, we are motivated by what we value. As you continue on in the semester and work toward personal and professional growth and change, consider the following ideas:

▶ Examine your personal values and beliefs to determine if you need to make cultural adjustments.

▶ Listen to people and try to understand them before you form opinions about them.

▶ Stand up against intolerance and bigotry of any kind.

▶ Help others understand the importance of organizing against hate crimes.

▶ Develop relationships with people from a variety of backgrounds.

▶ Learn to appreciate and celebrate differences.

▶ Maintain close friendships with people who share your values and beliefs and with people who bring new and different ideas to the mix.

"To be nobody but yourself—in a world which is doing its best, night and day, to make you like everybody else—means to fight the hardest battle which any human being can fight, and never stop fighting."

—e. e. cummings

KNOWLEDGE *in* BLOOM

Cultural Research and Understanding Project

Each chapter-end assessment is based on *Bloom's Taxonomy of Learning.* See the inside front cover for a quick review.

UTILIZES LEVELS 1–6 OF THE TAXONOMY

Level 1 Question: Identify one culture, subculture, or religion that you are not a part of that you would like to research. You may use interviews, books, journals, the Internet, or newspapers as your resources.

The culture, subculture, or religion that I have chosen is: _____

I chose this topic because: _____

_____

_____

_____

Level 2 Question: What are the facts that you learned through researching this topic?

_____

_____

_____

_____

_____

_____

What is one value that this culture or religion embraces?

_____

_____

_____

_____

_____

_____

_____

Level 3 Question: Prepare a statement that identifies one thing that people from this culture or religion believe that is different from what you have been taught.

_____

_____

_____

_____

_____

Level 4 Question: Analyze the characteristics of the culture or religion you are researching and compare them to the characteristics of your own culture or religion.

_____
_____
_____
_____
_____
_____
_____

Level 5 Question: Determine what your opinions are of this religion or culture and justify your reasons for having these opinions.

_____
_____
_____
_____
_____
_____

Level 6 Question: After conducting your research, prepare a brief presentation with at least five positive points that you can share with your classmates about the religion or culture you studied. List the five points here.

_____
_____
_____
_____
_____
_____

SQ3R *Mastery* STUDY SHEET

EXAMPLE QUESTION: *(from page 35)* Define ethnocentrism.	**ANSWER:**
EXAMPLE QUESTION: *(from pages 40–41)* What is the difference between age and generational diversity?	**ANSWER:**
AUTHOR QUESTION: *(from page 34)* What does globalization have to do with diversity appreciation?	**ANSWER:**
AUTHOR QUESTION: *(from page 38)* Identify and discuss three different cultural dimensions.	**ANSWER:**
AUTHOR QUESTION: *(from page 36)* Define xenocentrism	**ANSWER:**
AUTHOR QUESTION: *(from page 43)* What is the difference between discrimination and prejudice?	**ANSWER:**
AUTHOR QUESTION: *(from page 43)* Why is it important to have an open mind?	**ANSWER:**
YOUR QUESTION: *(from page ___)*	**ANSWER:**
YOUR QUESTION: *(from page ___)*	**ANSWER:**
YOUR QUESTION: *(from page ___)*	**ANSWER:**
YOUR QUESTION: *(from page ___)*	**ANSWER:**
YOUR QUESTION: *(from page ___)* Finally, after answering these questions, recite this chapter's major points in your mind. Consider the following general questions to help you master this material.	**ANSWER:**

▶ What was it about?
▶ What does it mean?
▶ What was the most important thing I learned? Why?
▶ What are the key points to remember?

CHAPTER 3
CHALLENGES TO COMMUNICATION

OBJECTIVES

Studying this chapter will allow you to:

- ► Explain three types of needs we seek to satisfy through communication.
- ► Understand the process and strategies involved in saving face when confronted with failed expectations.
- ► Define several types of deception: equivocation, concealment, half-truths, diversions, and lies.
- ► Explain the difference between aggressive and assertive messages.
- ► Identify ways for a listener to improve understanding.
- ► Identify ways for a speaker to improve representation.
- ► Discuss various methods of managing conflict.

Scenario 1: The discussion during a group meeting has grown very heated. Everyone is tired, and the group does not seem to be getting anywhere. You suggest that the group adjourn and start fresh the next day. Another group member immediately chastises you, saying. "You're an idiot!! You've made no contributions the whole time, and now you try to boss us around. What a jerk you are." You shout back that the other person is an idiot and that you have been listening very closely to what is going on. You continue that your being quiet doesn't mean you can't suggest that the group adjourn. You turn to the other group members to see their reactions.

Scenario 2: Your boss asks you to help a new employee, Chris, learn some of the procedures that need to be followed on the job. You explain to Chris in great detail how things work. While you talk, Chris nods understandingly but says little. You ask Chris if she understands what you've said. She says, "Yeah, I, um, think so." A week later your boss complains to you that you did a poor job of training Chris. Chris has not followed any of the procedures correctly. You are exasperated.

Scenario 3: You and a friend decide to go out Saturday night. You are ready to go at eight, but your friend has not shown up. Around half past nine, your friend calls and says he's at a party and can't get away; he'll see you Monday. On Monday, you tell your friend that you no longer want to be friends. He asks why. You start telling him how selfish and immature he is, but he interrupts and claims that you are being unreasonable. For an hour you go back and forth, arguing about what happened and about the future of the relationship. Eventually, your friend apologizes and vows to be more diligent in following through on commitments. You accept the apology and express your willingness to continue the friendship.

Earlier chapters offered seven reasons why we communicate. The first reason was to satisfy needs. Each of the three scenarios represents a different kind of challenge that we encounter in our effort to satisfy three particular types of needs: identity, instrumental, and relational.[1]

Satisfying **identity needs** involves using communication to present who you are to other people, to have that presented self accepted and confirmed by other people, and to confirm other people's identities. Rejection of a presented self thwarts your effort to satisfy your identity needs. In the first scenario, your identity needs are challenged by the group member who criticizes you and calls you names. Your "face" is being threatened by what the other group member has declared about you. People often respond to attacks with counterattacks and attempts to defend or justify their behaviors. Sometimes people even lie. You can address the challenge of dealing with aggressive behavior, attacks to your face, and lying by improving your communication skills.

The second scenario reflects communication that is used to meet **instrumental needs**—that is, to accomplish a task or perform a job. However, the new employee does not understand your instructions, and so the task is not performed correctly. Even though you ask if she understands you, Chris probably does not want her face threatened by having to admit that she doesn't understand. She wouldn't want to threaten your face either by telling you that your explanation isn't clear. In general, we are able to satisfy our instrumental needs through understanding and through effective use of persuasive strategies. However, satisfying instrumental needs can be hampered by problems in perception, listening, expressing ideas, and strategic decisions.

The third scenario focuses on satisfying your need for healthy relationships. Communication is used to satisfy **relational needs** through the management of relationships from initiation to termination. In this scenario, communication is used to maintain the relationship by effectively managing a conflict. This involves satisfying both your identity and your relational needs. Ineffective use of communication, on the other hand, can intensify conflicts.

These scenarios reflect the types of challenges we must deal with in our interactions with other people. Knowing how to communicate effectively can help us resolve many problems and satisfy our needs. However, communication can also be a problem in and of itself or can worsen a problem. One popular myth is that we could solve all our problems with other people if we would just sit down and talk. Indeed, there are some problems that can be helped by constructive communication. However, there are also times when communication is the wrong action to take.

For instance, if you are having a major fight with a friend, it might be best to retreat awhile, cool down, and distance yourselves from the situation. If you continue to talk, you both might regret things spoken in a fit of anger. Communication has to be used strategically to be effective. Knowing *when* to say something is just as important as knowing *how* to say it.

This chapter will examine a variety of factors that inhibit our ability to satisfy our needs. To use communication effectively to satisfy our needs, we must overcome the challenges created by threats to our face, by misunderstandings and misrepresentations, and by conflict. By the end of this chapter, you will have gained a variety of suggestions on how to recognize and adapt to such communication challenges.

THE CHALLENGE OF MAINTAINING FACE

Each time you communicate with other people, you present a conception of yourself (face), and you seek confirmation and acceptance of that presented self.[2] As you stand in front of an audience to give a presentation, for example, you have a particular image you are trying to convey. You want the audience to confirm and accept that image. You probably want to be seen as intelligent, articulate, informed, and likable. What happens, though, when you get lost in the middle of your presentation? You start muttering and apologizing as you search for your next point. You feel embarrassed by your behavior.

In situations like this, you have threatened your own face; that is, you have displayed behaviors that contradict the image you were trying to present. Apologies are a way of helping us **save face,** that is, restore the image that we were originally trying to convey. In our example, you find your place in the speech again and continue on, trying to do better and forget what happened. When you finish your presentation, the audience applauds, and your friends tell you that you did a great job and that they found the presentation very informative.

Why do your listeners make a point of complimenting you and ignoring your stumbles? Because, generally, other people will try to help us **maintain face** by providing support, confirmation, and acceptance of the self-conception we are presenting. Some of the ways people can help us maintain face involve expressions of understanding, friendly advice, pardons, compassion, offers of help, and laughing with us.[3] By not raising the issue of your getting lost in the middle of your presentation, your listeners are helping you maintain your image as an articulate and intelligent speaker. Obviously, this example depends on your having a self-concept that includes being articulate and intelligent. If that is not how you think of yourself, getting lost in the speech might not be a threat to your face.

There are times when rather than helping us maintain our face, people threaten and challenge it. Face-threatening acts include name-calling, arguing, disapproval, criticism, ridicule, teasing, insults, accusations, disagreements, contradictions, reprimands, complaints, blatant noncooperation, threats, orders, and ignoring. However, when people make face-threatening statements, they put their own face on the line as well. For example, suppose I accuse you of not turning in an assignment, but in fact you did turn it in and I simply misplaced it. My accusation threatens your face, and you are likely to try to save face by a strong declaration that you turned in the assignment. By accusing you, I have put my face on the line—my self-concept of being a diligent and fair instructor. After finding your paper, I have to come back to you and admit my error, which causes me to lose some face. I will probably present some excuse for my error in an attempt to minimize my loss of face.

One way we protect ourselves from face threats is to use powerless language. We can "waffle" a bit in presenting our face, so it becomes more difficult to threaten. Statements like "I might be wrong, but. . . . " or "I think, maybe, we could do it this way" are a way of presenting an idea without commitment or ownership. If someone says, "No, we shouldn't do it that way," we can save face by saying, "Yeah, I didn't think that was the best way either."

The audience's positive reaction to the speaker helps the person maintain a positive face.

We can also indicate that we are aware of a social code and ask for indulgence while we violate it.[4] My family has a rule about not burping loudly at the table. One of my sons is particularly adept at shaking the walls with his belches. He knows the rule and abides by it; however, he occasionally asks permission to violate the rule and let it rip, which is sometimes granted. He knows that if he did not ask permission and just belched loudly, he would be acting impolitely and disrespectfully, which is not the face he wishes to present.

Failure Events

Human communication and interactions are filled with expectations about behaviors. Failing to fulfill an obligation or expectation produces a **failure event.**[5] Failure events relate to communication in two ways: First, failure events occur in your communication behavior; and second, communication can be used as a tool for managing failure events.

Imagine that your boss expects you to deliver a well-prepared presentation to a group of managers. When you are ill prepared, it is a failure event. Your friends expect that when you say you will help decorate for a party, you will be there. Not showing up is a failure event. So what will you do in these two failure events? Part of your reaction depends on the other people. You may choose not to say or do anything if your boss or friends don't mention your failure. On the other hand, if you know that the other people are really upset, you may choose not to wait for them to say something—you may raise the issue yourself and apologize.

Failure events involve threats to people's face, and the management of failure events is an exercise in "face work." Giving an ill-prepared presentation could reflect an image of some-

ASK YOURSELF

Cultures differ in terms of the importance of face. Think about your own cultural background. How important is it in your culture to save face and to help others do so? What factors in your upbringing have influenced the way you think about face?

Compare your thoughts with those of your classmates. To what degree do you find differences by race, sex, age, or hometown?

one who is unprofessional and incompetent, and thus it would threaten your face (unless that's how you want to be perceived). Your boss's face is also threatened by your action. Your boss's abilities to make decisions, judge personnel, and manage effectively are undermined by your performance.

It is challenging to resolve such situations while preserving both parties' face. Sometimes one person's face is maintained through the loss of the other person's face.[6] Apologizing to your boss helps your boss maintain face but causes some loss of face for you. Potentially, neither of you would suffer a loss of face if your reason for being ill prepared was out of your control, such as a computer crash that destroyed all your material right before your presentation.

REPROACHES

A failure event may be followed by a reproach. A **reproach** is an indication by someone (usually the person toward whom the failure event is directed) that a failure event has occurred. The reproach can be either implicit or directly stated.

Reproaches fall along a continuum from mitigating to aggravating.[7] A **mitigating reproach** reflects only mild irritation with the failure event (for instance, stating rather matter-of-factly, "I thought you were going to be here ten minutes ago"). An **aggravating reproach** is a severe, intense declaration of the occurrence of a failure event (such as loudly stating, "Once again, you've kept me waiting! Do you think I don't have anything better to do? You are so irresponsible!").

ACCOUNTS

Usually, a reproach is followed by an account. An **account** is a stated response to a reproach by the person accused of the failure event. Early researchers identified five types of accounts: apology, excuse (the most common), justification, denial, and silence.[8]

- ▶ An **apology** is a statement in which the person admits the failure event, accepts responsibility for it, and expresses regret.

- ▶ An **excuse** reflects an admission that the failure event occurred but contends that nothing could have been done to prevent it (because, for example, it occurred through unfortunate circumstances).

- ▶ **Justification** involves accepting responsibility for the failure event but then trying to redefine the event as not being a failure.

- ▶ **Denial** involves stating that a failure event never took place.

- ▶ **Providing no account,** or **silence**, occurs when an individual either offers no response or ignores the reproach by changing the subject.

Examples of these five types of accounts are given in Table 3.1. Which of the accounts do you think would create the most negative reaction from a reproacher? Which would evoke the most positive reaction?

Like reproaches, accounts can be placed on a continuum of mitigating to aggravating. Table 3.1 lists them in this order, with apology being the most mitigating and silence, or no account, the most aggravating. There is also a connection between how aggravating an account is and how threatening it is to each participant's face. For example, an apology causes the greatest loss of face for the accounter while preserving the most face for the reproacher. Silence, on the other hand, protects the accounter's face the most, but represents the greatest threat to the reproacher's face.[9] In general, mitigating reproaches are likely to evoke mitigating accounts, while aggravating reproaches are likely to evoke aggravating accounts.[10]

Maintaining Face:
Sex Differences in Communication Styles

A popular author of gender and communication texts, Deborah Tannen explains some of the differences in the way men and women respond to face-threatening situations such as apologizing, fighting, and criticism. As you read this article, see if the descriptions match the way you read to these face-threatening situations.

Unfortunately, women and men often have different ideas about what's appropriate, different ways of speaking. Many of the conversational rituals common among women are designed to take the other person's feelings into account, while many of the conversational rituals common among men are designed to maintain the one-up position, or at least avoid appearing one-down. As a result, when men and women interact—especially at work—it's often women who are at the disadvantage. Because women are not trying to avoid the one-down position, that is unfortunately where they may end up. Here are the biggest areas of miscommunication:

APOLOGIES

Women are often told they apologize too much. The reason they're told to stop doing it is that, to many men, apologizing seems synonymous with putting oneself down. But there are many times when "I'm sorry" isn't self-deprecating, or even an apology; it's an automatic way of keeping both speakers on an equal footing. For example, a well-known columnist once interviewed me and gave me her phone number in case I needed to call her back. I misplaced the number and had to go through the newspaper's main switchboard. When our conversation was winding down and we'd both made ending-type remarks, I added, "Oh, I almost forgot—I lost your direct number, can I get it again?" "Oh, I'm sorry," she came back instantly, even though she had done nothing wrong and I was the one who'd lost the number. But I understood she wasn't really apologizing; she was just automatically reassuring me she had no intention of denying me her number.

Even when "I'm sorry" is an apology, women often assume it will be the first step in a two-step ritual: I say "I'm sorry" and take half the blame, then you take the other half. At work, it might go something like this:

A: When you typed this letter, you missed this phrase I inserted.

B: Oh, I'm sorry. I'll fix it.

A: Well, I wrote it so small it was easy to miss.

When both parties share blame, it's a mutual face-saving device. But if one person, usually the woman, utters frequent apologies and the other doesn't, she ends up looking as if she's taking the blame for mishaps that aren't her fault. When she's only partially to blame, she looks entirely in the wrong. . . .

Unfortunately, not apologizing can have its price too. Since so many women use ritual apologies, those who don't may be seen as hard-edged. What's important is to be aware of how often you say you're sorry (and why), and to monitor your speech based on the reaction you get.

(continued)

Maintaining Face:
Sex Differences in Communication Styles

CRITICISM

A woman who co-wrote a report with a male colleague was hurt when she read a rough draft to him and he leapt into a critical response—"Oh, that's too dry! You have to make it snappier!" She herself would have been more likely to say, "That's a really good start. Of course, you'll want to make it a little snappier when you revise."

Whether criticism is given straight or softened is often a matter of convention. In general, women use more softeners. I noticed this difference when talking to an editor about an essay I'd written. While going over changes she wanted to make, she said, "There's one more thing. I know you may not agree with me. The reason I noticed the problem is that your other points are so lucid and elegant." She went on hedging for several more sentences until I put her out of her misery: "Do you want to cut that part?" I asked—and of course she did. But I appreciated her tentativeness. In contrast, another editor (a man) I once called summarily rejected my idea for an article by barking, "Call me when you have something new to say."

Those who are used to ways of talking that soften the impact of criticism may find it hard to deal with the right-between-the-eyes style. It has its own logic, however, and neither style is intrinsically better. People who prefer criticism given straight are operating on an assumption that feelings aren't involved: "Here's the dope. I know you're good; you can take it." . . .

FIGHTING

Many men expect the discussion of ideas to be a ritual fight—explored through verbal opposition. They state their ideas in the strongest possible terms, thinking that if there are weaknesses someone will point them out, and by trying to argue against those objections, they will see how well their ideas hold up.

Those who expect their own ideas to be challenged will respond to another's ideas by trying to poke holes and find weak links—as a way of helping. The logic is that when you are challenged you will rise to the occasion: Adrenaline makes your mind sharper; you get ideas and insights you would not have thought of without the spur of battle.

But many women take this approach as a personal attack. Worse, they find it impossible to do their best work in such a contentious environment. If you're not used to ritual fighting, you begin to hear criticism of your ideas as soon as they are formed. Rather than making you think more clearly, it makes you doubt what you know. When you state your ideas, you hedge in order to fend off potential attacks. Ironically, this is more likely to invite attack because it makes you look weak.

Although you may never enjoy verbal sparring, some women find it helpful to learn how to do it. An engineer who was the only woman among four men in a small company found that as soon as she learned to argue she was accepted and taken seriously. . . .

THERE IS NO "RIGHT" WAY TO TALK. When problems arise, the culprit may be style differences—and all styles will at times fail with others who don't share or understand them, just as English won't do you much good if you try to speak to someone who knows only French. If you want to get your message across, it's not a question of being "right"; it's a question of using language that's shared—or at least understood.

Source: Deborah Tannen, Excerpted from Deborah Tannen, *Talking from 9 to 5: How Women's and Men's Conversational Styles Affect Who Gets Heard, Who Gets Credit, and What Gets Done at Work* (New York: William Morrow, 1994). Text: Copyright © 1994 by Deborah Tannen. By permission of William Morrow and Company, Inc.

TABLE

3.1 *Examples of the Five Types of Accounts*

Reproach: *"Your presentation today really needs some work. You didn't seem very prepared."*

Apology	"You're right. I'm sorry. I've already got some ideas for improving it."
Excuse	"Yeah, I know. My computer crashed while I was putting together my notes. I lost a lot of what I was planning to use."
Justification	"Well, I had a choice: finish the research report that the president wanted, or prepare for this presentation. You know how the president feels about late reports."
Denial	"Hey, everybody else seemed to like it. I think it went really well."
No account	"So next week we're going to be working on that new computer project, right?"

THE GIVE-AND-TAKE OF FAILURE EVENTS

After an account is given, it is up to the reproacher to decide whether the account is acceptable and whether to dismiss the failure event. When the account is rejected, we often try to provide another account. We might initially give an excuse for our failure event, but if the reproacher doesn't buy the excuse, we might decide to apologize. A give-and-take occurs that sometimes develops into a conflict.

Each party must decide how far to push his or her point of view. A number of factors influence this process, such as the perceived severity of the failure event, the importance of other issues (such as the relationship), and the consequences for future behavior.

EMBARRASSMENT

Sometimes we fail to meet our own expectations for our behaviors (we threaten our own face) and thus feel embarrassed.[11] For example, walking into class and spilling a can of soft drink all over the place means you have threatened your own face by appearing clumsy and uncoordinated. Research on how we manage embarrassing situations indicates that we use the account strategies already discussed, plus four additional strategies: humor, remediation, escape, and aggression:[12]

▶ *Humor* involves laughing off the issue or making light of it. After spilling your soft drink, you might say something like "I didn't really need the caffeine anyway."

▶ Through *remediation*, people make restitution, repair the damage, or simply re-collect themselves. Using this strategy, you might quickly get some paper towels and wipe up the spilled soda, particularly if no one else is around to know that you have made the mess.

▶ *Escape* allows people to distance themselves from the situation. If you were the only person in the room when you spilled the soft drink, you could use escape as a strategy by leaving the room and coming back later. Upon your return, you would act as if you didn't have anything to do with the spill.

▶ Finally, *aggression* involves a verbal or physical attack on the other people involved. You might lash out at the other students who watched you spill your drink: "What's the matter? Haven't you seen anybody spill something before?" A particularly aggressive response might be to knock over other students' drinks as a way of disguising the initial embarrassment.

ASK YOURSELF

Think about a recent significant event in which you failed to meet someone else's expectations and were reproached. How did the other person reproach you? How did this reproach affect you, and what account did you give?

How else might the other person have reproached you, and in that case, how would you have reacted?

MANAGING FAILURE EVENTS AND EMBARRASSMENT

Your communication interactions are filled with failure events and embarrassing situations. Understanding the likely patterns in these events can help you use communication to manage them better.

You can handle failure events better if you appreciate, for example, how your reproaches affect other people. If you threaten a person's face too aggressively, you are unlikely to gain admission of guilt, apology, or restitution. Thus, you need to consider what your goal is in reproaching the other person. Reproaches can be used to correct behavior that you find inappropriate, unsatisfactory, or damaging. But reproaches that are presented simply to belittle the other person are unproductive and can ultimately backfire.

Likewise, in providing an account to another person, you should examine your culpability. You should also consider the reproacher's objectives and desires so that you can understand his or her reason for the reproach. Sometimes it is best simply to admit your failure and make a genuine effort to correct it.

In many situations, unfortunately, attempts to save face lead to lying or deceit. You might create false excuses or justifications to gain acceptance of your account and get yourself off the hook. In the next section, we'll look at different types of deception and some of the reasons people resort to them.

Deception

One of the unique characteristics of human communication is that we can manipulate symbols and create messages that are false, misleading, and deceptive. We cannot believe everything we hear, and consequently we must evaluate messages for their veracity. Guarding against deception in communication is a regretful necessity.

Deception can be thought of as the intentional disguising, avoiding, hiding, or falsifying of the truth. There are a number of types of deceptive communication, including equivocation, concealment (secrets), half-truths, diversions, and lies.

EQUIVOCATION

Given the ambiguity of language, messages are often equivocal—that is, suggestive of more than one interpretation. The term equivocation, however, adds the sense of intention, or purpose. **Equivocation** involves purposely sending vague, unclear, or ambiguous messages.

Politicians are often stereotyped as exemplars of equivocation. The rest of us, too, use equivocation as a way of avoiding the truth, often because we are afraid of hurting another person's feelings. For example, a friend going out on a date asks you, "What do you think of my new outfit?" You think to yourself that the outfit is unflattering, but you don't want to threaten your friend's face. On the other hand, you don't want to threaten your own face by lying (after all, you have an honest relationship). So what do you say? You probably equivocate, saying something like "It's interesting." You are being deceptive because you are not disclosing your true reaction; however, you are not telling an outright lie if you think the outfit is indeed interesting.

Sometimes other people realize that we are sending ambiguous messages. In that case, they have two options. They can move on to another topic, realizing that we are trying to help them save face. Or they can ask us to give them more specific feedback. In the situation of your friend's new outfit, your friend may use a "disclaimer" that in essence gives you permission to threaten her face: "No, really, tell me what you think, I know this might not be my best look." At this point, you may be more "honest" but still try to limit the threat to your friend's face by saying something like "I think your blue jeans and navy blue sweater are a better look."

CONCEALMENT

In our example of equivocation, your response was meant to hide your true reaction to your friend's new outfit. A similar technique is **concealment,** which involves holding back information so that the other person reaches erroneous conclusions.

Suppose you are in an employment interview. As the interviewer examines your transcript, she comments, "Wow, you got an A in statistics, that's really good, we need people with good math and statistics skills." You remain silent, concealing the fact that the course involved hardly any math and that everyone in the class got an A because the instructor was an easy grader. This is deception by concealment.

HALF-TRUTHS

Half-truths are similar to concealment in that some information is withheld. **Half-truths** involve leaving out information or modifying or qualifying the message to lessen the impact or reaction. Suppose your computer crashes for an hour one night while you are working on a class assignment. After you get it running again, you decide to go out with some friends. The next day you tell your professor, "My computer crashed last night in the middle of working on today's assignment, so I don't have it done. Can I turn it in tomorrow?" Your statement is only half true; it is deceptive because you are intentionally trying to create the impression that the computer failure prevented you from finishing the assignment.

Some half-truths are created by qualifying. For example, a boss might mislead her employees about a cutback in funds that she knows is going to happen by saying, "I know some of you are upset about these proposed cutbacks, but you know, sometimes the company ends up not making the cuts, so don't panic."

DIVERSIONS

Sometimes deception involves simply dodging the matter. **Diversions** are attempts to change the focus of the communication to another topic to avoid discussing the issue at hand. After outlining a quality-control plan that requires employees to meet in groups to develop their ideas, a manager fields the following question: "Will we be meeting on company time or on our own time to discuss our ideas for improvements?" The manager uses diversion to respond: "That's a good question. There will be lots of opportunities to improve the production facilities, for example. . . ." The manager at first seemed willing to address the question, but actually diverted the answer to a side issue. The manager was hoping to deceive the listeners into believing that the question was answered.

Unless we are effective listeners, we might not even realize that someone hasn't responded to our query. And even if we do realize, we are usually hesitant to requestion the speaker after a diversion because that would challenge the speaker's face and potentially our own. How would you tactfully get someone who is using diversions back on track? Which of the following two follow-ups to the manager's response would be more effective?

A. "You didn't answer my question. Are we doing this on our own time or not?"

B. "I'm not sure I understood you. Are you saying we will be doing this on our own time?"

Statements that are qualified and that put the responsibility for misunderstanding on you rather than on the other person are less threatening to the other person. Therefore, option B would be the better choice.

LIES

Lies are probably viewed more negatively than any other form of deception because there is little doubt about the speaker's intention. **Lies** are the deliberate presentation of false information. Lies are probably the most common form of deception.[13] Lies take on many forms, and they are sometimes categorized by their degree of falseness or harm.

The term **white lie,** for instance, is used to describe a lie that is viewed as fairly close to the truth and fairly insignificant in its impact. Sometimes we lie as part of teasing, kidding, joking,

ASK YOURSELF

Think about an instance of deception you have engaged in recently. What type did you use? Why did you do it? What were the effects for you? What were the effects for the other person? Did you get caught?

bluffing, or playing a hoax. We kid others with statements like "You know those new CDs you lent me? Did you know they melt?" After watching for a horrified reaction, the "teaser" usually breaks out laughing and admits, "I was just kidding."

We also lie through exaggeration or embellishment, overstating the case or adding information that is inaccurate. The famous line in fishing, "You should have seen the one that got away—it was this big" (at which point the speaker's arms spread wide apart), is a good example of exaggeration. Exaggeration is generally used to emphasize a particular point, ensure the listener's attention, add credibility to a story, impress the listener, or heighten the effect. A narrow escape from a wild bear sounds much more exciting if the teller says the bear was only two feet away rather than admitting that it was thirty feet away.

Exaggerations are not to be taken lightly when the intention is to deceive and gain advantage over the listener. Commercials are monitored for false claims in which the value of a product is exaggerated. Almost every week an investigative report on *60 Minutes* or *20/20* details exaggerated claims for get-rich schemes or products such as miracle-cure mineral waters.

REASONS FOR DECEPTION

Research shows that deception is fairly pervasive in our communication.[14] Most of the time we use it for selfish reasons, such as the following:

▶ We sometimes use deception to gain or protect resources. Those resources can be material things, such as money or possessions. But resources can also include relationships and self-esteem.

▶ We might use deception to improve our ability to persuade or gain compliance from other people. One research study found distinct differences in the way truthful and deceptive persuaders tried to get something from someone.[15] Deceptive persuaders offered more explanations and rationales for granting the request than did the truthful persuaders. On the other hand, truthful persuaders were more likely to use reward or punishment as a means of persuasion.

▶ We use deception to protect ourselves. For instance, after a failure event, we might lie to save face. We might falsify information in our excuse or justification to reduce the damage to our face. We also try to protect ourselves by avoiding conflicts through deception. The manager who used diversion when responding to an employee's question was probably motivated by a desire to avoid conflict.

LEMONT BROWN *by Darrin Bell*

▶ We might use deception for our amusement. Deceptive teasing or kidding allows us to gain some pleasure from watching other people's reactions. The TV shows *Candid Camera* and *Bloopers* often involve filming people's reactions to a deceptive situation for the entertainment of the audience.

▶ Finally, we use deception to protect others (although there is often a degree of self-serving in such acts as well). For example, we might not reveal information to friends that we expect would upset or depress them.

DETECTING DECEPTION

Research on detecting deception has produced contradictory results.[16] Some research suggests that as relationships become more intimate, we develop a truth bias; that is, we are more apt to believe what we are told by those closest to us. One study found that being a participant in an interaction decreases our ability to detect deception as compared to those who simply observe the interaction.[17] In contrast, other researchers in a noninteractive study found that lovers could tell when their partners were lying 65 to 70 percent of the time.[18]

In some research studies, ironically, "experts" (such as military intelligence officers) were less accurate in determining truth than were novices.[19] Nonetheless, other research has found that deception detection training is sometimes effective. One study, evaluating a training program that had participants focus on six behavioral causes of deception, found that the training did increase the participants' accuracy in judging other people's statements.[20]

We do tend to give some clues when we are telling lies. **Leakages** are subtle behavioral changes that accompany deception. The degree to which these leakages occur depends on the level of anxiety felt by the deceiver: the less anxiety, the less leakage. This is one reason that lie detection machines are not infallible.

Leakages involve various types of behavior. Compared to nondeceivers, deceivers generally exhibit more adaptors (such as scratching, rubbing, picking, handling a pencil), hand gestures, and speech errors. Deceivers also pause more often, take a longer time to respond to questions, and provide shorter responses.[21]

What happens when we suspect that someone isn't being honest with us? If it's an interpersonal encounter, we might decide to probe for more information to determine the person's veracity. Our probing behavior, though, can potentially alert the deceiver to our suspicions, thus causing the deceiver to alter his or her behavior to cover up.[22]

Aggressive Versus Assertive Message

We have discussed teasing as both a face-threatening act and a form of deception. Teasing can also have another impact, that of making the recipient feel put down and belittled. When this is the speaker's intent, teasing becomes an aggressive message.

Aggressive messages are verbal attacks on the self-concepts (face) of individuals for the purpose of making them feel less favorable about themselves.[23] Four reasons have been identified for the use of verbal aggressiveness: frustration (a response to having goals blocked), social learning (the way someone has learned to deal with situations), psychopathology (lashing out at other people who symbolize unresolved personal issues), and argumentative skill deficiency (lack of verbal skills to constructively deal with issues)[24]. Most of us have been outargued or otherwise frustrated in our interaction with someone, and we may have responded by verbally attacking the other person through name-calling, putdowns, insults, and so on. Such attacks to another person's face often result in a corresponding attack on our own face and/or escalation of the interaction into a conflict.

How aggressive are you? Complete the following Test Yourself to see what the aggressiveness scale indicates about you. How does your score compare with the way you generally regard your level of aggressiveness?

ASK YOURSELF

Under what circumstances do you feel deception is acceptable? Within which of the following categories of communication do you feel deception is least unethical? Most unethical? Explain.

interpersonal communication
presentational communication
interviewing
organizational communication
small group communication
mass communication

CONNECT YOURSELF

A significant problem in communicating with strangers on the Internet is the presentation of false information and the attempt to detect it. Log on to a chat session for a while and see what cues you can identify that might lead you to believe a deception is occurring. What can you do to determine if other people on the Net are being honest with you? How important is honesty over the Internet?

Test Yourself

This verbal aggressiveness scale is concerned with how we try to get people to comply with our wishes. Indicate how often each statement is true for you personally when you try to influence other people. Use the following scale: (1) almost never true, (2) rarely true, (3) occasionally true, (4) often true, (5) almost always true.

_____ 1. I am extremely careful to avoid attacking individuals' intelligence when I attack their ideas.

_____ 2. When individuals are very stubborn, I use insults to soften the stubbornness.

_____ 3. I try very hard to avoid having other people feel bad about themselves when I try to influence them.

_____ 4. When people refuse to do a task I know is important, without good reason, I tell them they are unreasonable.

_____ 5. When others do things I regard as stupid, I try to be extremely gentle with them.

_____ 6. If individuals I am trying to influence really deserve it, I attack their characters.

_____ 7. When people behave in ways that are in very poor taste, I insult them in order to shock them into proper behavior.

_____ 8. I try to make people feel good about themselves even when their ideas are stupid.

_____ 9. When people simply will not budge on a matter of importance I lose my temper and say rather strong things to them.

_____ 10. When people criticize my shortcomings, I take it in good humor and do not try to get back at them.

_____ 11. When individuals insult me, I get a lot of pleasure out of really telling them off.

_____ 12. When I dislike individuals greatly, I try not to show it in what I say or how I say it.

_____ 13. I like poking fun at people who do things which are very stupid in order to stimulate their intelligence.

_____ 14. When I attack peoples' ideas, I try not to damage their self-concepts.

_____ 15. When I try to influence people, I make a great effort not to offend them.

_____ 16. When people do things which are mean or cruel, I attack their character in order to help correct their behavior.

_____ 17. I refuse to participate in arguments when they involve personal attacks.

_____ 18. When nothing seems to work in trying to influence others, I yell and scream in order to get some movement from them.

_____ 19. When I am not able to refute others' positions, I try to make them feel defensive in order to weaken their positions.

_____ 20. When an argument shifts to personal attacks, I try very hard to change the subject.

Scoring instructions: Sum the scores of the 20 items after reversing the scoring for items 1, 3, 5, 8, 10, 12, 14, 15, 17, and 20 (change 1 to 5, 2 to 4, 4 to 2, and 5 to 1).

One study found the average score to be 49.10. How does your score compare to this number? A score greater than 59 probably indicates strong verbal aggressiveness. A score less than 39 probably reflects verbal nonaggressiveness.

Source: From D. A. Infante and C. J. Wigley, III, "Verbal Aggressiveness: An Interpersonal Model and Measure," _Communication Monographs,_ 53 (1986): 61–69. Reprinted with permission.

We sometimes use aggressive messages in the mistaken belief that we are simply asserting our own rights. However, we can assert our rights without attacking others. **Assertive messages** are messages in which we argue for our own rights while recognizing the rights of others. Assertive messages involve a forthright yet socially appropriate expression of our rights and feelings.

Being assertive is a complex task that requires the ability to express one's self verbally and nonverbally in such a way as to minimize hostility or defensiveness on the part of other people. Let's go back to the employee who asked the manager about the quality-control plan. Underlying the interaction is the question of whether the employee is going to have to forfeit his or her own time. An assertive response would be: "I would not be happy if I had to do this on my own time. I believe that my time is *my* time, not the company's. However, I'd be happy to participate while I'm on the clock." This statement includes an honest expression of feelings, a claim of personal rights, and a recognition of the manager's rights.

You might choose not to be assertive because you are concerned about how you will be seen. You wouldn't want to voice an assertive message that conveyed an image contrary to your positive face. Also, you might be concerned about the threat to another person's face caused by your assertive message. The key is to make statements that are both consistent with your face and minimally damaging to the other person.

How would you handle the following situation? You are in a busy restaurant and your order is messed up. You get a spinach salad when you ordered a tossed salad. Do you go ahead and eat the salad, or do you call the waiter over to correct your order? If you don't ask to have the order corrected, why not? If you do ask, are you aggressive (hostile) or assertive (recognizing that the waiter is busy)? Telling the waiter that the order is incorrect challenges the waiter's face. He wants to be seen as a good waiter and get a good tip. How can you help him maintain his image as a good waiter while getting what you want?

THE CHALLENGE OF MISUNDERSTANDINGS AND MISREPRESENTATIONS

Two people never really have a 100 percent overlap in the meaning they assign to messages. But the fact that you and I don't share exactly the same meanings doesn't mean that we can't communicate effectively. Human communication is flexible enough to tolerate most deviations from shared meaning without causing significant breakdowns in our interactions. Misunderstandings occur only when the differences reach a critical threshold.

Misunderstandings are instances in which a hearer's inability to comprehend the message results in confusion, failure events, conflict, or incorrect responses. Misunderstandings are problems in the way the hearer decodes messages or interprets perceptions. In addition to difficulties with the language in the message, misunderstanding can occur at several other levels:

▶ *Misunderstanding intentions.* You might understand the words people have spoken but misunderstand their intentions. For example, Lincoln asks Myron to leave. Myron doesn't leave, and Lincoln becomes irritated and says, "Why aren't you leaving like I asked you?" Myron responds, "I thought you were kidding. I didn't really think you meant it." Myron understood Lincoln's words but misunderstood his intentions.

▶ *Misunderstanding the relationship.* You may believe that a certain relationship exists between you and the person speaking to you, but that person may have a contrary perception. In this case, you have a misunderstanding of the relationship.

▶ *Misunderstanding the situation.* Showing up in shorts and a T-shirt for a Sunday afternoon brunch at which everyone else is in skirts and suits reflects a misunderstanding of the situation. Usually, this kind of misunderstanding results in socially inappropriate behavior.

▶ *Misunderstanding the culture.* Misunderstanding the cultural factors that underlie another person's behavior can lead to incorrect attribution of meaning, as you saw earlier.

Speakers themselves also contribute to incomprehension. **Misrepresentations** are instances in which a speaker produces an incomprehensible message. Like misunderstandings, misrepresentations lead to confusion, failure events, conflict, and incorrect responses. Suppose you have been invited back to your elementary school to give a presentation to the sixth graders about college life. During part of your presentation, you say, "Higher education exposes you to a heterogeneous group of pedagogical purveyors who enjoin you to ratiocinate in neoteric ways." Do you think the sixth graders will understand what you have said? You have chosen language beyond their level of understanding and created incomprehension. A more

ASK YOURSELF

Suppose you are interacting with someone from another country who is not particularly fluent in your language. What can you do to minimize misunderstanding? What can you do to minimize misrepresentation?

effective statement would have been, "In college you have a lot of different teachers who make you think in new ways."

Some of the other ways speakers create misunderstandings are through the use of confusing nonverbal communication, insensitive or threatening statements, and lack of clear explanation. Sometimes the message might be clear but the speaker has caused the listener to quit listening. There are ways in which both listeners and speakers can reduce the amount of misunderstanding and misrepresentation. Underlying such efforts must be a desire by the listener to achieve understanding and a desire by the speaker to have the message accurately received. The following sections offer suggestions for making yourself both a better listener and a better speaker.

Improving Understanding: Things a Listener Can Do

Thus far, you have read about a number of factors that interfere with your ability to accurately receive, decode, and interpret what you perceive. The problems include perceptual distortion, the ambiguity of words and nonverbal cues, and confusion about intentions. In this section, you'll find a number of suggestions for reducing misunderstandings. Ultimately, of course, the success of any of these suggestions rests on your desire and commitment to work actively toward better understanding.

IMPROVE PERCEPTION

Understanding requires gathering complete and accurate information. If your field of perception is too narrow, you will miss information. Challenge yourself to look beyond the obvious.

Perhaps you are listening to a speaker who talks in a quiet monotone. As a result, you conclude that the speaker must not have anything important to say and you tune out. Such behavior could cause you to miss important information. Rather than tuning out, seek additional information. Make more observations before reaching conclusions. You will need to monitor and correct for perceptual biases. Are you attending only to the first and last information you receive? Are you drawing conclusions too quickly? Are you weighting negative information too heavily? What preconceptions did you bring to the situation? Are you focusing too much on irrelevant points (the speaker's monotone, fidgeting, poor eye contact, and so on)?

IMPROVE LISTENING

Part of misunderstanding stems from a failure to hear the complete message. The intermittent nature of listening almost ensures that you will miss part of the message. The question is whether you miss critical elements during your "vacation" time. You need to minimize the amount of time that your focus wanders away from the message.

You can consciously remind yourself to return your focus to the speaker and to ignore both external and internal distractions. You can also use your vacation time to focus on other aspects of what is being said that will aid you in understanding. You can organize what you are hearing so that it is easier to retain and recall. You can compare what is being said with how it is being said, seeking to capture deeper meanings.

Finally, you can apply active listening skills, putting yourself in the role of cocreating understanding. Ask yourself what you understand. Tell the other person what you understand. Tell the speaker what you think has been said in your own words (paraphrasing). Don't just parrot back the words, but rephrase them. In that way, you add your interpretation to what was said and allow the other person to correct you if necessary.

IMPROVE SELF-UNDERSTANDING

Understanding your own self helps to ensure understanding others. That is, a clear understanding of your psychological context helps you identify the factors that might distort what you hear—for example, your culture, your emotional state, your needs.

It is important to be conscious of your biases and how they affect your interpretations. You should examine and compensate for any communication preconceptions you might have. You need to identify your tendencies to impose expectations on what is actually heard and observed.

Finally, you can try to desensitize yourself to words that might create overemotional reactions, interfering with your comprehension of the message.

IMPROVE SOCIAL DECENTERING (PERSPECTIVE TAKING)

Social decentering is a way to help you understand other people's attributions of meaning. Social decentering involves knowing people's psychological contexts—their backgrounds, needs, cultures, and so forth. This enhances your ability to understand their meanings and behaviors.

You also need information about the situation. Understanding where people are "coming from" and the influence of the situation lets you put yourself in their shoes. You can comprehend their messages because you understand their feelings, thoughts, and behaviors. In one episode of the TV show *Star Trek: Deep Space Nine,* an electronic alien entity invaded the space station's computer system and began shutting down life-support systems. The entity had been alone on a spacecraft for decades. The alien's behavior was seen as hostile, and the more the protagonists tried to defeat it, the more aggressive it became. The solution to saving the station came when the engineering chief realized that the creature was like a puppy dog, longing for attention and caring. Imagining how attention craved the alien "puppy" must have been, cooped up on the spacecraft, the engineering chief created an electronic "doghouse" where the alien could be played with and cared for. An initial misunderstanding of behavior was corrected by the use of imagination-based social decentering. You can do the same thing when interacting with people.

ADMIT AND CORRECT MISUNDERSTANDINGS

You must judge the significance of a misunderstanding and decide if it should be corrected. If you decide that it could cause problems, then the misunderstanding should be addressed as soon as possible. Waiting often intensifies the problems and makes addressing the misunderstanding a more burdensome task.

What do these two people need to know about one another to enhance their understanding of one another's messages?

We sometimes ignore a misunderstanding or delay addressing it because we are afraid of losing face or of threatening another person's face. Don't be afraid to admit confusion or misunderstanding. People generally prefer to work on achieving shared understanding during the initial interaction, rather than correct errors caused by the misunderstanding at a later time.

Improving Representation: Things a Speaker Can Do

Just as you can work to improve your comprehension of messages as a listener, you can work to improve the degree to which your own messages are understood. Again, there is an assumption here that you want your message to be understood rather than to baffle your listeners. A sincere commitment to improving the comprehensibility of your messages relies on understanding your listeners, being sensitive to feedback, creating clear messages, and double-checking that listeners understand.

IMPROVE SOCIAL DECENTERING

How will the other person interpret what you are saying? What other interpretations are possible besides the one you intend? Your goal is to get your message through clearly. Are the words you choose or the accompanying behaviors you display creating any "noise," or interference, that will cause miscomprehension for the listener?

The more you know about your listener, the more effectively you can choose language that will be understood. Most of us intuitively change the words we use when talking to children because we realize they won't understand many of our "adult" words. With other adults, however, egocentric communication is a significant contributor to misrepresentation. We fail to recognize that the listener is different from us and has different reactions to what we say. Consequently, we may use language that, from the other person's perspective, is ambiguous or misleading. Our intercultural interactions are often marred by a failure to appreciate the effects of culture on another person's understanding of our messages.

You can engage in social decentering by listening to your message from the other person's perspective. Suppose you want your roommate to turn down the stereo so you can study. You could say, "Hey! I'm trying to study." But your roommate enjoys having the stereo playing loudly when studying and therefore doesn't comprehend your statement as a request to turn down the stereo. You failed to take your roommate's perspective when considering how your message would be heard. Taking into account your roommate's habits means creating a more developed request: "I'm studying for a big exam tomorrow and I really can't study very well with the stereo on. Would you be willing to listen through the headset?"

IMPROVE PERCEPTION OF FEEDBACK

Speakers sometimes ignore the fact that they are receiving continual reactions to their messages. You need to monitor the feedback you receive from those with whom you are interacting. This includes watching nonverbal behaviors and being sensitive to the undertones of verbal messages.

In scenario 2 at the beginning of this chapter, the employee you are training gives contradictory feedback, nodding her head to show understanding while responding to your question about whether she understands you by saying, "Yeah, I, um, think so." The way the scenario is written, the hesitancy and uncertainty the employee conveys is not picked up. How close is this to your real behavior?

To improve your skills, you need to be sensitive to the verbal and nonverbal feedback you receive that might indicate miscomprehension. You may need to ask listeners more than once if they really understand you. And you need to ask in such a way that they know you are receptive to questions and it's okay to admit confusion. One rule of presentational speaking is this: After asking if there are any questions, slowly count to three before continuing. The use of silence and waiting is one way to signal that you really are open to questions. Teachers sometimes think that all the students must have understood what was said at a lecture because there were no questions. Effective teachers, however, are constantly scanning the students' faces for signs of confusion.

ASK YOURSELF

Which of the skills for improving understanding are your strongest? Which skills need the most improvement? How might you go about improving them?

Similarly, which of the skills for reducing misrepresentation are your strongest? Which need the most improvement? How might you go about improving them?

IMPROVE MESSAGE DELIVERY

You have many options for encoding your messages, and this means that some messages will be more comprehensible than others. Several points germane to this principle have already been covered, such as adapting the language and avoiding ambiguous or equivocal language. Here are some other suggestions.

▶ Organize information in a manner that facilitates retention.

▶ Keep your message interesting so that listeners will be less likely to tune out.

▶ Repeat what you have said.

▶ Rephrase what you have said and say it again.

▶ Try to keep your nonverbal behaviors consistent with your verbal message, avoiding contradictory cues that create confusion.

▶ Use nonverbal cues to emphasize important points.

▶ Include examples relevant to your listener.

SEEK PARAPHRASES

A final way you can help comprehension is by asking your listener to paraphrase what you have said. Listeners may be reluctant to volunteer a restatement of what you have just said, so they may need encouragement from you. Sometimes, however, asking for paraphrasing can put people on the spot. There is an implicit threat to face: "All right now, let's see if you were really listening." You have witnessed teachers calling on students who aren't paying attention, a technique that usually results only in laughter and embarrassment. The request for paraphrasing needs to be made in a way that minimizes threat to face. You might say something like "I don't know if I said that very clearly. Why don't you tell me what you heard, and I'll try to clear up any parts that might be confusing."

THE CHALLENGE OF MANAGING CONFLICTS

Misunderstanding and misrepresentation can lead to conflicts as individuals try to allocate blame for problems or deal with the fallout from the miscomprehension. The manifestations of conflict can vary, but there are fundamental commonalities, which we will review here. Later in the text, you'll find more specific advice that is appropriate for each communication category. In general, conflicts need to be managed in such a way as to reduce the debilitating effects they have on effective and healthy communication.

Defining Conflict

Conflict is the interaction of interdependent people over real or falsely perceived incompatible goals and/or interference from each other in achieving goals.[25] This definition may seem complicated, so let's take it apart and examine each component.

CONFLICT INVOLVES INTERACTION

You may be upset with a decision made by your boss, but it is not a conflict unless you actually raise the issue with your boss, directly interacting with your boss about the decision. Your feelings may affect your communication with your boss, but unless you voice your concerns, what occurs is more appropriately considered negative, hostile, aggressive, or defensive communication rather than conflict.

There are many cases in which we decide we are better off ignoring an issue of potential conflict or finding some alternative way of reaching our goals. We are likely to apply social exchange principles to reach a decision about whether to initiate a conflict. That is, we evaluate the value of winning the conflict (achieving our goal) as well as our potential for winning the conflict (likelihood of success). We weigh these against the costs of engaging in the conflict—the damage that might be caused and the cost to us if we lose. We then decide whether the rewards outweigh the costs. There are times, however, when we act more impulsively and charge right into conflict situations. Also, we are sometimes drawn into a conflict by other people's actions.

The management of conflict can vary. It can be direct and focused on resolving the matter, or it can be indirect and sustained. Once the conflict is initiated, the parties involved may attempt to resolve it with dispatch, or they may continue the conflict for some time because of a failure to find a way of overcoming the issues (as in a feud). Sometimes conflicts are best managed by simply deciding to move on without reaching any final resolution. In that case, the parties recognize each other's points of view and accept that their views are different; they agree to disagree.

CONFLICT INVOLVES PEOPLE WHO ARE INTERDEPENDENT

The second part of the definition, interdependence, means that the conflicting parties are dependent on each other for something. Differences in their level of dependence can have a dramatic effect on their actions. A student's conflict with an instructor, for example, usually reflects a significant difference in dependence, with the student being more dependent than the instructor. As a result, the student is limited in the strategies or actions that can be used to resolve the conflict.

Sometimes only one party is dependent on the other. In such cases, there is no *interdependence*, and conflict doesn't really happen, though hostility and frustration certainly do. Perhaps you have been in a romantic relationship that you wanted to maintain (making you dependent on the other person), but your partner was no longer interested (no dependence). In this circumstance, your attempts to raise issues of conflict would usually be ignored by your partner, who would feel no compulsion to deal with the issues.

CONFLICT INVOLVES THE PARTIES' GOALS

The last part of the definition of conflict focuses on goals. Goals can be classified as indivisible or opposing. **Indivisible goals** are goals that only one party can attain. In essence, they are winner-take-all goals. Most sports, for example, allow only one person or team to be victorious, so the goal of winning the game is an indivisible one. **Opposing goals** are goals that prevent each other from being attained. When one party sees his or her goals blocked by the goals of the other party (or both parties see their goals blocked by the other's goals), it is a case of opposing goals. Parents attempting to accomplish their goal of protecting their children may set a curfew of eleven o'clock for a sixteen-year-old. The young person, who has the goal of having a good time with friends, wants to stay out till one o'clock. The ensuing conflict occurs because the teenager and the parents perceive themselves as having opposing goals.

A distinction is made between real and falsely perceived goal differences. *Real goal differences* exist when the parties are vying for a goal that is indeed indivisible or for separate goals that are truly blocked by each other. *Falsely perceived differences* exist when the parties see their goals as being in conflict although in reality they share similar goals. Conflicts over falsely perceived differences usually occur because people have misunderstood or misrepresented their goals or the situation.

Resolution of falsely perceived goal differences is usually easier to manage than resolution of real differences, and it often depends on the methods for improving comprehension skills that were discussed earlier. You and a friend might have a conflict over plans for Saturday night. You want to go dancing at a club, but your friend wants to go to a movie. You see your goals as opposing one another. One solution would be for each of you to do your own thing, but this is usually not desirable because the underlying goal that you both share is to spend time together. Another solution is to recognize that your goals don't have to be perceived as opposing; you could actually do both activities. You could go to a movie and then go out dancing afterward. (Of course, this is an expensive solution and might conflict with a goal of fiscal restraint. I don't have all the answers!)

Categories of Conflict

Conflict can occur anytime people communicate, because communication involves attempting to achieve goals. Most of the time, fortunately, our goals are compatible or the differences are not significant enough to warrant conflict.

When conflicts do occur, they can appear in any number of communication categories.

▶ Intrapersonal conflicts occur when we have to make decisions for which there are several choices. For example, do you go to a party tonight or study for tomorrow's exam? This creates a conflict between the goal of having a good time and the goal of being a good student. In a sense, the parties to the conflict are different aspects of your self.

▶ Interpersonal conflicts are probably the most common. They occur in interpersonal relationships in which interdependence is a defining element.

▶ In small groups, conflict occurs among group members (intragroup conflict, which is a form of interpersonal conflict) and among groups (intergroup conflict).

▶ Organizational conflicts include interpersonal conflicts and group conflicts as well as interorganizational conflicts (between organizations). If an environmental group challenges a manufacturing company's plans to build a factory in a wetland, the result is interorganizational conflict.

▶ In mass communication, the conflicts are generally interorganizational conflicts in which one organization, such as a consumers advocacy group, challenges a mass media organization. For instance, a consumers group might challenge television networks in connection with the TV rating system, children's programming, or the preponderance of sex and violence on TV.

▶ In presentational communication, you may think conflicts are unlikely, but speakers often find themselves confronted by resistant or belligerent audiences and even hecklers. Many presentations also involve question-and-answer periods that have the potential to spawn conflicts.

Conflict Management Styles

Good conflict management does not necessarily mean that the conflict is resolved. Rather, it means that we choose the best option for handling a conflict—that is, the way that best protects our interests. The basic options, which we can call *conflict management styles,* include avoidance, accommodation, competition, compromise, and collaboration.

Figure 3.1 shows how these styles differ in terms of concern for your own goals (competitiveness) and concern for the other person's goals (cooperativeness). The competitive axis ranges from having no real concern for your own goals to an extremely strong commitment to getting what you want. The cooperative axis ranges from no concern for the other person's goals to a strong desire to provide the other person what he or she wants. The five styles reflect different combinations of the two types of concern. The conflict management style you choose depends on the nature of the conflict, your needs, and your relationship to the other party.

▶ *Avoidance* involves strategically evading direct discussion of the conflict. This might be the most useful strategy when a situation becomes emotionally charged. Avoidance lets you put the conflict aside until everyone is calm. You also might use avoidance when the issues are not particularly important and when focusing on the conflict could damage the relationship.[26]

▶ *Accommodation* means that you let the other party fulfill his or her goal while your immediate goal is set aside. This strategy would be effective when the issue is not as important for you as you perceive it is for the other person. Accommodation is also a good way to show your reasonableness and commitment to the health of the relationship. Accommodation on one issue can be used as a strategy for gaining accommodation by the other person on a later issue: "I let you have your way last time, now it's my turn."

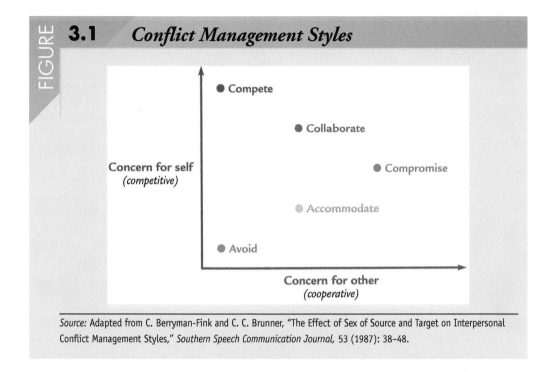

FIGURE 3.1 *Conflict Management Styles*

Source: Adapted from C. Berryman-Fink and C. C. Brunner, "The Effect of Sex of Source and Target on Interpersonal Conflict Management Styles," *Southern Speech Communication Journal*, 53 (1987): 38–48.

▶ *Competition* is an appropriate strategy when you really are dealing with an indivisible goal that is important to you and when the relationship is much less important. Competition sends a clear message about your commitment to the goal, and it works best when there is a need for quick, decisive action.

▶ *Compromise* is also an effective way to reach quick decisions and overcome stalemates. It is particularly useful when the parties are fairly equal in power. You may also decide on compromise if you are losing a competition. Compromise lets both parties feel as though they have fulfilled part of their goals (though it also means they have given up part of their goals).

▶ *Collaboration* is an attempt to reach an agreement in which both parties' goals are fulfilled. The earlier example of going to a movie and then dancing is an example of collaborative management of a conflict. Collaboration takes time, energy, and respect by each party for the other party's goals; therefore, its application is limited.

General Conflict Management Skills

Each conflict presents unique challenges. There are, however, some general guidelines you can follow to manage conflict more effectively. One critical factor is to maintain effective communication. You have probably witnessed more than one conflict, such as a labor-management dispute or an interpersonal confrontation, in which communication broke down and the conflicting parties refused even to talk with each other. Keeping communication flowing during a conflict requires managing emotions, managing the information, and managing the flow of the conflict itself.

MANAGING EMOTIONS

Conflicts threaten your negative face by preventing you from accomplishing your goals. Conflicts can also include direct threats to your positive face ("You're an idiot, and you don't know what you are talking about!"). Threats to either your positive or your negative face evoke emotions, and becoming too emotional can hamper your ability to manage a conflict effectively. Here's an example of such a process:

ASK YOURSELF

How ethical is it to use deception as a way of resolving conflict? Or to overstate your needs in hopes of reaching a compromise that gives you what you really wanted all along? Or to use face-threatening tactics as a way to resolve a conflict in your favor?

JACKIE	We really need to add another salesperson to my district. I can't get the coverage I need with just the four people I have.
JACE	Everybody thinks they need more staff. Maybe your staff is full of goof-offs and deadbeats.
JACKIE	(raising her voice) You're an idiot! My people are working their butts off. You just don't want me to be successful.
JACE	(also raising his voice) Then maybe it's their manager that's the problem!
JACKIE	(louder) Are you saying I'm not doing my job? You're a moron!!
JACE	(also louder) You can't call me names. *You're fired!!*

In this scenario, both parties should have called time out and broken off the interaction when their emotions started to get out of control. The use of avoidance would have helped both Jackie and Jace calm down. Both individuals had their face threatened and responded by further threatening the other's face, rather than helping each other maintain face.

The following suggestions can help you manage the destructive impact of unbridled emotions:

▶ Avoid aggressive messages—name-calling, personal attacks, and other direct face-threatening acts.

▶ Avoid emotional exaggerations and extremes. It's okay to be intense—emotions are unavoidable—but you don't have to be belligerent.

▶ Describe your emotions and ask the other people to describe their emotions when the situation calls for it. There are times when emotions are part of the conflict and need to be discussed. Hiding or ignoring emotions can result in destructive, volcanic eruptions of emotion.

▶ Listen to and watch yourself. What emotions are you displaying? How will the other person respond to those displays? You've probably been told things like "Don't look at me that way!" or "Quit smiling at me, I'm really upset." Our nonverbal cues can heighten emotional tension.

▶ Choose a time and place that are most conducive to a relaxed interaction. Being called into the dean's office in school or the boss's office at work can immediately raise a person's anxiety. Likewise, trying to discuss a conflict with people at the end of the day when they are tired or when they are swamped with work increases the likelihood of emotional interference.

MANAGING INFORMATION

We also manage conflicts by the way we manage information. Jace's comment about Jackie's sales staff evoked her defensiveness. Jace should have been aware that his offhand remark would upset her. He should have either stated the issue in a more constructive manner or dealt with the issue of Jackie's staff on another occasion. A number of rules apply to managing information during a conflict.

1. *Plan your message.* You can more easily state your concern about a point of conflict if you have planned in advance what you are going to say, rather than addressing the issue on the spur of the moment. Planning the message lets you consider how the other person might react and lets you choose language that is least likely to evoke a strong emotional reaction.

2. *Approach the issue from a problem-oriented perspective rather than an evaluative one.* Evaluative statements evoke defensiveness, whereas statements that focus on specific behaviors or issues tend to be supportive.27 Jace could have approached the issue of Jackie's sales staff in a problem-oriented manner by saying, "Why don't we look at what your current staff is doing and see if there are any ways to improve their effectiveness?"

3. *Separate the issues from the person, and deal only with the issues.* We sometimes are lured into criticizing and evaluating the individual rather than dealing with the point of conflict. Jace and Jackie needed to deal with the issues of Jackie wanting to be more successful and Jace feeling the need to keep employee costs down. Instead, Jackie began focusing on Jace and drifted away from her own needs and goals.

4. *Seek information to understand the conflict more fully.* This includes seeking in formation from outside sources and directly from the other party. It also means listening effectively to what the other party is telling you and applying active listening skills.

5. *Share information with the other party.* Hiding information undermines trust and encourages the other party to hide information from you as well. Openly sharing information helps the other party learn about your position and establishes a climate of cooperation.

MANAGING THE CONFLICT

Managing emotions and information puts you in a position to manage the conflict effectively. Each of the five styles mentioned earlier is a possible way of managing conflicts. There are also rules you can follow to improve the process for all the parties.

1. *Define and focus on the problem.* This might seem like an obvious thing to do, but we often lose sight of the issues during conflicts. In addition, the parties in the conflict often have different definitions of the problem. In either case, it becomes important to mutually define the problem. In defining the problem, both parties need to present their goals and needs. Both parties need to listen to and appreciate the needs and goals of the other person. Sometimes we dismiss the other person's goals because we don't see them as valid or important. Such judgments only serve to heighten tensions and raise the ire of the other party.

2. *Analyze the problem.* Analysis of the problem again involves both parties' presenting their perspective on what created the problem, the impact of the problem, and the reasons the problem persists. This discussion should include an attempt to find similarities between the conflicting parties. In the conflict described earlier, Jackie and Jace both want to see high sales and good profits in Jackie's territory. In analyzing the problem, they would have realized that Jackie saw the problem as too large a territory for the number of staff, and Jace saw the problem as an inefficient staff. This would have led them to explore the question of staffing efficiency.

ASK YOURSELF

Think of a current conflict you are having. What are your goals and needs? What are the other party's goals? What commonalities are there in your goals and interests? What do you see as the underlying causes of the conflict? How would the other party describe the causes of the conflict? What would happen if you approached this person using the method we have just described?

3. *Define a mutually acceptable goal.* The conflict is practically over once this step is accomplished. However, this is much easier said than done. At this point, both parties must be willing to cooperate in defining a goal that is acceptable to both. This can be accomplished by integrating the goals and needs of both parties, often creatively. Jackie and Jace probably could agree on the goal of maximizing sales while minimizing costs in her district.

4. *Generate multiple solutions to the problem.* Once a common goal has been identified, the parties should work to generate a number of alternative solutions. At times we are sucked into focusing on only one solution—just as Jackie saw the addition of a staff member as the only solution to her problem. Even if one solution seems apparent, try to generate as many other possibilities as you can. Valuable, innovative ideas often arise during the process of brain-storming alternatives. The best solution might be one that has integrated components of various alternatives.

5. *Select the best solution.* Once a list of alternative solutions has been generated, the parties can begin to analyze each choice in terms of how well it fulfills their mutually agreed-on goal. At this point, details are needed about how to implement the solution and monitor its effectiveness, as well as agreement on what steps to take if the selection does not seem to be working.

Remember, the challenges to communication discussed in this chapter apply to all communication situations. Each time we interact with others, we risk threats to our face, the possibility of miscomprehension, and the development of conflict. Fear of such possibilities should not cause us to avoid communication; rather, knowledge of how to manage these challenges should lead us to be more effective in our dealings with other people.

SUMMARY

This chapter has focused on three aspects of communication that are particularly challenging: maintaining face (self-image), dealing with misunderstandings and misrepresentations, and managing conflict. These challenges directly relate to the three basic types of communication needs (identity, instrumental, and relational). We enter communication interactions with a need to have our identity accepted and confirmed, but often we find it threatened. Our instrumental needs are met by using communication to accomplish and perform tasks. Finally, we have relational needs that are satisfied through communication with other people.

A variety of communication events pose threats to our face. We then use communication to try to save, maintain, or restore our face. Sometimes we cause failure events when we act in an unexpected manner or fail to meet an obligation. These events threaten both our face and that of the other people involved. Another person might point out our failure through a reproach, and we then respond with an account. Reproaches and accounts affect each other and vary in terms of how threatening they are.

Our face is also threatened by other people's deception. Deception occurs when a person intentionally tries to hide or falsify the truth. It can take the form of equivocation, concealment, half-truths, diversions, or lies. Deception is used for a variety of reasons, including gaining resources, gaining compliance, protecting face, having fun, and protecting others. Sometimes we can detect deception when we are able to observe leakages, the subtle behavioral cues that accompany deception.

Some attacks on our face come from aggressive messages, such as name-calling and insults—messages designed intentionally to threaten our face. In contrast to aggressive messages, assertive messages can be used to present a claim for one's own rights while acknowledging the rights of others.

Another major challenge to effective communication stems from misunderstandings and misrepresentations. Both of these communication events result in miscomprehension by the listener of what the speaker is trying to communicate. Misunderstanding is listener based, while misrepresentations are speaker-based. Misunderstanding can be minimized through improved perception, improved listening, better self-understanding, improved social decentering, and admitting to and correcting misunderstandings. Misrepresentation can be minimized through improved social decentering, improved perception of listeners' feedback, improved message delivery, and asking for paraphrased feedback from listeners.

The final section of this chapter focused on conflict. The definition of conflict includes the following components: interaction; interdependence of the parties; and real or false perception of incompatible goals and/or interference in achieving goals. Goals can be classified as either indivisible (winner-take-all) or opposing. Conflict management styles include avoiding, accommodating, competing, compromising, and collaborating, and these five styles vary in terms of concern for self and concern for the other person.

Conflict management involves effectively managing emotions, information, and the conflict itself. Among the rules for managing emotions are avoiding aggressive messages, choosing a place and time conducive to a relaxed interaction, and being willing to discuss emotions. Information management involves planning a problem-oriented message, separating the issue from the person, and directly seeking and openly sharing information. Managing the conflict requires defining and analyzing the problem, finding a mutually acceptable goal, and then generating and selecting the best solutions.

understanding, improved social decentering, and admitting to and correcting misunderstandings. Misrepresentation can be minimized through improved social decentering, improved perception of listeners' feedback, improved message delivery, and asking for paraphrased feedback from listeners.

The final section of this chapter focused on conflict. The definition of conflict includes the following components: interaction; interdependence of the parties; and real or false perception of incompatible goals and/or interference in achieving goals. Goals can be classified as either indivisible (winner-take-all) or opposing. Conflict management styles include avoiding, accommodating, competing, compromising, and collaborating, and these five styles vary in terms of concern for self and concern for the other person.

Conflict management involves effectively managing emotions, information, and the conflict itself. Among the rules for managing emotions are avoiding aggressive messages, choosing a place and time conducive to a relaxed interaction, and being willing to discuss emotions. Information management involves planning a problem-oriented message, separating the issue from the person, and directly seeking and openly sharing information. Managing the conflict requires defining and analyzing the problem, finding a mutually acceptable goal, and then generating and selecting the best solutions.

KEY TERMS

identity needs The needs we satisfy when we present who we are to other people, have that presented self accepted and confirmed by other people, and confirm other people's identities.

instrumental needs The needs we satisfy when we accomplish tasks or perform jobs.

relational needs The needs we satisfy when we manage our relationships.

save face Restore the image that we were originally trying to convey before our face was threatened.

maintain face Prevent loss of face. Other people can help us maintain face by providing support, confirmation, and acceptance of the self-conception we are presenting.

failure event An instance of failure to fulfill an obligation or expectation.

reproach An indication by someone that a failure event has occurred.

mitigating reproach A reproach that reflects only mild irritation with a failure event.

aggravating reproach A severe, intense declaration of the occurrence of a failure event.

account A stated response to a reproach by the person accused of the failure event.

apology A statement in which the person admits a failure event, accepts responsibility for it, and expresses regret.

excuse An admission that a failure event occurred combined with an assertion that nothing could have been done to prevent it.

justification Accepting responsibility for a failure event but then trying to redefine the event as not being a failure.

denial Stating that a failure event never took place.

providing no account Either offering no response to a reproach or ignoring it by changing the subject; silence.

silence Either offering no response to a reproach or ignoring it by changing the subject; providing no account.

deception The intentional disguising, avoiding, hiding, or falsifying of the truth.

equivocation Deception by purposely sending vague, unclear, or ambiguous messages.

concealment Deception through the holding back of information so that the other person reaches erroneous conclusions.

half-truths Deceptions that leave out information or modify or qualify the message to lessen the impact or reaction.

diversions Deceptions that change the focus of the communication to another topic to avoid discussing the issue at hand.

lies Deception through the deliberate presentation of false information.

white lie A lie that is viewed as fairly close to the truth and fairly insignificant in its impact.

leakages Subtle behavioral changes that accompany deception.

aggressive messages Verbal attacks on the self-concepts (face) of individuals for the purpose of making them feel less favorable about themselves.

assertive messages Messages in which we argue for our own rights while recognizing the rights of others.

misunderstandings Instances in which a hearer's inability to comprehend a message results in confusion, failure events, conflict, or incorrect responses.

misrepresentations Instances in which a speaker produces an incomprehensible message.

conflict The interaction of interdependent people over real or falsely perceived incompatible goals and/or interference from each other in achieving goals.

indivisible goals Goals that only one party can attain.

opposing goals Goals that prevent each other from being attained.

REVIEW QUESTIONS

1. Define identity, instrumental, and relational needs.
2. Explain the process of dealing with a failure event.
3. Explain the differences between the different types of deception.
4. Distinguish between an aggressive message and an assertive message.
5. Identify several ways of improving understanding and representation.
6. Explain how conflict management involves the management of emotions, information, and the conflict itself.

CHAPTER 4
TIME AND MONEY

ajid was working one part-time job in the evenings, as an assistant manager at Radio Shack, and another on weekends, doing bookkeeping at his cousin's auto body shop. The income from both jobs was enough for tuition, rent, food, and other expenses. However, the time commitment was too much. Without evening and weekend time to study, he couldn't keep up with the work in his 12 credits of classes, and his grades were suffering.

When Sajid lost his job in the electronics store, he considered it a mixed blessing. He knew he would have money problems. However, he also knew that he would have the time to catch up on his schoolwork. He feels like it is impossible to have both the time *and* the money he needs to get through school.

IN THIS CHAPTER . . .

You explore answers to the following questions:

Get the most out of your actions by starting with clear goals and a plan. Thinking ahead about your time and your budget will mean fewer obstacles in your path.

▶ **Powerful questions about thinking before you act** (from page 83)

▶ **Real people think before they act** (from page 84)

▶ **Habit summary** (from page 97)

▶ **Test prep: Start it now** (from page 104)

WHAT DO TIME AND MONEY HAVE TO DO WITH COLLEGE SUCCESS?

A student like Sajid might have the skill and talent to succeed in school. He might have chosen the college and major that are a good fit. He might have a strong support system, an organized study area, top-notch computer equipment, and the best of intentions. However, if he doesn't have the time to study or the money to pay his tuition and expenses, he will face obstacles that are hard to overcome.

Time and money are valuable resources. You need time to attend classes, study, and work on projects and papers. You need money to pay for tuition, books, and other expenses. These resources are linked; for example, many students need time to work, so that they can earn the money to pay for expenses.

Making Money Costs You Time

Look at money and what you buy with it in terms of the time you spend earning it. For example, you are thinking about purchasing a new $200 cell phone. If you have a job that pays $10 an hour after taxes, you have to work 20 hours to buy that phone. Ask yourself: Is it worth it? If the answer is no, use the money for something that matters more to you.

Considering the time you have to spend earning money can hit home when you look at where your money goes from day to day. Cutting back on regular expenses can make a significant difference (see Key 4.1). If it takes you a month of work to earn $1,000 at your part-time job, you need to decide whether you would rather spend that money on coffee or put it toward next term's tuition.

The bad news is time flies. The good news is you're the pilot.
—Michael Altschuler, motivational speaker

KEY 4.1 *Put Your Wallet Away Today and Earn Money for Tomorrow*

DAY-TO-DAY EXPENSE	APPROXIMATE COST	POTENTIAL SAVINGS IF INVESTED*
Gourmet coffee	$4 per day, 5 days a week, totals $20 per week	$80 per month; $1040 for the year. With interest from a savings account earning 3% would be $1, 071.
Cigarettes	$5 per day, 7 days a week (for a pack-a-day habit), totals $35 per week	$140 per month; $1,820 for the year. With interest from a savings account earning 3% would be $1,874.
Ordering in meals	$15 per meal, twice per week, totals $30 per week	$120 per month; $1,560 for the year. With interest from a savings account earning 3%, would be $1,606.

*Monthly cost = weekly cost × 4 weeks
Yearly cost = weekly cost × 52 weeks

Managing Time and Money May Mean Taking Longer to Graduate

Managing your key resources—time and money—is a crucial part of your job as a student. Time is a finite resource—everyone has the same 24 hours in a day, every day—and money is limited for nearly every student. The key is to make smart decisions about how you spend each of them. Such decisions may involve adjustments in when you take courses and for how long.

The reality for many college students is that they do not have enough money to go to college full time, straight through the two or four years it takes to graduate. For example, statistics show that public college students working toward a four-year degree take, on average, more than six years to finish.[1] Students like Sajid have a variety of choices, including:

▶ Going part time in order to maintain a work schedule while having enough time to study.

▶ Working full time over a summer—or, if necessary, while "stopping out" (leaving school temporarily) for a year—in order to put money away for tuition.

▶ Taking some or all courses online in order to have more flexibility with a work schedule.

▶ Transferring to a school with cheaper tuition or one that doesn't require living on campus.

Students all over the country are turning to solutions like these to afford college.

Going to college may cost more hours of work than almost any other purchase, and it takes hours away from your day that you might otherwise spend earning money. However, you are spending tuition and time in order to better your chances of long-term financial success. If you look at the statistics in Key 4.2, you will see that college graduates tend to earn more in the workplace than non-graduates. However long it takes you to attain your degree or certificate, you are making a sound investment in your future.

As you read through the rest of the chapter, remember that how you spend both time and money reflects what you value. Therefore, if along the way you find that the way you use either or both of these precious resources is causing problems, look carefully at how you can adjust your choices to align with your most important values.

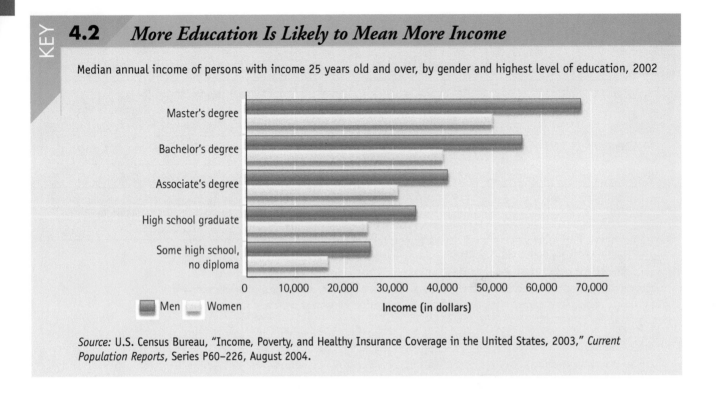

KEY **4.2** *More Education Is Likely to Mean More Income*

Median annual income of persons with income 25 years old and over, by gender and highest level of education, 2002

Source: U.S. Census Bureau, "Income, Poverty, and Healthy Insurance Coverage in the United States, 2003," *Current Population Reports*, Series P60–226, August 2004.

WHAT KIND OF TIME AND MONEY MANAGER ARE YOU?

Successful time and money management is based on self-knowledge, so start by thinking about how you interact with these resources.

For each question, circle the number in the range that most applies to you.							
My energy is best in the . . .	morning	1	2	3	4	5	evening
I tend to be . . .	always on time	1	2	3	4	5	always late
I focus best . . .	for long periods	1	2	3	4	5	for short periods
I'm most likely to . . .	save money	1	2	3	4	5	spend money
I put money toward . . .	things now	1	2	3	4	5	future needs
I would borrow money . . .	anytime	1	2	3	4	5	never

Identify Your Time-Related Needs and Preferences

Body rhythms and habits affect how each person deals with time. Some people are night owls; others are at their best in the morning. A mismatch between your habits and your schedule causes stress that may affect your grades. Take the following steps to identify how you can make time work for you rather than against you:

CREATE A PERSONAL TIME "PROFILE"
Ask yourself the following questions:

► At what time of day do I have the most energy? The least energy?

► Do I tend to be early, on time, or late?

► Do I focus well for long stretches or need regular breaks?

CONSIDER YOUR PROFILE WHEN CREATING A SCHEDULE FOR EXAMPLE:

▶ Early birds may try to schedule early classes; people whose energy peaks later may look for classes in the afternoons or evenings.

▶ People who tend to be late might want to determine what situations contribute to this tendency (early classes, back-to-back classes, etc.) and try to avoid them.

▶ If you focus well for long stretches, you can handle classes back to back; if you tend to need breaks, try to set up a schedule with time between class meetings.

Note Your Unique Way of Managing Money

The way you interact with money is as unique as you are: You might be a spender or a saver. You might focus on money in the present tense, or you might look primarily to the future. You might charge everything, only purchase things that you can buy with cash, or do something in between. You might search actively for college loans or try to avoid borrowing altogether.

How you handle money and the level of importance it has for you affects your decisions about college, major, and career. Among the factors that influence you as a money manager are:

▶ **Your values.** You tend to spend money on what you think is most important.

▶ **Your personality.** Thinkers may focus on planning, Organizers may balance bank accounts down to the penny, Givers may prioritize spending money to help others, Adventurers may spend impulsively and deal with the consequences later.

▶ **Your culture.** Some cultures see money as a collective resource to be shared within families; others prize individual accumulation as a sign of independence. Some cultures tend to avoid borrowing; others use credit and loans freely.

▶ **Your family and peer group.** You tend to either follow or react against how your parents and immediate family handle money. Your friends also influence you.

Money coach Connie Kilmark notes that you cannot change how you handle money until you analyze your attitudes and behaviors. "If managing money was just about math and the numbers, everyone would know how to manage their finances sometime around the fifth grade," she says.[2] Once you take a hard look at your approach to money, you can make real-life money decisions based on what works best for you.

Now that you have a better idea of your tendencies, take a closer look at time, the resource accessible to everyone.

HOW CAN YOU MANAGE YOUR TIME?

Consider each day as a jigsaw puzzle: You have all the pieces (seconds, minutes, hours) in a pile, and your task is to form a picture of how you want your day to look. Start by building the schedule that works best for you.

Build a Schedule

Schedules help you gain control of your life in two ways: They provide segments of time for things you have to do, and they remind you of events, due dates, responsibilities, and deadlines. Start by recording your schedule in a planner.

CHOOSE A PLANNER

Planners help you keep track of events, commitments, and tasks. You can choose a notebook planner (which devotes a page to each day or shows a week's schedule on a two-page spread) or an electronic planner or "smartphone" such as a BlackBerry or iPhone (which allows you to perform functions like scheduling events and due dates, making lists, and creating an address book). You might also consider online calendars, such as Google calendar, which can "communicate" with your phone or other electronic planning device.

Though electronic devices are handy and have a large data capacity, they cost more than the paper versions, and their small size means they are easy to lose. Which tool should you choose? The one that you are most likely to use every day. An inexpensive notebook, used conscientiously, may work as well for some people as a top-of-the-line electronic device.

Coordinating your schedule with classmates, work colleagues, and friends is a crucial task. These students use electronic devices to update contact information.

© Michael Newman/
PhotoEdit

SCHEDULE AND PRIORITIZE TASKS, EVENTS, AND COMMITMENTS

Everything that has a date, a time, or a deadline goes in your planner. However, not every item has the same level of importance, and you need to spend the bulk of your time on your **priorities**. As you get ready to enter items into your planner, think through your responsibilities using three priority levels:

Priority 1 items are the most crucial. They include:

▶ Class meeting times and dates

▶ Exam and quiz dates

▶ Due dates for papers, projects, lab assignments, and presentations

▶ Work shifts

▶ Child-care responsibilities (pickups, times during which you are responsible for children)

Priority 2 items are important but more flexible parts of your routine. These include:

▶ Blocks of study time

▶ Meetings for study groups, tutoring, discussion groups, clubs, support groups

▶ Steps that are part of a major task, such as dates you want to complete project research

▶ Personal needs (medical appointments, food shopping, cooking, workout time)

Priority 3 items are lowest in importance. These include:

▶ Social activities and events

▶ Leisure-time activities (downloading new tunes, getting in touch with a friend)

▶ Maintenance tasks (cleaning out a closet, organizing a room)

Next, use the following steps to lay everything out in your planner:

PUT IN PRIORITY 1 ITEMS FIRST. Enter your class and work times for the entire term all at once. Your syllabus will tell you when readings and assignments are due and when quizzes and tests will take place.

NEXT, SCHEDULE PRIORITY 2 ITEMS AROUND PRIORITY 1 ITEMS. Start by blocking out study time where available on your schedule, being sure to indicate the specific material you plan to study. According to one formula, you should spend at least two hours studying and working on assignments for every credit hour. That means that if you take 12 credits, you should study about 24 hours a week outside of class. Although this may not be easy, especially if you have a job, a family, or both, do whatever you can to put in the hours. After you schedule your study time, include other Priority 2 items.

FINALLY, INSERT PRIORITY 3 ITEMS WHEN YOU CAN. You may not want to put these into your schedule ahead of time. One strategy is to keep a separate list of these tasks so that you can refer to it when free time pops up.

Priorities
tasks or intentions that are more important than others.

Once your schedule is filled out, decide on a visual way to indicate priority level. Some people use numbers or letters (A, B, C). Some write different priority items in different-colored pens (red for Priority 1, blue for Priority 2, etc.). Electronic planners may allow you to color-code or flag items according to priority.

Key 4.3 shows parts of a daily schedule and weekly schedule.

Make Your Schedule Work for You

Once your schedule is written, it's time to put it to use. These six strategies will help.

PLAN REGULARLY. Set aside regular periods: each day to plan the next day and the weekend to plan the next week. Keep your planner with you at all times, and check it periodically.

LOOK AT YOUR TERM OR SEMESTER ALL AT ONCE. Don't be fooled—finals week is *not* the only busy week you'll face. If you map out your biggest responsibilities from the beginning to the end of the term, you can see where your work-heavy weeks will come up and can plan how to handle those ahead of time. For example, a student who has three tests and a presentation all in one week in November may have to adjust a work schedule, arrange extra child care, or simply schedule extra blocks of study time to handle the load.

> ## By the way...
> according to a 2007 survey, nearly 50% of college freshmen add a job to their scheduled weekly responsibilities in order to earn money to pay for tuition.[3]

KEY 4.3 *Note Daily and Weekly Tasks*

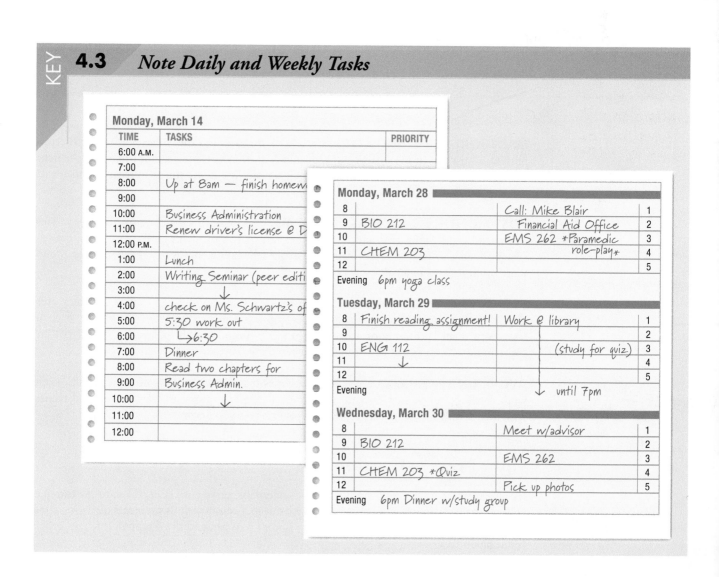

Monday, March 14

TIME	TASKS	PRIORITY
6:00 A.M.		
7:00		
8:00	Up at 8am — finish homew	
9:00		
10:00	Business Administration	
11:00	Renew driver's license @ D	
12:00 P.M.		
1:00	Lunch	
2:00	Writing Seminar (peer editi	
3:00	↓	
4:00	check on Ms. Schwartz's of	
5:00	5:30 work out	
6:00	↳6:30	
7:00	Dinner	
8:00	Read two chapters for	
9:00	Business Admin.	
10:00	↓	
11:00		
12:00		

Monday, March 28

8		Call: Mike Blair	1
9	BIO 212	Financial Aid Office	2
10		EMS 262 *Paramedic	3
11	CHEM 203	role-play*	4
12			5
Evening	6pm yoga class		

Tuesday, March 29

8	Finish reading assignment!	Work @ library	1
9			2
10	ENG 112	(study for quiz)	3
11	↓		4
12			5
Evening		↓ until 7pm	

Wednesday, March 30

8		Meet w/advisor	1
9	BIO 212		2
10		EMS 262	3
11	CHEM 203 *Quiz		4
12		Pick up photos	5
Evening	6pm Dinner w/study group		

TAKE ACTION: Make a To-Do List

Make a to-do list for your busiest day this week. Include all the tasks and events you know about, including attending class and study time, and the activities you would like to do (exercising, lunch with a friend) if you have extra time. Then use a coding system (and your naturalistic intelligence) to categorize your list according to priority.

Date:_____

1. _____   7. _____

2. _____   8. _____

3. _____   9. _____

4. _____   10. _____

5. _____   11. _____

6. _____   12. _____

After examining this list, record your daily schedule in your planner (if you have a busy day, you may want to list Priority 3 items separately to complete if time permits). At the end of the day, evaluate this system. Did the list help you to manage your time and tasks effectively? If you liked it, use a to-do list on a daily and weekly basis.

MAKE AND USE TO-DO LISTS. Use a *to-do list* to record the things you want to accomplish on a busy day or for a particular challenge like exam week or a major project. Write items on separate paper, prioritize the list, and then transfer the items you plan to accomplish each day to open time slots in your planner.

POST MONTHLY CALENDARS AT HOME. Use a monthly wall calendar for an overview of your major commitments and upcoming events. If you live with family or friends, create a group calendar to stay on top of plans and avoid scheduling conflicts. Try having each person write commitments in a particular color.

SCHEDULE LEISURE TIME. Taking time off—to watch a show, chat online, get some exercise, take a nap—will refresh you and actually improve your productivity when you get back on task. Even small 10-minute breathers within study sessions can help, because you often can't concentrate well for extended periods of time without a break.

AVOID TIME TRAPS. Carefully limit activities that take time that you need for study and work. Surfing the Internet, instant messaging, playing computer or video games, and talking with friends on your cell phone can eat up hours before you know it.

Fight Procrastination

It's human and common to leave difficult or undesirable tasks until later. Taken to the extreme, however, **procrastination** can develop into a habit that causes serious problems including stress from a buildup of responsibilities, work that is not up to par, and the disappointment of others counting on you.

Procrastination
the act of putting off
a task until another
time.

Among the reasons people procrastinate are:

▶ **Perfectionism.** Habitual procrastinators often measure their value by their ability to achieve.[4] To the perfectionist procrastinator, a failed project equals a failed person. For that reason, not trying at all is better than an attempt that falls short of perfection.

▶ **Fear of limitations.** Procrastinators can blame a failure on waiting too long, not on any personal shortcoming. If you don't try, you don't have to face your limitations.

▶ **Being unsure of the next step.** If you get stuck and don't know what to do, sometimes it seems easier to procrastinate than to make the leap to the next level of your goal.

▶ **Facing an overwhelming task.** Some big projects can immobilize you. If a person facing such a task fears failure, she may procrastinate to avoid confronting the fear.

The following strategies will help you avoid procrastination:

▶ **Analyze its effects.** Ask yourself what is likely to happen if you put something off. Realizing that procrastination will hurt you more than help you is often the first step to facing your responsibilities.

▶ **Set reasonable goals.** Unreasonable goals can immobilize you. Set manageable goals, and allow enough time to complete them.

▶ **Break tasks into smaller parts.** If you concentrate on one small step at a time, the task may become less burdensome. Setting time limits for each task may help you feel more in control.

▶ **Get started whether or not you "feel like it."** The motivation techniques might help you take the first step. Once you start, you may find it easier to continue.

▶ **Ask for help.** Once you identify what's holding you up, see who can help you face the task. Another person may come up with an innovative way to get you moving.

▶ **Don't expect perfection—ever.** Most people learn by starting at the beginning, making mistakes, and learning from those mistakes. It's better to try your best than to do nothing at all.

▶ **Reward yourself.** When you accomplish a task, take a break, see a movie, and tell yourself that you are making progress.

INSIDE TIPS

FROM JOYCE, TECHNOLOGY COACH Technology can save you a tremendous amount of time, but it can also be an enormous time drain, as when you start texting friends or surfing YouTube on a study break and look up to see that an hour has passed. Control your social tech time by scheduling it tightly. Assign yourself 25 minutes of reading and 5 minutes of computer time every half-hour, for example. Set an alarm so you know when to get back on task.

Be Flexible

No matter how well you think ahead, sudden changes can upend your plans if you are inflexible. Change is a fact of life, and although you can't always choose your circumstances, you can make decisions about how you handle them.

For changes that occur periodically—the need to work an hour overtime at your after-school job, a meeting that tends to run late—think through a backup plan ahead of time. For surprises, the best you can do is to be ready to brainstorm and rely on your internal and external resources. If you have to miss a class, for example, ask to see a classmate's notes. When change involves more serious problems—your car breaks down, a family member gets sick—use problem-solving skills to help you

POWERFUL QUESTIONS

Think about what leads you to procrastinate—a particular kind of assignment, a certain course, instructions from a person you find difficult. What do you tend to do, and what happens because of it? Now think about how this chapter's Habit for Success can help you improve the situation.

How can thinking before you act—or fail to act—help you face your responsibilities? Name one upcoming task on which you commit to *not* procrastinating—and get on it.

Real People
Think Before They Act

© Summer Dilworth

**DOCTOR SAMPSON DAVIS
DOCTOR RAMECK HUNT
DOCTOR GEORGE JENKINS**
Graduates of Seton Hall University

Source: The Three Doctors, LLC.

Thinking before taking action propelled these three friends from difficult circumstances to successful medical and dental careers—and to a lifelong quest to help others realize their dreams.

Before they met as young teenagers, each had grown up in Newark, New Jersey, in struggling families.

George spent his early years living in and around the projects with his mother and brother. His father left when George was 2. From the age of 11, Sam, his five siblings, and his mother lived on welfare after Sam's father left. Rameck lived with his grandmother. His father was in and out of jail, and both of his parents were fighting drug addictions.

STOP AND THINK

George, Sam, and Rameck grew up facing enormous challenges. What difficulties have you faced that made it hard to focus on your schoolwork?

Because of their academic abilities, each boy caught the attention of teachers. Sam and George were tested and admitted in the seventh grade to University High School in Newark, a magnet school for high achievers in math and science. Rameck joined them in ninth grade.

When they were juniors, they went to a presentation about an opportunity at Seton Hall University called the Pre-Medical/Pre-Dental Plus Program, which provided financial support to poor students who showed promise. Thinking about his childhood dream of becoming a dentist, George convinced his two friends to apply to the program, and they made a pact that they "would apply to Seton Hall, go to college together, then go to medical [and dental] school and stick with one another to the end . . . . We . . . headed back to class, without even a hint of how much our lives were about to change."

Real People
Think Before They Act

STOP AND THINK

Have you had a moment, like George, Sam, and Rameck, when something you heard or read opened you to new possibilities? What happened, and how did it change your attitude and goals?

Although all three got into the program, life continued to present challenges. Rameck and Sam both did time in juvenile detention after which they redoubled their efforts at school. Ultimately they attended Seton Hall University together.

Later, George was accepted into the University of Medicine and Dentistry, and Rameck and Sam were accepted into the Robert Wood Johnson Medical School. Through the next few years, they continued to keep one another focused on the goal ahead. Sam failed his medical boards the first time out, but with his friends' support he passed with flying colors on his next attempt.

As they passed each hurdle, the men saw more and more how important their mutual support had been to their achievements. During their residencies, they created The Three Doctors Foundation, dedicated to exposing poor children to colleges, professional people, and the working world as well as providing financial assistance. Their pact to help one another has become a pact to help many more.

THINK ABOUT GEORGE, SAM, AND RAMECK AND THINK ABOUT YOURSELF

▶ Which of the actions of the three doctors was successful because they thought carefully before acting? Why is this habit so crucial when you are making a big move in your life?

▶ First, think of a choice you made without thinking beforehand. What would you do differently now? Then, describe a choice you have coming up, and discuss how you plan to get the best results.

After graduating from college, Andrea Jung took a sales management job, figuring it would give her a strategic advantage when she went to law school. However, she thrived in the sales world. Thinking carefully, she shifted her course and stayed in sales, which led her up the ladder. She eventually became the first female CEO of Avon and has spearheaded a movement to address and combat violence against women around the world.

© Jennifer Graylock/
AP Images

85

through. Your academic advisor, counselor, dean, financial aid advisor, and instructors may have ideas and assistance.

Change is a reality for money management as well as time management. Staying in control of your money will help you make adjustments when sudden expenses pop up.

HOW CAN YOU MANAGE YOUR MONEY?

According to the American Psychological Association, nearly three out of four Americans cite money as the number one stressor in their lives.[5] Adding college expenses to the basic cost of living means that, for the vast majority of college students, money is tight. Soaring college costs far outpace the cost of living. From 1997 to 2007, the cost of living rose 24%. In contrast, college costs increased by more than 80%. This steep rise places a burden on students and their families to find a way to pay for college.[6]

Finances can be especially problematic for self-supporting students who may have to come up with funds for tuition, books, and other college fees. Additionally, many older students—and even a few traditional-aged ones—are responsible for living expenses and supporting children or other family members on top of school costs. The more complicated the situation, the more it can distract you from your work and your academic goals.

Your challenge is to come up with enough money to pay for college and expenses, without working so many hours that you have no time to study (remember Sajid?) or taking out so many loans that you can't dig out of debt for years. The answer may involve some combination of applying for financial aid, holding a job, effective budgeting, and avoiding credit card debt.

Explore and Apply for Financial Aid

Financing your education—alone or with the help of your family—involves gathering financial information and making decisions about what you can afford and how much help you need. Some roadblocks stand in the way of getting help. Your challenge is to find a way around them:

STUDENTS DON'T APPLY. One recent report indicated that almost 40% of full-time community college students do not fill out a federal aid application, including 29% of students with incomes under $10,000 per year. These students may be intimidated by the application process or simply believe that they won't qualify for aid.[7]

THE ECONOMY HAS AN EFFECT. When the economy is struggling, private banks are less likely to grant loans, and federal programs like the Pell Grants (see Key 4.5) have less money. Also, in tough economic times, more students apply for grants like the Pell, with the result that more people will get smaller pieces of the pie.[8]

COLLEGES VARY IN WHAT THEY OFFER. State colleges provide fewer opportunities for aid when their funding is reduced. Additionally, concerned about students' ability to pay back loans, some smaller colleges stop offering federal loans to their students.[9]

TYPES OF AID

Aid comes in the form of student loans, grants, and scholarships. *Almost all students are eligible for some kind of need-based or merit-based financial assistance.*

STUDENT LOANS. Student loan recipients are responsible for paying back the amount borrowed, plus interest, according to a payment schedule that may stretch over a number of years. The federal government administers or oversees most student loans. To receive aid from a federal program, you must be a citizen or eligible non-citizen and be enrolled in a program that meets government requirements. Key 4.4 describes the main student loan programs to which you can apply.

	KEY **4.4**	*Get the Details on Federal Student Loan Programs*

LOAN	DESCRIPTION
Perkins	Low, fixed rate of interest. Available to those with exceptional financial need (determined by a government formula). Issued by schools from their allotment of federal funds. Grace period of up to nine months after graduation before repayment, in monthly installments, must begin.
Stafford	Available to students enrolled at least half-time. Exceptional need not required, although students who prove need can qualify for a subsidized Stafford loan (the government pays interest until repayment begins). Two types of Staffords: the direct loan comes from federal funds, and the FFEL (Federal Family Education Loan) comes from a bank or credit union. Repayment begins six months after you graduate, leave school, or drop below half-time enrollment.
PLUS	Available to students enrolled at least half-time and claimed as dependents by their parents. Parents must undergo a credit check to be eligible, or may be sponsored through a relative or friend who passes the check. Loan comes from government or a bank or credit union. Sponsor must begin repayment 60 days after receiving the last loan payment.

GRANTS. Unlike student loans, grants do not require repayment. Grants, funded by federal, state, or local governments as well as private organizations, are awarded to students who show financial need. Key 4.5 describes federal grant programs. Additional information about both grants and loans is available in *The Student Guide to Financial Aid*, which you can find at your school's financial aid office, request by phone (800-433-3243), or access online at www.ed.gov/prog_info/SFA/StudentGuide/.

SCHOLARSHIPS. Scholarships are awarded to students who show talent or ability in specific areas (academic achievement, sports, the arts, citizenship, or leadership). They may be financed by government or private organizations, employers (yours or your parents'), schools, religious organizations, local and community groups, credit unions, or individuals.

LOOKING FOR AID
Take the following five actions in your quest to pay for college.[10]

ASK, ASK, ASK. Visit the financial aid office more than once. Ask what you are eligible for. Alert the office to any money problems, such as a change in your financial situation. Search libraries and the Web, including your school's Web site, for information on everything that is possible.

APPLY FOR GOVERNMENT AID. Fill out the Free Application for Federal Student Aid (FAFSA) form electronically. The form can be found through your college's financial aid office or Web site, or via the U.S. Department of Education's Web site at www.ed.gov/finaid.html. The U.S. Education Department has an online tool called FAFSA Forecaster, which you can use to estimate how much aid you qualify for. You will need to reapply every year for federal aid. This is a free form—if you hear about services that charge a fee for completing your FAFSA for you, avoid them.

GET HELP. Consider asking a parent or relative to co-sign on a loan application or to loan you money directly. Web sites such as www.fynanz.com or www.GreenNote.com can help you

KEY **4.5** *Get the Details on Federal Student Loan Programs*

GRANT	DESCRIPTION
Pell	Need-based; the government evaluates your reported financial information and determines eligibility from that "score" (called an expected family contribution, or EFC). Available to undergraduates who have earned no other degrees. Amount varies according to education cost and EFC. Adding other aid sources is allowed.
Federal Supplemental Educational Opportunity (FSEOG)	Need-based; administered by the financial aid administrator at participating schools. Each participating school receives a limited amount of federal funds for FSEOGs and sets its own application deadlines.
Work-study	Need-based; encourages community service work or work related to your course of study. Pays by the hour, at least the federal minimum wage. Jobs may be on campus (usually for your school) or off (often with a nonprofit organization or a public agency).

create a legal document formalizing the agreement between you and the person offering the loan.

CONSIDER A RANGE OF OPTIONS. Look at loans from all kinds of private lenders in addition to federal loans. Compare loans using Web sites like www.estudentloan.com. Consider transferring to a less expensive school. You may be able to get a comparable education while escaping post-graduation debt.

APPLYING FOR AID

The number one rule is to apply—and apply by the deadline or, even better, early. The earlier you complete the process, the greater your chances of being considered for aid, especially when you are vying for part of a limited pool of funds. Here are some additional tips from financial aid experts Arlina DeNardo and Carolyn Lindley of Northwestern University:[12]

> **Know what applications you need to fill out.** FAFSA is required at all colleges, but some also require a form called the CSS/Financial Aid Profile.

> **Note the difference between merit-based and need-based aid.** While some aid is awarded based on financial need, other aid is merit-based, meaning that it is linked to specifics such as academic performance, a particular major, or ethnic origin.

> **Be aware of the total cost of attending college.** When you consider how much money you need, add books, transportation, housing, food, and other fees to tuition.

> **If you receive aid, pay attention to the award letter.** Know whether the aid is a grant or a loan that needs to be repaid. Follow rules such as remaining in academic good standing. Note reapplication deadlines and meet them (many require reapplication *every year*).

Finally, don't take out more money than you need. If you max out on your total aid too early in your college career, you could run into trouble as you approach graduation. Look at your needs year by year, and make sure you are only taking out what is absolutely necessary.

By the way . . .

according to a recent survey, although 78% of students indicate that the financial aid office is one of the most important resources on campus, only 17% report using it frequently.[11]

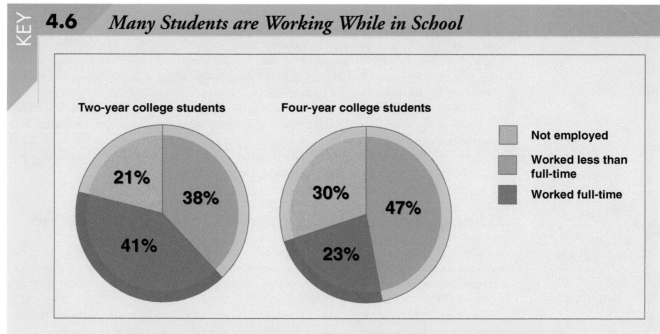

KEY 4.6 *Many Students are Working While in School*

Two-year college students

- 21%
- 38%
- 41%

Four-year college students

- 30%
- 47%
- 23%

Not employed

Worked less than full-time

Worked full-time

Source: U.S. Department of Education, National Center for Educational Statistics, *Profile of Undergraduates in U.S. Postsecondary Educational Institutions: 2003–2004* (NCES 2006-184), June 2006, p.13.

Juggle Work and School

More than two-thirds of college students have some kind of job while in school. Key 4.6 shows the percentages of part-time and full-time college students who work.

If, like Sajid, you want to or need to work, try to do it in a way that allows you to focus on schoolwork.

ESTABLISH YOUR NEEDS

Think about what you need from a job before you begin your job hunt. Ask questions like these:

▶ How much money do I need to make—weekly, per term, for the year?

▶ What time of day is best for me? Should I consider night or weekend work?

▶ Can my schedule handle a full-time job, or should I look for part-time work?

▶ Do I want hands-on experience and/or connections in a particular field?

▶ What do I like and dislike doing?

▶ Does location matter? Where do I want to work, and how far am I willing to commute?

▶ How flexible a job do I need?

▶ Can I, or should I, find work at my school or as part of a work-study program?

ANALYZE EFFECTS OF WORKING WHILE IN SCHOOL

Working while in school can have both pros and cons. Here are some possibilities for each:

▶ **Pros:** general and career-specific experience; developing future contacts; enhanced school performance (working up to 15 hours a week may help you use your time more effectively)

▶ **Cons:** time commitment that reduces available study time; reduced opportunity for social and extracurricular activities; having to shift gears mentally from work to classroom; stretching yourself too thin and being tired all the time

IDENTIFY OPTIONS, MAKE A CHOICE, AND EVALUATE

Use what you learned about yourself when you apply for jobs. Continue to evaluate after you start a job. If the benefits you anticipated aren't there, or aren't enough, consider other possibilities at work or at school. Sajid might find, for example, that one job gives him enough money if he goes to school part time. He's okay with taking longer to get a degree because he realizes that he will almost certainly fail if he continues what he is doing.

Connect with your school's job placement office, career center and counselors, or Web site job board as you search for the right position. Keep in mind that work-study positions have many advantages for students: They are located on campus, and they don't involve weekend or holiday hours. Finally, if you do get a job off campus, make sure your employer knows that you are a student and that your schedule may change every term.

Manage Income and Expenses Through Budgeting

Budget
a plan to coordinate resources and expenditures; a set of goals regarding money.

Creating a practical monthly **budget** that works means that you gather information about your resources (money flowing in) and expenditures (money flowing out) and analyze the difference. Next, you come up with ideas about how you can make changes. Finally, you adjust spending or earning so that you come out even or ahead.

Your biggest expense right now is probably the cost of your education. However, that expense may not hit you fully until after you graduate and begin to pay back your student loans. For now, include in your budget only the education costs you are paying while you are in school.

FIGURE OUT WHAT YOU EARN

Add up all of the money you receive during the year—the actual after-tax money you have to pay your bills. Common sources of income include:

- ▶ Take-home pay from a regular full-time or part-time job during the school year
- ▶ Take-home pay from summer and holiday employment
- ▶ Money you earn as part of a work-study program
- ▶ Money you receive from your parents or other relatives for your college expenses
- ▶ Loans, scholarships, or grants

If you have saved money for college, decide how much you will withdraw every month for school-related expenses.

FIGURE OUT WHAT YOU SPEND

Start by recording every check or electronic withdrawal going toward fixed expenses like rent, phone, and Internet service. Then, over the next month, record personal expenditures in a small notebook. Indicate any expenditure over $5, making sure to count smaller expenditures if they are frequent (for example, a bus pass for a month, coffee or lunch purchases per week).

Some expenses, like automobile and health insurance, may be billed only a few times a year. In these cases, divide the yearly cost by 12 to see how much you pay each month. Common expenses include:

- ▶ Rent or mortgage
- ▶ Tuition that you are paying right now (the portion remaining after all forms of financial aid)
- ▶ Books, lab fees, and other educational expenses
- ▶ Regular bills (electric, gas, oil, phone, water)
- ▶ Food, clothing, toiletries, and household supplies
- ▶ Child care
- ▶ Transportation and auto expenses (gas, maintenance, monthly bus or train pass)

- Credit cards and other payments on credit (car payments)
- Insurance (health, auto, homeowner's or renter's, life)
- Entertainment (cable TV, movies, restaurants, books and magazines, music downloads)
- Computer-related expenses, including the cost of your online service
- Miscellaneous unplanned expenses

Use the total of all your monthly expenses as a baseline for other months, realizing that your expenditures will vary depending on what is happening in your life and even the season (for example, the cost to heat your home may be much greater in the winter than in the summer).

EVALUATE THE DIFFERENCE

Focusing again on your current situation, subtract your monthly expenses from your monthly income. Ideally, you have money left over—to save or to spend. However, if you are spending more than you take in, ask some focused questions.

© Shutterstock

- **Examine expenses.** Did you forget to budget for recurring expenses such as dental visits? Was your budget derailed by an emergency expense such as a major car repair?
- **Examine spending patterns and priorities.** Did you overspend on entertainment or clothes? Are you being hit by high interest payments or late fees on your credit card? Did you really need that new iPod, cell phone, car stereo, hair color, or movie club membership?
- **Examine income.** Do you bring in what you need? Do you need to look for another source of income—a job or financial aid?

ADJUST EXPENSES OR EARNINGS

If you need to make changes, brainstorm solutions that involve either increasing resources or decreasing spending. To increase resources, consider taking a part-time job, increasing hours at a current job, or finding aid. To decrease spending, look at what expenses you can trim or cut out. In addition, save money in day-to-day ways such as the following:

- Share living space
- Take advantage of free on-campus entertainment (movies and events)
- Rent movies or borrow them from friends or the library
- Eat at home more often
- Use grocery and clothing coupons
- Take advantage of sales, buy store brands, and buy in bulk
- Find discounted play and concert tickets for students
- Walk or use public transport
- Bring lunch from home
- Shop in secondhand stores or swap clothing with friends
- Bring coffee from home instead of buying it at expensive coffee shops
- Reduce credit hours
- Ask a relative to help with child care or create a babysitting co-op
- Cut back on air conditioning and use compact flourescent bulbs (CFLs)

Key 4.7 shows a sample budget of an unmarried student living with two other students in off-campus housing with no meal plan. Included are all regular and out-of-pocket expenses with the exception of tuition, which the student will pay back after graduation in student loan payments. In this case, the student is $523 over budget, having spent more than $300 this month on miscellaneous expenses such as clothing, downloadable music, and a new cell phone. How would you make up the difference?

KEY

4.7   *How One Student Mapped Out a Monthly Budget*

▶ Wages: $12 an hour (after taxes) × 20 hours a week = $240 a week × 4 1/3 weeks (one month) = $1,039

▶ Monthly withdrawals from savings (from summer earnings) = $200

▶ Total income per month = $1,239

MONTHLY EXPENDITURES

School-related expenses (books, supplies, any expense not covered by financial aid)	$80
Public transportation	$90
Phone	$92
Food (groceries and takeout)	$285
Credit card payments	$100
Rent (including utilities)	$650
Entertainment (music, movies, tickets to events)	$90
Miscellaneous expenses, including clothing and personal items	$375
Total monthly spending:	**$1,762**
$1,239 (income) − $1,762 (expenses) = −$523	*$523 over budget*

Credit card offers pop up everywhere, as these women applying for Walmart cards know. Think carefully before applying for any type of card.

© Bob Daemmrich/PhotoEdit

Consider your dominant multiple intelligences when planning your budget. For example, whereas logical–mathematical learners may take to a classic detail-oriented budgeting plan, visual learners may want to create a budget chart, or bodily–kinesthetic learners may want to make budgeting more tangible by dumping receipts into a big jar and tallying them at the end of the month. See the multiple intelligence strategies grid on the next page for MI-related ideas about how to manage your money.

Manage Credit Card Use

Credit card companies target college students with dozens of offers. Credit cards are a handy alternative to cash and can help build a strong credit history if used appropriately, but they also can plunge you into debt, affecting your credit rating and making it difficult to get loans or finance car or home purchases. Tough economic times often mean heavier reliance on credit to get by. Recent statistics show how college students use credit cards:[14]

▶ 84% of college students hold at least one credit card. The average number of cards is 4.6 and 50% have four or more.

▶ Students who hold credit cards carry an average outstanding balance of $3,173.

▶ 92% of students report charging school supplies or other education expenses. Nearly 30% report using cards to pay tuition.

Multiple Intelligence Strategies for Money Management

Briefly describe a money management problem you have.

_____

_____

Now, brainstorm potential solutions to your problem, linking each solution to an intelligence. Use the right-hand column to record your ideas.

INTELLIGENCE	SUGGESTED STRATEGIES	USE MI STRATEGIES TO COME UP WITH SOLUTIONS
Verbal–Linguistic	■ Talk over your financial situation with someone you trust. ■ Write out a detailed budget outline. If you can, store it on a computer file so you can update it regularly.	
Logical–Mathematical	■ Focus on the numbers; using a calculator and amounts as exact as possible, determine your income and spending. ■ Calculate how much money you'll have in 10 years if you start now to put $2,000 in a 5% interest-bearing IRA account each year.	
Bodily–Kinesthetic	■ Consider putting money, or a slip with a dollar amount, each month in envelopes for various budget items—rent, dining out, etc. When the envelope is empty or the number is reduced to zero, spending stops.	
Visual–Spatial	■ Set up a budgeting system that includes color-coded folders and colored charts. ■ Create color-coded folders for papers related to financial and retirement goals—investments, accounts, etc.	
Interpersonal	■ Whenever money problems come up, discuss them right away with a family member, partner, or roommate. ■ Brainstorm a five-year financial plan with one of your friends.	
Intrapersonal	■ Schedule quiet time to plan how to develop, follow, and update your budget. Consider financial-management software, such as Quicken. ■ Think through where your money should go to best achieve your long-term financial goals.	
Musical	■ Include a category of music-related purchases in your budget—going to concerts, buying CDs—but keep an eye on it to make sure you don't go overboard.	
Naturalistic	■ Analyze your spending by using a system of categories. Your system may be based on time (when payments are due), priority (must-pay bills vs. extras), or spending type (monthly bills, education, family expenses).	

TAKE
ACTION: Map Out Your Budget

Use your logical–mathematical intelligence to see what you take in and spend and to decide what adjustments you need to make. Consider using an online calculator—such as www.calculatorweb.com—for this task.

Step 1: Estimate your current expenses in dollars per month, using the following table. This may require tracking expenses for a month, if you don't already have a record.

EXPENSE	AMOUNT SPENT
Rent/mortgage or room and board payment	$
Utilities (electric, heat, gas, water)	$
Food (shopping, eating out, meal plan)	$
Telephone (land line and mobile phone)	$
Books, lab fees, other educational expenses	$
Loan payments (educational or bank loans)	$
Car (repairs, insurance, payments, gas)	$
Public transportation	$
Clothing/personal items	$
Entertainment	$
Child care (caregivers, clothing/supplies, etc.)	$
Medical care/insurance	$
Other	$
TOTAL MONTHLY EXPENSES	$

Step 2: Calculate your average monthly income. If it's easiest to come up with a yearly figure, divide by 12 to derive the monthly figure. For example, if you have a $6,000 scholarship for the year, your monthly income would be $500 ($6,000 divided by 12).

INCOME SOURCE	AMOUNT RECEIVED
Regular work salary/wages (full-time or part-time)	$
Grants or work-study programs	$
Scholarships	$
Assistance from family members	$
Other	$
TOTAL	$

TAKE ACTION: Map Out Your Budget (continued)

Step 3: Subtract the grand total of your monthly expenses from the grand total of your monthly income

INCOME PER MONTH	$
Expenses per month	– $
CASH FLOW	$

Step 4: If you have a negative cash flow, you can increase income, decrease spending, or both. List two workable ideas about how you can get your cash flow back in the black.

1. _____

2. _____

Often cash-poor, college students charge books and tuition on cards (or "plastic") as well as expenses like car repair, food, and clothes. Before they know it, their debt becomes unmanageable. It's hard to notice trouble brewing when you don't see your wallet taking a hit.

HOW CREDIT CARDS WORK

Every time you charge a purchase, you create a debt that must be repaid. The credit card issuer earns money by charging interest on unpaid balances. Here's an example: Say you have a $3,000 unpaid balance on your card at an annual interest rate of 18%. If you make the $60 minimum payment every month, it will take you eight years to pay off your debt, *assuming that you make no other purchases*. The effect on your wallet is staggering:

▶ Original debt—$3,000
▶ Cost to repay credit card loan at an annual interest rate of 18% for 8 years—$5,760
▶ Cost of using credit—$5,760 – $3,000 = $2,760

As you can see, by the time you finish, you will repay nearly *twice* your original debt.

The first step in avoiding debt is to know as much as you can about credit cards, starting with the important concepts in Key 4.8 on the next page.

MANAGING CREDIT CARD DEBT

Think before you act in order to avoid debt. Ask questions before charging: Would I buy it if I had to pay cash? Can I pay off the balance in full at the end of the month? If I buy this, what else will I have to give up? The majority of American citizens have some level of debt, and many people go through periods when they have a hard time paying bills. If you use credit wisely while in school, however, you will build good habits that can improve your financial future.

A few basics will help you stay in control.

"Money is only a tool. It will take you wherever you wish, but it will not replace you as the driver."

—Ayn Rand, writer and philosopher

KEY

4.8 *Be a Smart Credit Consumer*

WHAT IS THIS?	WHAT DO YOU DO WITH IT?
Annual percentage rate (APR) is the amount of interest charged on the money you don't pay off in any given month. The higher your APR, the higher your finance charges.	Shop around for low rates (check www.studentcredit.com). Look for fixed rates. Watch out for low rates that skyrocket to more than 20% after a few months or a couple of late payments.
Cash advance is an immediate loan, in cash, from the credit card company.	Use a cash advance only in emergencies. Finance charges begin immediately, and you may also have to pay a transaction fee.
Credit limit is the top amount your card company allows you to charge, including all fees and cash advances.	Card companies generally set lower credit limits for students, but your limit may rise if you pay bills on time. Avoid charging up to the limit, so that you have credit available for emergencies.
Finance charges include interest and fees and are calculated each month.	The only way to avoid a finance charge is to pay your balance in full by the due date.
Minimum payment is set by the card company and refers to the smallest amount you can pay by the statement due date.	Make the minimum payment at the very least—not doing so may hurt your credit report. Remember that the more you can pay each month, the less you spend on fees.

Creditor
A person or company to whom a debt is owed, usually money.

▶ **Choose your card wisely.** Students are often eligible for lower interest rate cards, cards with no annual fee, cards with useful rewards, or cards with a grace period (no penalty for late payments up to a certain number of days).

▶ **Pay bills on time, and make at least the minimum payment.** Remind yourself a week or so before the due date by creating an e-mail alert through your card account, making a note in your planner, or setting an alarm on your electronic planner.

▶ **Stay on top of problems.** If you get into trouble, call the **creditor** and see if you can set up a payment plan. Then, going forward, try to avoid what got you into trouble. Organizations such as the National Foundation for Credit Counseling (www.nfcc.org) can help you solve problems.

▶ **Reduce the load.** Cut up a credit card or two if you have too many.

HABIT FOR SUCCESS

THINK BEFORE YOU ACT

Below are examples of how you can put this habit into action in different situations. Use the three spaces to add your own ideas for actions you can accomplish now or in the future. Be specific, and be realistic.

Before quitting a job you are unhappy with, think about finding another job so you won't have trouble paying your bills.

Before you buy a used car, research Blue Book values and prices from different dealerships.

Before agreeing to a weekly Wednesday afternoon basketball game, plan out how much time you need to study for finals.

Think Before You Act Habit for Success

Before getting a new pet, think over whether you have the time and resources to care for it properly.

Look carefully at the commuting time when considering a job or local college.

BUILDING
SKILLS: For Successful Learning

NOTE THE IMPORTANT POINTS

What do time and money have to do with college success?

Explain how your two key resources—money and time—are connected.

_____

_____

WHAT KIND OF TIME AND MONEY MANAGER ARE YOU?

Briefly describe yourself as a time manager.

_____

_____

Briefly describe yourself as a money manager.

_____

_____

HOW CAN YOU EFFECTIVELY MANAGE YOUR TIME?

Describe how to build a useful schedule.

_____

_____

Name three strategies that can help you put your schedule to work.

1. _____

2. _____

3. _____

BUILDING SKILLS: For Successful Learning (continued)

HOW CAN YOU MANAGE YOUR MONEY?

Describe two actions you can take to find financial aid.

1. _____

2. _____

Define what it means to "budget."

_____

CRITICAL THINKING: Applying Learning to Life

DISCOVER HOW YOU SPEND YOUR TIME

Use the tables here to record data. Answer questions and write additional thoughts on separate paper or in a computer file.

Everyone has exactly 168 hours in a week. How do you spend yours? To warm up, make guesses, or estimates, about three particular activities. In a week, how much time do you spend . . .

1. Studying? _____ hours

2. Sleeping? _____ hours

3. Interacting with media and technology (computer, online services, cell phone, video games, television) for non-study purposes? _____ hours

   Now, to find out the real story, record how you spend your time for seven days. The chart on pages 100–101 has blocks showing half-hour increments. As you go through the week, write in what you do each hour. Include sleep and leisure time. Record your *actual* activities instead of the activities you wished you did. There are no wrong answers.

CRITICAL
THINKING: Applying Learning to Life (continued)

TIME	Monday ACTIVITY	Tuesday ACTIVITY	Wednesday ACTIVITY	Thursday ACTIVITY
6:00 A.M.				
6:30 A.M.				
7:00 A.M.				
7:30 A.M.				
8:00 A.M.				
8:30 A.M.				
9:00 A.M.				
9:30 A.M.				
10:00 A.M.				
10:30 A.M.				
11:00 A.M.				
11:30 A.M.				
12:00 P.M.				
12:30 P.M.				
1:00 P.M.				
1:30 P.M.				
2:00 P.M.				
2:30 P.M.				
3:00 P.M.				
3:30 P.M.				
4:00 P.M.				
4:30 P.M.				
5:00 P.M.				
5:30 P.M.				
6:00 P.M.				
6:30 P.M.				
7:00 P.M.				
7:30 P.M.				
8:00 P.M.				
8:30 P.M.				
9:00 P.M.				
9:30 P.M.				
10:00 P.M.				
10:30 P.M.				
11:00 P.M.				
11:30 P.M.				
12:00 A.M.				
12:30 A.M.				
1:00 A.M.				
1:30 A.M.				
2:00 A.M.				

CRITICAL THINKING: Applying Learning to Life (continued)

TIME	Friday ACTIVITY	Saturday ACTIVITY	Sunday ACTIVITY
6:00 A.M.			
6:30 A.M.			
7:00 A.M.			
7:30 A.M.			
8:00 A.M.			
8:30 A.M.			
9:00 A.M.			
9:30 A.M.			
10:00 A.M.			
10:30 A.M.			
11:00 A.M.			
11:30 A.M.			
12:00 P.M.			
12:30 P.M.			
1:00 P.M.			
1:30 P.M.			
2:00 P.M.			
2:30 P.M.			
3:00 P.M.			
3:30 P.M.			
4:00 P.M.			
4:30 P.M.			
5:00 P.M.			
5:30 P.M.			
6:00 P.M.			
6:30 P.M.			
7:00 P.M.			
7:30 P.M.			
8:00 P.M.			
8:30 P.M.			
9:00 P.M.			
9:30 P.M.			
10:00 P.M.			
10:30 P.M.			
11:00 P.M.			
11:30 P.M.			
12:00 A.M.			
12:30 A.M.			
1:00 A.M.			
1:30 A.M.			
2:00 A.M.			

(continued)

CRITICAL
THINKING: Applying Learning to Life (continued)

After a week, add up how many hours you spent on each activity (round off to half-hours—that is, mark 40 minutes of activity as a half-hour, and 45 minutes as one hour). Log the hours in the boxes in the table below using tally marks, with a full mark representing one hour and a half-size mark representing one-half hour. In the third column, total the hours for each activity. Leave the "Ideal Time in Hours" column blank for now.

ACTIVITY	TIME TALLIED OVER ONE-WEEK PERIOD	TOTAL TIME IN HOURS	IDEAL TIME IN HOURS
Example: Class	꤯꤯꤯ Ⅱ	16.5	
Class			
Work			
Studying			
Sleeping			
Eating			
Family time/child care			
Commuting/traveling			
Chores and personal business			
Friends and important relationships			
Telephone time			
Leisure/entertainment			
Spiritual life			
Other			

Add the totals in the third column to find your grand total. Use a separate sheet of paper to answer the following questions:

▶ What surprises you about how you spend your time?

▶ Where do you waste the most time? What do you think that is costing you?

▶ On what activities do you think you should spend more or less time?

▶ What are you willing to do to make a change?

Go back to the chart and fill in the "Ideal Time in Hours" column. Finally, write a short paragraph describing the time-management changes you plan to make to move closer to spending your time the way you want to.

TEAM BUILDING: Collaborative Solutions

BRAINSTORM DAY-TO-DAY WAYS TO SAVE MONEY

▶   Gather in a group of three or four. Together, think about the ways you spend money in a typical month. Come up with three areas of spending that you have in common.

▶   On your own, take five minutes to brainstorm ideas about how to reduce spending in those areas. What expense can you reduce or do without? Where can you look for savings? Can you exchange a product or service for one that a friend can provide?

▶   Come together to share your ideas. Discuss which ones you would be most able and likely to put into action. Write your five most workable ideas here.

1. _____

2. _____

3. _____

4. _____

5. _____

On your own, give these a try and see how they can help you put some money toward your savings. To make the experiment tangible, put cash into a jar once a week in the amount you've saved by making these changes. See how much you have at the end of one month—and bank it.

Test Prep: START IT NOW

THINK BEFORE YOU ACT TO PREPARE FOR MIDTERM/EXAM WEEK

It is never too early to get on top of what you will need to do to prepare for a big exam week (choose either midterm or finals week, depending on which is more challenging for you). Look at your schedule now, and note the date exactly three weeks before your first exam. Write that date here.

_____

Your goal is to find *three hours per day for each day of those three weeks* to study for your exams. First, subtract the hours allotted to Priority 1 activities—class, work, caring for children or others, and sleep. Then look at what is left. For each day in the three-week calendar here, write the date and indicate your planned study hours in whatever form you can manage them—for example, "2–5 p.m." or "10–11 a.m. and 9–11 p.m.," or even "1–2 p.m., 5–6 p.m., and 9–10 p.m."

Month: _____

SUN	MON	TUES	WED	THURS	FRI	SAT

Enter this schedule into your planner, and do your best to stick to it. Life may get in the way of several of your study sessions, but commit to finding other times for them rather than giving them up entirely.

Time for a Change: TAKE STEPS TO IMPROVE A HABIT FOR SUCCESS

First: Write one of your three **strongest** Habits for Success here. _____

_____

Why does it work for you? Name a result of this habit that helps you solve problems and move toward important goals. _____

_____

Now: Write one of your three **least developed** Habits for Success here. _____

_____

Why do you want to develop this habit—in other words, what positive effect do you think it will have on your ability to solve problems

and achieve goals? _____

_____

Focus on this challenging habit more carefully. Answer the following questions on a separate piece of paper or computer file.

▶ Name two specific, short-term actions you can take to power up this habit.

▶ Name a support person and describe your plan for communicating your progress and getting encouragement (for example, have your person call, e-mail, or text you on a regular basis to check up on particular actions you've committed to taking).

Remember, the way to make a habit stick is to do it over and over again over a period of at least 21 days. *Right now,* commit to checking your progress on a regular basis over the next three weeks, using whatever method you prefer. Describe the method you will use to track your habit development.

▶ What will you use? (Example: date book, electronic planner, cell phone alarm, e-mail alert)

▶ When and how often will you use it? (Example: every day at bedtime, every other day when I get up, twice a week after a particular class)

It's time for a change—put your plan in motion *today.*

CHAPTER 5
SETTING AND REACHING GOALS

USING VALUES, STRESS MANAGEMENT, AND TEAMWORK RESOURCES

L idia is experiencing overload. She is a full-time office assistant during the week and spends nights and weekends taking college accounting courses. With a toddler, a 10-year-old, and a husband who works nights, child care is a major problem. Her mother watches the kids on Mondays and Tuesdays, but she works too.

Lidia often has to drop everything in the middle of a study session to deal with her kids. She can't afford full-time child care, so she tries to find help day by day. She is trying to keep this up for another two years until her oldest can babysit his younger brother. In the meantime, she worries that she will be unable to stay on the path toward completing her courses and earning a degree.

IN THIS CHAPTER . . .

You explore answers to the following questions:

WHY ARE VALUES THE FOUNDATION OF SUCCESSFUL GOAL SETTING?

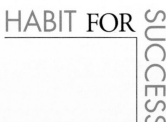

Core Values
the principles and qualities that inform your beliefs and actions.

To set the goals that are best for you—and, even more importantly, to move ahead toward achieving them—you need to identify the **core values** that motivate you. This chapter will show you how to set S.M.A.R.T. goals (specific, measurable, attainable, relevant, and linked to time frame) based on these values. It will also give you tools to manage the stress that can hinder your efforts to reach your target, and strengthen your ability to work with others so you can achieve goals faster and more efficiently than you could if you worked alone.

For the best chance at success, your core values should guide the goals you set and the choices you make. Lidia's choice to pursue a degree reflects her belief that a college education will help her get ahead, and focusing on child care shows that she prioritizes the needs of her family. Discovering what matters to *you* ensures that the changes you make in your life in the goal-setting process are meaningful and will keep you motivated.

Your values help you to:

▶ **Understand what you want out of life.** Your top goals reflect what you value most.

▶ **Define your educational path.** Values help you to explore what you want to learn, your major, and career goals.

▶ **Create "rules for life."** Values form the foundation for decisions and behavior. You will return repeatedly to them for guidance, especially when dealing with new problems.

Values are influenced by family, friends, culture, media, school, work, neighborhood, religion, world events, and more. Your strongest values are often linked to childhood experiences and family, but values may shift as you acquire knowledge and experiences and build new relationships. For example, a student whose family and friends were there for him after a serious accident may place greater value on relationships than he did before the accident.

Values form the bedrock of meaningful goals. The stronger the link between your values and your long-term goals, the happier, more motivated, and more successful you are likely to be in setting and achieving those goals.

"A goal without a plan is just a wish."
—Larry Elder, radio talk show host

TAKE ACTION: Explore Your Core Values

Rate each of the following values on a scale from 1 to 5, 1 being least important to you and 5 being most important.

Knowing myself_____

Self-improvement_____

Political involvement_____

Leadership and teamwork skills_____

Getting a good job_____

Pursuing an education_____

Having a family_____

Helping others_____

Being liked by others_____

Taking risks_____

Being with friends_____

Political involvement_____

Being organized_____

Spiritual/religious life_____

Health and fitness_____

Participating in an online community_____

Having time to read_____

Time to myself_____

Lifelong learning_____

Competing and winning_____

Financial stability_____

Making a lot of money_____

Creative/artistic pursuits_____

Other (write below)_____

_____

Write your top three values here:

1. _____

2. _____

3. _____

Often, musical choices reflect values. Putting your musical intelligence to work, find a song that inspires you. Now imagine that you're creating a CD for a friend with that song on it. Write a quick note about why you included the song on the CD. Be sure to mention how it connects to one or more of your top values.

_____

_____

_____

HOW DO YOU SET AND ACHIEVE GOALS?

Goal
an end toward which you direct your efforts.

When you set a **goal**, you focus on what you want to achieve and create a path that can get you there. Learning to set and achieve goals isn't just important for students. It is essential in your personal life and career.

Setting goals involves defining what you are aiming for in both long-term and short-term time frames. *Long-term* goals are broader objectives you want to achieve over a long period of time, perhaps a year or more. *Short-term* goals are smaller steps that move you toward a long-term goal, making it manageable and achievable, piece by piece (see Key 5.1).

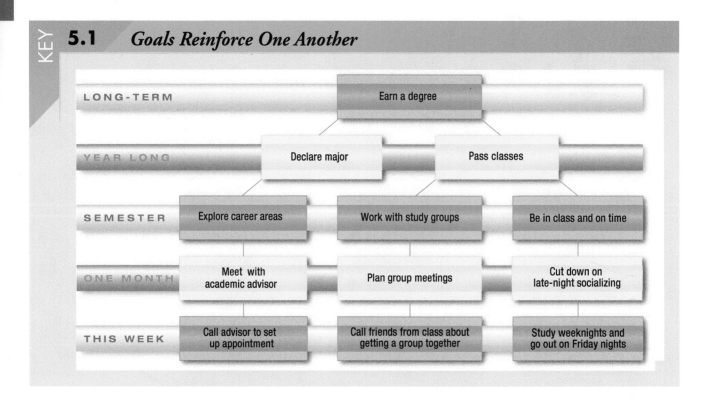

LONG-TERM		Earn a degree		
YEAR LONG		Declare major	Pass classes	
SEMESTER	Explore career areas	Work with study groups		Be in class and on time
ONE MONTH	Meet with academic advisor	Plan group meetings		Cut down on late-night socializing
THIS WEEK	Call advisor to set up appointment	Call friends from class about getting a group together		Study weeknights and go out on Friday nights

Set Long-Term Goals

Take a moment to imagine: What do you want your life to look like in 5 years? In 10 years? In 20? What degree do you want to earn, what kind of job do you want, where do you want to live? Your answers to questions like these help you identify your long-term goals.

Some long-term goals have an open-ended time frame. For example, if as a nursing student, your long-term goal is to stay on top of developments in medicine, you will pursue this goal throughout your professional life. Other goals, such as completing the required courses for your degree, have a more definite end and often fewer options for getting there.

One way to make long-term goals real is to put them in writing. For example:

My goal is to become a nurse practitioner, emphasizing preventative medicine, who works in a clinic in an underserved community.

To determine your long-term goals, think about what you want to accomplish while in school and after you graduate. For example, it is no surprise that Lidia, who values financial stability, is motivated to do well in her accounting courses.

Set Short-Term Goals

Lasting as short as an hour or as long as several months, *short-term* goals help you narrow your focus and encourage progress toward bigger dreams. The student aiming to be a nurse practitioner might set supporting short-term goals like these for her second year of college:

Choose courses that keep me on track to complete pre-med requirements. Locate a medical practice serving an underprivileged community and apply for a

---

By the way...

focusing on one goal at a time increases your chance of success. Studies show that switching back and forth too often, or trying to accomplish more than one goal at a time, reduces focus and can actually increase stress.[1]

summer internship. Research graduate schools that offer a nurse-practitioner degree.

Getting more specific, this student may set these short-term goals for the next six months:

- ▶ I will learn the names and functions of every human bone and muscle.
- ▶ I will work with a study group to understand the muscular-skeletal system.

These goals can be broken down into even shorter time frames. Here are one-month goals:

- ▶ I will work with on-screen tutorials of the muscular-skeletal system.
- ▶ I will spend three hours a week with my study partners.

Your short-term goals may last a week, a day, or even a couple of hours. Here's how Lidia might use smaller short-term goals to support a month-long goal to set up weekend child care:

- ▶ **By the end of today:** Text and e-mail friends to see if they know of available sitters or are looking to pick up some extra cash themselves
- ▶ **One week from now:** Have at least two potential sitters to contact
- ▶ **Two weeks from now:** Have spoken to potential sitters and evaluated the possibilities
- ▶ **Four weeks from now:** Have plan in place for regular help for at least one weekend day

Your Syllabus: A Powerful Goal-Achievement Tool

Remember: For each course you take, your syllabus provides a clear layout of the goals you will target throughout the term and when you need to achieve them. Keep paper syllabi where you can refer to them frequently, and bookmark electronic syllabi if your instructors post them on-line. Key 5.2 shows a portion of an actual syllabus with important items noted.

Set Up a Goal-Achievement Plan

At any given time, you are working toward goals of varying importance. Prioritize goals so you can put the bulk of your energy and time toward those that matter most. Then draw up a plan, using the S.M.A.R.T. system to make your goals Specific, Measurable, Attainable, Relevant, and attached to a Time Frame (see Key 5.3).

Step 1: Define an attainable, relevant goal. *What do you want?* Is it attainable (within reach)? Is it relevant (connected to your needs)? To develop an attainable, relevant goal, consider your hopes, interests, abilities, and values. Then, reflect on whether your goal is possible, given your resources and circumstances. Write out a clear description of your goal.

Step 2: Define a specific path. *How will you get there?* Brainstorm different paths. Choose one; then map out its specific steps. Focus on behaviors and events that are under your control.

Step 3: Set a timetable. *When do you want to accomplish your goal?* Schedule steps within a realistic time frame. Create specific deadlines for each step you defined in Step 1. Charting your progress will help you stay on track.

Step 4: Measure your progress. *What safeguards will keep you on track?* Will you record your progress in a weekly journal? Report to a friend? Use an alarm system on your smartphone to remind you to do something? Create a measurement system to evaluate your progress.

Step 5: Get unstuck. *What will you do if you hit a roadblock?* The path to a goal is often rocky and stressful. Anticipate problems and define **specific** ways to alter your plans if you run into trouble (stress management strategies are presented later in the chapter). Reach

5.2   *A Syllabus Helps You Stay on Schedule and Fulfill Responsibilities*

ENG 122 Spring 2007

Instructor: Jennifer Gessner
Office Hours: Tue & Thur 12:30–1:30 (or by appointment) in DC 305
Phone: 303-555-2222
E-mail: jg@abc.xyz

How to connect with the instructor

Required Texts: *Good Reasons with Contemporary Arguments,* Faigley and Selzer
A Writer's Reference, 5th ed., Diana Hacker

Books and materials to get ASAP

Required Materials:

- a notebook with lots of paper
- a folder for keeping everything from this class
- an active imagination and critical thinking

Course Description: This course focuses on argumentative writing and the researched paper. Students will practice the rhetorical art of argumentation and will gain experience in finding and incorporating researched materials into an extended paper.

Course coverage, expectations, responsibilities

Writer's Notebook: All students will keep, and bring to class, a notebook with blank paper. Throughout the semester, you will be given writing assignments to complete in this book. You must bring to class and be prepared to share any notebook assignment. Notebook assignments will be collected frequently, though sometimes randomly, and graded only for their completeness, not for spelling, etc.

Grading:

- Major Writing Assignments worth 100 points each.
- Final Research Project worth 300 points.
- Additional exercises and assignments range from 10 to 50 points each.
- Class participation: Based on the degree to which you complete the homework and present this in a thoughtful, meaningful manner in class.
- Attendance: Attendance is taken daily and students may miss up to three days of class without penalty, but will lose 5 points for each day missed thereafter.
- Late work: All work will lose 10% of earned points per class day late. No work will be accepted after five class days or the last class meeting.

How grades are determined for this course

Final Grade: The average of the total points possible (points earned divided by the total possible points). 100–90% = A; 89–80% = B; 79–70% = C (any grade below 70% is not passing for this class).

Academic Integrity: Students must credit any material used in their papers that is not their own (including direct quotes, paraphrases, figures, etc.). Failure to do so constitutes plagiarism, which is illegal, unethical, <u>always recognizable</u>, and a guaranteed way to fail a paper. The definition of plagiarism is "to steal and use (the writings or ideas of another) as one's own."

Reflects schools academic integrity policy

Week 4
2/1   The Concise Opinion.
            HW: Complete paper #1 Rough Draft (5–7 pages double-spaced)

2/3   How Professionals Argue
            HW: Read Jenkins Essay (p 501 of *Good Reasons)* and Rafferty Essay (p 525); compare argumentative style, assess and explain efficacy of arguments.

Topics of that days class meeting

Notice of due date for paper draft

Notice of reading assignments to complete

Week 5
2/15   Developing an Argument
            Essay Quiz on Jenkins and Rafferty Essays
            HW: Chap 5 of *Good Reasons;* based on components of a definition of argument, write a brief explanation of how your argument might fit into this type.

2/17   Library Workday: Meet in Room 292
            PAPER #1 DUE

Notice of quiz

Notice of final due date for paper

Source: Jennifer Gessner, Community College of Denver.

KEY 5.3   *Make Your Goals S.M.A.R.T.*

Goal: To raise my algebra grade from a C to a B.

MY GOAL IS . . .	MEANING . . .	EXAMPLE
Specific	Name exactly how you will achieve your goal.	I will accomplish my goal by studying algebra at least an hour a day and working with a tutor once a week.
Measurable	Find ways to measure your progress over time.	I will look at my weekly quiz grades to see if I am making progress. I will also use the exercises in my text to take practice tests and use the answer key to grade my work.
Attainable	Set a goal that challenges you but isn't too far out of your reach.	Algebra is tough for me, but I know that I can manage to pull up my grade.
Relevant	Define a goal that is meaningful to you and your needs.	I need to pass this required course to move ahead in my major.
Time Frame	Set up a time frame for achieving your goal and the steps toward it.	I will do an extra problem set every Monday and Thursday night. I will get my grade point up by the end of the term.

out to friends, family, and college personnel who can help you. Be ready to brainstorm other ideas if your plans don't work.

Step 6: Action time. Follow the steps in your plan until you achieve your goal.

Staying motivated on your way to a goal can be tough when you have years of work ahead of you. (As a student just beginning college and with your degree years away, you know what that feels like.) Your challenge is to find ways to "keep your eyes on the prize." You might visualize yourself accomplishing your goal or remind yourself of what you stand to gain when you complete your goal. Checking off short-term goals and seeing them as signs of progress will also help. Lidia, for example, might keep a photo of her kids in her notebook to remind herself of how getting a degree will help her support her family.

It will take work and persistence to pursue your goals. The changes—positive or negative— that happen along the way are likely to cause some stress. If managed well, however, it shouldn't stop you from reaching your goals. Next, we examine potential sources of stress and strategies for dealing with them.

TAKE
ACTION: Create a SMART Goal Achievement Plan

Name a general area in which you want to change or improve this year.

_____

Using the S.M.A.R.T. system and your visual intelligence, define a goal in this area by filling in this think link and the table underneath it.

6. Action time — Put your plan in motion.

5. Get unstuck — Think of a potential roadblock you might hit as you try reach your goal. Name two **specific** ways you can get back on track if this roadblock occurs.

_____

_____

4. Be accountable — Describe the system you will use to stay on track and **measure** your progress.

_____

_____

3. Set a timetable — What is a realistic **time frame** within which you can accomplish this goal?

_____

2. Define a path — What are the **specific** steps? _____

_____

_____

1. Define your goal — Be **specific**. What exactly do you want to accomplish?

_____

Why is this goal **relevant**—how does it relate to what you need?

_____

What makes it **attainable**—enough of a challenge to motivate but not so tough that you give up?

_____

Define your path within the time frame from number 3. Use this grid to assign estimated dates to specific steps.

Step					
Date done					

WHAT ARE WAYS TO MANAGE STRESS AS YOU PURSUE YOUR GOALS?

If you feel **stress** as you try to reach your goals, you are not alone. Stress levels among college students have increased (see Key 5.4). Handling stress involves identifying and defusing stress triggers, keeping your body and mind healthy so that you can handle increased pressures, and avoiding poor personal health choices that take you off your path.

For Lidia, and almost every other student, dealing with stress is an everyday challenge that can take a toll on your health and on your ability to achieve your goals. However, some amount of stress gives you energy to do well on tests, finish assignments on time, or prepare for a class presentation. Key 5.5 shows that stress can be helpful or harmful, depending on how much you experience. A manageable balance empowers you to forge ahead.

Stress
physical or mental strain produced in reaction to pressure.

Identify and Address Stress Triggers

When psychologists T. H. Holmes and R. H. Rahe measured the intensity of people's reaction to specific changes, they found that stress is linked to both positive *and* negative events. On page 117 is an adaptation, designed for college students, of the Holmes-Rahe scale. It delivers a "stress score," based on events in the past year, that indicates your likelihood of experiencing a

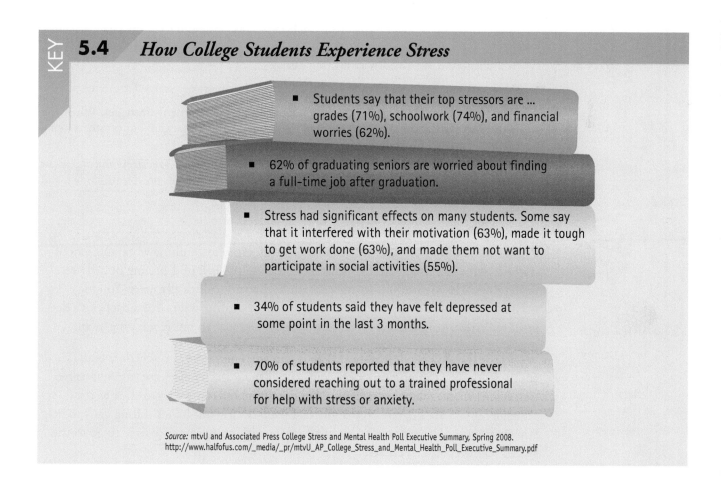

KEY 5.4 *How College Students Experience Stress*

- Students say that their top stressors are ... grades (71%), schoolwork (74%), and financial worries (62%).

- 62% of graduating seniors are worried about finding a full-time job after graduation.

- Stress had significant effects on many students. Some say that it interfered with their motivation (63%), made it tough to get work done (63%), and made them not want to participate in social activities (55%).

- 34% of students said they have felt depressed at some point in the last 3 months.

- 70% of students reported that they have never considered reaching out to a trained professional for help with stress or anxiety.

Source: mtvU and Associated Press College Stress and Mental Health Poll Executive Summary, Spring 2008. http://www.halfofus.com/_media/_pr/mtvU_AP_College_Stress_and_Mental_Health_Poll_Executive_Summary.pdf

KEY | **5.5**   *Stress Levels Can Help or Hinder Performance*

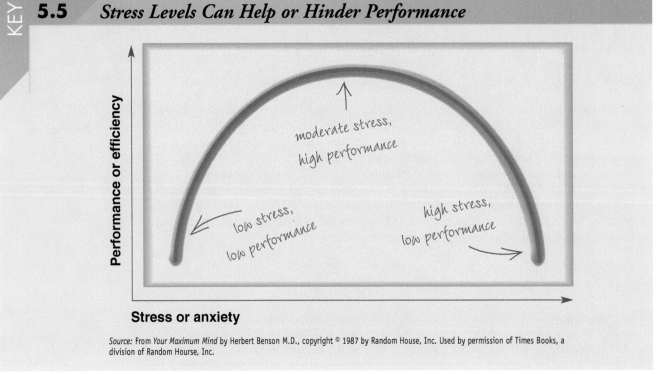

Source: From *Your Maximum Mind* by Herbert Benson M.D., copyright © 1987 by Random House, Inc. Used by permission of Times Books, a division of Random Hourse, Inc.

stress-related health problem. Understanding your stress score can guide your actions in two ways:

▶ Seeing what you face on a regular basis can help you decide how to handle ongoing pressures.

▶ In a high-stress period of your life, understanding what's causing the pressure can help you re-evaluate and, if necessary, adjust your goals.

How can you cope with stress and prevent it from derailing your plans? First, remember:

▶ **The goal-setting strategies in this chapter are stress-management strategies.** When you set SMART goals and pursue them step by step with focus, reaching out to others along the way for help, you reduce stress.

▶ **The time-management strategies you learned in Chapter 4 are stress-management strategies.** When you create and follow a schedule, complete items on your to-do list, and avoid procrastinating, you reduce stress.

Here are some additional ways to keep stress under control:

BE REALISTIC ABOUT COMMITMENTS. Students who combine work and school may become overloaded and fall behind, increasing the risk of dropping out. If you need to work to pay tuition, set up a schedule you can realistically meet. You may need more than two years (for an associate's degree) or four years (for a bachelor's degree) to graduate, but taking extra time is much better than not graduating at all.

WORK WITH YOUR PERSONALITY. If you are a night person, schedule your course work in the afternoon or evening—or, if there's no choice, use external (three alarm clocks) and internal strategies ("I'm determined to do well") to stick to the schedule. If you are fidgety, keep a squeezable object in your hands during class to help you stay focused. If you need to blow off steam with exercise, make time to go to the athletic center between classes.

Activity

To determine your stress score, add up the number of points corresponding to the events you have experienced in the past 12 months.

1 Death of a close family member_____100	17 Increase in workload at school _____ 37
2 Death of a close friend _____ 73	18 Outstanding personal
3 Divorce _____ 65	achievement _____ 36
4 Jail term _____ 63	19 First quarter/semester in college _____ 36
5 Major personal injury or illness_____ 63	20 Change in living conditions _____ 31
6 Marriage _____ 58	21 Serious argument with an
7 Firing from a job _____ 50	instructor _____ 30
8 Failing an important course _____ 47	22 Lower grades than expected _____ 29
9 Change in health of a family	23 Change in sleeping habits _____ 29
member _____ 45	24 Change in social activities _____ 29
10 Pregnancy _____ 45	25 Change in eating habits _____ 28
11 Sex problem _____ 44	26 Chronic car trouble _____ 26
12 Serious argument with close	27 Change in the number of
friend _____ 40	family gatherings _____ 26
13 Change in financial status _____ 39	28 Too many missed classes _____ 25
14 Change in major _____ 39	29 Change of college _____ 24
15 Trouble with parents _____ 39	30 Dropping more than one class _____ 23
16 New girlfriend or boyfriend _____ 37	31 Minor traffic violations _____ 20

Total: _____

If your score is 300 or higher, you are at high risk for developing a health problem. If your score is between 150 and 300, you have a 50–50 chance of experiencing a serious health change within two years. If your score is below 150, you have a 30% chance of a serious health change.

Source: Paul Insel and Walton Roth, *Core Concepts in Health,* 4th ed., Palo Alto, CA: Mayfield Publishing Company, 1985, p. 29.

HAVE SOME FUN. Doing things you enjoy, such as meeting up with friends on a Thursday night for pizza, will take the edge off of stress. Put fun on your schedule so you are sure to have time.

ACTIVELY MANAGE YOUR SCHEDULE. Get in the habit of checking your planner throughout the day. Also, try not to put off tasks. If you can take even one tiny step toward a goal, do it.

TRY RELAXATION TECHNIQUES. Techniques that will help you relax and increase your awareness of your physical body can help calm you. These include various breathing techniques (some based in yoga), progressive relaxation (tensing and relaxing different muscles one by one), and visualization (focusing on a place that you find calming).

CHECK THINGS OFF. Use a physical action when you complete a task—check off the item, delete it from your task list, crumple up the Post-It note. A physical act can relieve stress and highlight the confidence that comes from getting something done. Consider listing the courses you need to complete your degree and checking off those you complete every term.

MANAGE FAMILY RESPONSIBILITIES. Students with elderly parents, relatives with health-care issues, or young children often have to juggle family responsibilities as they try to study (see Key 5.6 for helpful suggestions on child-care issues).

KNOW WHEN YOU NEED HELP—AND ASK FOR IT. Trying to do it all on your own may not be possible and can actually make things worse. Call on family and friends to take the pressure off. Switch shifts at work to free up study time, ask a friend

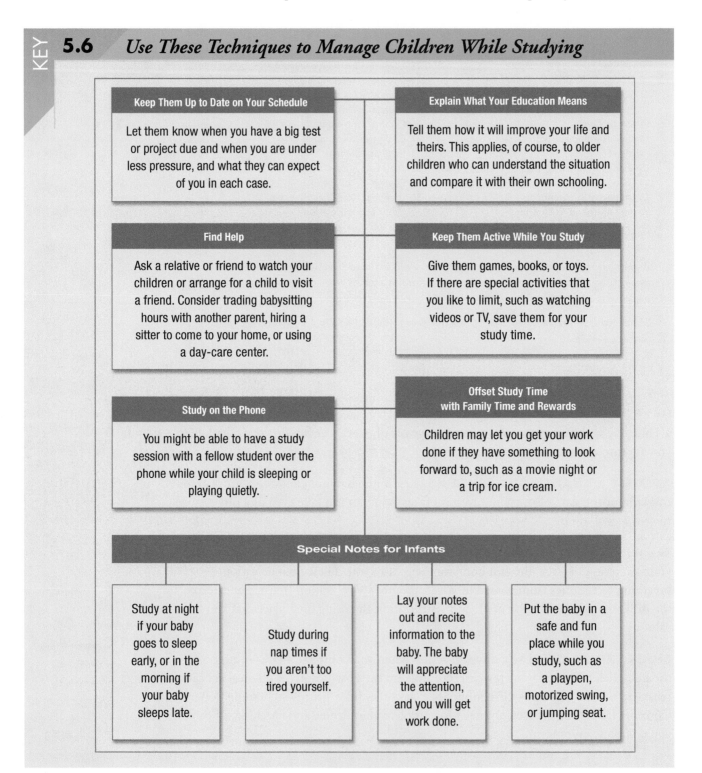

KEY **5.6**   *Use These Techniques to Manage Children While Studying*

Keep Them Up to Date on Your Schedule

Let them know when you have a big test or project due and when you are under less pressure, and what they can expect of you in each case.

Explain What Your Education Means

Tell them how it will improve your life and theirs. This applies, of course, to older children who can understand the situation and compare it with their own schooling.

Find Help

Ask a relative or friend to watch your children or arrange for a child to visit a friend. Consider trading babysitting hours with another parent, hiring a sitter to come to your home, or using a day-care center.

Keep Them Active While You Study

Give them games, books, or toys. If there are special activities that you like to limit, such as watching videos or TV, save them for your study time.

Study on the Phone

You might be able to have a study session with a fellow student over the phone while your child is sleeping or playing quietly.

Offset Study Time with Family Time and Rewards

Children may let you get your work done if they have something to look forward to, such as a movie night or a trip for ice cream.

Special Notes for Infants

Study at night if your baby goes to sleep early, or in the morning if your baby sleeps late.

Study during nap times if you aren't too tired yourself.

Lay your notes out and recite information to the baby. The baby will appreciate the attention, and you will get work done.

Put the baby in a safe and fun place while you study, such as a playpen, motorized swing, or jumping seat.

to take your kids the day before a test, or have a family member take your car for servicing. Because her mother already babysits when she can, Lidia might talk to a neighbor about trading child care in a pinch.

Keep Your Body Healthy

Even the most driven goal achiever has trouble moving ahead when illness or injury hits. If you do your best to eat well, get exercise and sleep, and avoid substances that can throw you off your game, you will be in shape to stay in motion.

EAT WELL

Eating well and getting exercise can be tough for students. The *food environment* in college is often filled with unhealthful choices,[2] and students tend to sit a lot, eat on the run, and get too busy to exercise. Healthy eating requires *balance* (varying your diet) and *moderation* (eating reasonable amounts). Here are some ways to incorporate both into your life:

▶ **Vary what you eat and reduce portion size.** The government "food pyramid" recommends certain amounts of food in particular food groups. (Go to www.mypyramid.gov.)

▶ **Limit fat, cholesterol, sugar, white flour, and alcohol.** Try to eliminate *trans fats*, which increase the risk of heart disease. Minimize candy, desserts, sugar-filled drinks, and alcohol, which is calorie-heavy.

▶ **If you need to lose weight, reach out.** A campus counselor can help you find a support group, such as Weight Watchers or an on-campus organization, which can help you stay on target. Set reasonable weight-loss goals and work toward them gradually.

EXERCISE REGULARLY

Being physically fit increases your energy, helps you cope with stress, and keeps you goal-directed. Here are some ways to make exercise a regular part of your life:

▶ Walk to classes and meetings. When you reach your building, use the stairs.

▶ Use your school's fitness facilities in between classes.

▶ Play team recreational sports at school or in your community.

▶ Find activities you can do on your own time, such as running or pick-up basketball.

▶ Work out with friends or family to combine socializing and exercise.

During solo exercise sessions, although your body is occupied, your mind is often free. Whether you are walking, using an elliptical trainer, or doing laps, you can brainstorm new goal-achievement strategies. Be open to the ideas that pop into your head.

GET ENOUGH SLEEP

Research indicates that eight to nine hours of sleep a night is ideal for students. But the average student sleeps only six to seven hours a night—and often gets much less.[3] Overwhelmed students often prioritize schoolwork over sleep, staying up regularly until the wee hours of the morning to study or pulling "all-nighters" to get through a tough project or paper.

INSIDE TIPS

FROM SARAH, SELF-MANAGEMENT COACH
You can't get new results with the same old behaviors. To reach new goals, you may need to change some personal health habits, such as how much sleep you get per night. Start small, and go step by step: Target one specific problem and decide on a concrete change that you think will help (go to bed an hour earlier, send your last text at 11 p.m., go without refined sugar). Put this change in place for a week. If it makes a difference, keep it up—and maybe add another.

More than just transportation, bicycling provides great exercise. As this bike rack shows, many students at this college use bicycles to get around.

© Shutterstock

Binge Drinking
having five or more drinks (for men) or four or more (for women) at one occasion.

Being sleep deprived hinders your ability to concentrate, raises stress levels, and makes you more susceptible to illness. For the sake of your health, your goals, and your GPA, find a way to get the sleep you need. Sleep expert Gregg D. Jacobs, Ph.D., has the following practical suggestions for improving sleep habits:[6]

▶ **Reduce consumption of alcohol and caffeine.** Caffeine may keep you awake, especially if you drink it late in the day. Alcohol can prevent you from sleeping deeply.

▶ **Nap.** Taking short afternoon naps can reduce the effects of sleep deprivation.

▶ **Be consistent.** Try to establish a regular sleep time and wake-up schedule.

▶ **Complete tasks an hour or so before sleep.** Give yourself a chance to wind down.

AVOID ALCOHOL AND DRUG ABUSE

Some students choose to use alcohol and other potentially addictive substances to alleviate stress temporarily or for other reasons. Actually, using these substances can affect your life in ways that *increase* stress. The abuse of these substances can have potentially serious consequences, including sending you way off the track that leads to your goals.

Alcohol is a depressant and the most frequently abused drug on campus. Of all alcohol consumption, **binge drinking** is associated with the greatest problems. Students who binge drink are more likely to miss classes or work, perform poorly, experience physical problems (memory loss, headache, stomach issues), become depressed, and engage in unplanned or unsafe sexual activity.[7] Even a few drinks affect muscle coordination and, more importantly, the ability to reason and make sensible decisions. All of these effects can send your stress level skyrocketing.

College students may use drugs to relieve stress, be accepted by peers, or just to try something new. In most cases, the negative consequences of drug use outweigh any temporary high. Drug use violates federal, state, and local laws, and you may be arrested, tried, and imprisoned for possessing even a small amount of drugs. You can jeopardize your reputation and your student status if you are caught using drugs or if drug use impairs your performance. Finally, long-term drug use can damage your body and mind. Every consequence of drug use has the potential to derail you from the goals that mean the most to you.

If you drink or take drugs, think carefully about the effects on your health, safety, and academic performance. Consider the positive and negative effects of your choice. If you believe you have a problem, reach out for help. Your college and community resources can help you generate options and develop practical plans for recovery.

Keep Your Mind Healthy

Although feeling anxious is normal at times, especially when you have a lot to do, some people react to high levels of stress in more serious ways. Mental health disorders interfere with your ability to reach your goals, and they can be caused or worsened by problematic health decisions. If you recognize yourself in any of the following descriptions, contact your student health center or campus counseling center for help or a referral to a specialist. These disorders include:

▶ **Panic disorder.** Specific situations bring on "panic attacks" that may include heart palpitations, rapid breathing, dizziness, and fear.

▶ **Post-traumatic stress disorder.** Past trauma (rape, war experiences, assault) triggers flashbacks, irritability, emotional distance, and sometimes violence.

▶ **Eating disorders.** *Anorexia nervosa* (severe restriction of eating), *bulimia* (eating excessive amounts of foods followed by purging), or *binge-eating disorder* (bingeing on foods without purging) cause serious health problems.

▶ **Clinical depression (depressive disorder).** At varying levels of severity, sometimes leading to threats of suicide.

Multiple Intelligence Strategies for Stress Management

Briefly describe a stress-related problem you have.

_____

_____

Now, brainstorm potential solutions to your problem, linking each solution to an intelligence. Use the right-hand column to record your ideas.

INTELLIGENCE	SUGGESTED STRATEGIES	USE MI STRATEGIES TO COME UP WITH SOLUTIONS
Verbal-Linguistic	■ Keep a journal of what situations, people, or events cause stress. ■ Write letters or e-mail friends about your problems.	
Logical-Mathematical	■ Think through problems using a problem-solving process, and devise a detailed plan. ■ Analyze the negative and positive effects that may result from a stressful situation.	
Bodily-Kinesthetic	■ Choose a physical activity that releases tension—running, yoga, team sports—and do it regularly. ■ Plan physical activities during free time—go for a hike, take a bike ride, go dancing with friends.	
Visual-Spatial	■ Enjoy things that appeal to you visually—visit an exhibit, see an art film, shoot photos with your camera. ■ Use a visual organizer to plan out a solution to a stressful problem.	
Interpersonal	■ Reach out for help to people who care about you and are supportive. ■ Shift your focus by listening to others who need to talk about their stresses.	
Intrapersonal	■ Schedule time when you can think through what is causing stress. ■ Allow yourself five minutes a day to meditate: Visualize positive resolutions to your stressful situation.	
Musical	■ Listen to music that relaxes, inspires, and/or energizes you. ■ Write a song about what is bothering you.	
Naturalistic	■ Try to categorize what's bothering you to identify solvable patterns. ■ If nature calms you, spend time outdoors, watch nature-focused TV, or read about nature or science.	

POWERFUL QUESTIONS

Consider whether the way you eat, exercise, sleep, or use drugs and alcohol are adding stress to your life and sidetracking you from your goals. If you are unhappy with where you are at, who can help you change?

Find Resources at Your School

that support student health—counseling, exercise facilities, health center, support groups, classes, and so on. Identify at least two people you might use as a resource, and write down the steps you will take to obtain the help you need.

Of these disorders, depression in particular has become fairly common on college campuses, due in part to the wide range of stressors that students experience. Recent research reports that nearly half of surveyed students reported feelings of depression at some point, with more than 30% saying that the level of depression made it difficult to function at times.[8] Key 5.7 shows possible causes of depression as well as some typical symptoms and offers helpful coping strategies.

At its worst, depression can lead to suicidal thoughts and attempts. A recent survey conducted by the American Psychological Association of students at 70 colleges and universities found that 15% of students had thought seriously about committing suicide, and 5% had made actual attempts. Many of these students reported that they did not seek help when in crisis.[9]

These disorders have the power to derail goals and dreams, so get medical care. The right help can change—or even save—your life.

Nearly all goals seem more reachable and less stressful when you work with others. As you will see next, getting the most out of your personal relationships requires both knowledge and skill.

KEY 5.7 *Know the Causes and Symptoms of Depression*

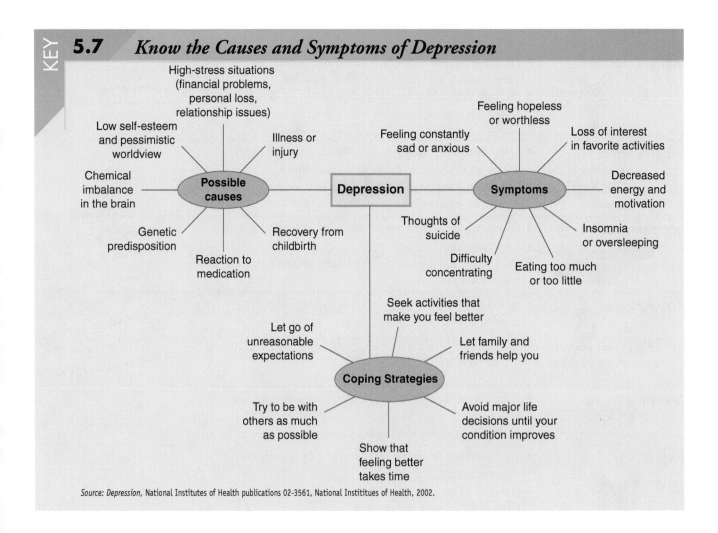

Source: Depression, National Institutes of Health publications 02-3561, National Instititues of Health, 2002.

HOW WILL LEARNING TO WORK WITH OTHERS HELP YOU REACH YOUR GOALS?

In school, as at work and in your personal life, being able to achieve your goals depends on your ability to relate effectively to others. Students taking the same course may work on projects together, create and perform a presentation, or form a study group that aims to prepare for an exam. Math and science instructors sometimes initiate student study groups, known as *peer-assisted study sessions* or *supplemental instruction,* to help students improve performance in those courses. Students in online courses may meet in chat rooms for virtual study group sessions or project work. No student is an island!

To work well with others on the way to your most important goals, you need to know:

▶ How emotions affect relationships

▶ How to value and benefit from diverse people and their perspectives

Start by examining how to manage your own emotions and understand the emotions of others.

> When you share an interest or goal with someone, personal differences may fade into the background. These students work together on an assignment.
>
> © Patrick White/ Merrill Education

Focus on Your Emotions

Psychologist Daniel Goleman says that **emotional intelligence** is essential to achieve your goals and helps you make the most of personal relationships. He believes that you can develop the ability to know yourself, manage your emotions, and understand the emotions of others.[10] The qualities of emotional intelligence are found in Key 5.8.

The key is staying aware of what your goals demand from your relationships. For example, succeeding in the classroom might require that you present yourself in appropriate ways both in the classroom and in meetings with your instructor. Lidia can use her emotional intelligence to get help from others with both academics and child care.

Here are some examples of how emotional intelligence can help you set and pursue goals:

▶ "Because I get bored quickly, I need to emphasize short-term goals."

▶ "Because I enjoy hands-on experiences, I will explore majors in the sciences that require lab courses."

▶ "My project partner is not himself today, so I'll reschedule our study session and see if he wants to go for coffee after class and talk instead."

You are building your emotional intelligence throughout your work in this text. Some of the Habits for Success—thinking before you act, for example, and being flexible—involve looking at your emotions and needs before deciding how to move ahead. Also, the self-assessments in each chapter help you learn more about who you are and how you react to a variety of situations.

Often the people you work with have different values and cultural backgrounds. In an increasingly global world, learning to appreciate that diversity and to understand and accept those who differ from you will help you work with others more successfully.

Emotional Intelligence
the ability to perceive, assess, and manage one's own emotions as well as understand the emotions of others.

KEY **5.8**   *Become More Emotionally Intelligent by Developing these Qualities*

Each quality is written as an affirmative statement. Make a commitment to live by them and to get in touch with how emotions affect you and others. Reaffirm each statement before joining a study group. If a problem arises and you have trouble controlling your feelings, go back to these qualities for direction.

PERSONAL COMPETENCE	SOCIAL COMPETENCE
Self-Awareness	*Social Awareness*
I know my emotions and how they affect me.	I sense the feelings and perspectives of others.
I understand my strengths and limits.	I help others reach their goals.
I am confident in my abilities.	I know how to relate to people from different cultures.
I am open to improvement.	I can sense how to serve the needs of others.
Self-Management	*Social Skills*
I can control my emotions and impulses.	I know how to work in a team.
I can delay gratification when there is something more important to be gained.	I can inspire people to act.
I am trustworthy.	I understand how to lead a group.
I can adapt to change and new ideas.	I know how to persuade people.
I persist toward my goals despite obstacles.	I can make positive change happen.

Source: Based on Daniel Goleman, *Working with Emotional Intelligence*, New York: Bantam Books, 1998, pp. 26–27.

Become Culturally Competent

Cultural Competence

the ability to understand and appreciate differences and to respond to people of all cultures in a way that values their worth, respects their beliefs and practices, and builds communication and relationships.

Most academic goals that you set will require you to work with other students, teachers, and administrators. Work goals will require you to work with clients, colleagues, and employers. Chances are that you will work with others who differ from you in ways both visible (race, ethnicity) and invisible (communication styles, values). The goal of **cultural competence** is to develop the ability to understand and appreciate diversity and adjust your behavior to improve how you get along with the people around you.

Building cultural competence means taking the following actions:[11]

1. Learn more about why and how people differ from you, and what tends to happen when differences in culture occur.

2. Become self-aware about your own perceptions and attitudes, including whether you have any **prejudices** or judge based on **stereotypes**. Challenge yourself to set them aside as you get to know and work with others.

3. Find ways to adjust to the differences of others that will create opportunities. Look past external characteristics, put yourself in other people's shoes, and recognize what you have in common with people everywhere.

For instance, if Lidia couldn't attend her study group as often because of family commitments, cultural competence could help both her and her study group to solve the problem. Realizing that she has responsibilities as a parent, a study group member could ask her to come up with a way to help the group when she's not there. She could then offer to work at home to combine notes from the text and class for a week. This contribution will help her and the group reach their goals of learning the course material.

Maximize Your Team Work

Whether you aim to complete a project or study for an exam, what can you gain from working with others?

Increased knowledge. When group members share knowledge, each member spends less time and energy learning the material. Another benefit: Talking about concepts or teaching them to others helps solidify what you know.

More motivation. Knowing that you are accountable to others and that they will see how prepared you are—or aren't—may encourage you to work hard.

Better teamwork skills. Nothing teaches you how to work effectively in groups better than experience. What you learn will be invaluable throughout college and in the workplace.

Strength from diversity. Working with students from a variety of backgrounds creates team strength. The more diverse the team, the more varied the approach to problem solving.

STRATEGIES FOR GROUP SUCCESS

The way a group operates may depend on members' personalities, motivation, and knowledge; what you are studying; group size; and where you are meeting. These general strategies will help all groups succeed:

► **Set long-term and short-term goals.** At your first meeting, decide what the group wants to accomplish. You may want to have an *agenda* (a meeting plan) for each meeting.

► **Set a regular schedule.** Determine how many meetings are needed and what members' schedules can handle. If you are studying for a final, you might start a month before the test with a weekly meeting. As test day nears, you may decide to meet more frequently.

► **Choose a leader for each meeting.** Rotating the leadership among members willing to lead helps everyone take ownership of the group.

► **Share the workload.** Your willingness to pitch in and work is more important than how much you know.

For groups with a study focus, here are further tips:

► **Create materials for one another.** Give each group member one topic to compile, photocopy, and review for the others.

► **Help each other learn.** Have group members teach each other information, work on problems, give feedback on responses to essay questions, or go through flash cards together.

► **Pool your note-taking resources.** Compare notes and fill in any information you don't have.

Study groups and other teams need both leaders *and* participants to accomplish their goals.[12] Lidia, who rarely has time or energy to take a leadership role, needs to understand that she is a crucial part of a group no matter which role she plays (see Key 5.9).

Prejudice
a preconceived judgment or opinion formed without just grounds or sufficient knowledge.

Stereotype
a standardized mental picture that represents an oversimplified opinion or uncritical judgment.

KEY 5.9   *The Group Process Needs Leaders and Participants*

For Participant

- Do your share of the work.
- Stay organized and focused.
- Be open and willing to discuss.
- Perform your responsibilities on schedule.

For Leader

- Define projects, and focus everyone's efforts.
- Assign work tasks, and set a schedule and deadlines.
- Set meeting and project goals.
- Keep everyone on target and moving ahead.
- Set a fair, respectful, and encouraging tone.
- Evaluate progress, and make changes if needed.

DEFUSE POTENTIAL PROBLEMS

As beneficial as it is to work in a team, issues can arise. Be prepared to address them if they happen to you:

▶ **People not pulling their weight.** At some point in almost every group, one or more people will not fulfill their responsibilities. If it's a one-time incident due to an illness or a personal problem, it's best to let it go. However, if it happens regularly, take action. Try reassigning tasks or having a group problem-solving session.

▶ **Trouble scheduling.** Finding a time and location that works for a group of people can be challenging. Coordinate everything on a group e-mail first. Once you find a time a day that works, schedule meetings consistently. You may want to rotate locations if there isn't one that is convenient for all group members.

▶ **Too much talking.** Although it may not be realistic to keep friends out of your study group, you can set boundaries. Set up some talking time at the end as a "reward" for accomplishing a goal.

Identifying your core values, setting goals that reflect them, learning techniques to manage the stress that can keep you from reaching your goals, and tapping the wisdom of the group will help you stay on target toward what you most want to achieve in college and beyond.

> *Sticks in a bundle are unbreakable.*
> *—Kenyan proverb*

Real People
Reach Out to Others

LOUISE GAILE EDROZO

Graduate of the Registered Nursing Program at Highline Community College, Des Moines, Washington

Gaile Edrozo was on track to earn a biology degree in a year's time and then begin medical school in her native Philippines. However, financial difficulties got in the way of her plans.

Aiming for more opportunity to work and earn a living, she and her family came to the United States in 2004. Because of her immigration status, she knew that she would be considered an international student when she started college.

STOP AND THINK

Have you experienced a sudden change, like Gaile's, that forced you to rethink your plans? What happened, and where did it take you?

As she and her family adjusted to living in Washington state, Gaile decided to explore nursing and enrolled as a nursing student at Highline Community College in the fall of 2004.

Gaile was on course to a meaningful, productive goal, but the cost of her education was too high for her family to manage. Even more frightening was the possibility that Gaile would lose her status in the U.S. if she were unable to stay in school and would have to return to the Philippines alone.

"My fears were so many I was drowning in them," says Gaile. "I wanted nothing more than to become a nurse, have a career I love, and help my family at the same time. I wanted it so much it hurt to think it could all be taken away—again."

STOP AND THINK

Gaile thought that academic success would be a key to many doors—and found that this was not true because of her immigration status. When have you thought that a skill or accomplishment was a sure thing only to find out that it wasn't enough? How did you react?

It was time to reach out for help. Gaile had heard about a course at Highline that helped students explore scholarship opportunities, prepare portfolio and résumé materials, and look at four-year institutions. She registered for Honors 100. In this course she met Dr. Barbara Clinton, her instructor and the head of the honors program at Highline.

(continued)

Real People
Reach Out to Others

With Dr. Clinton's help, Gaile was able to see the positive in her challenges, focus on what made her unique, and express those qualities in her portfolio and résumé so that they made a statement. When she shared her financial concerns, Dr. Clinton helped her find—and win—scholarships for which she was eligible. "The most beautiful thing is that Dr. Clinton did not stop helping me after the class was over. She became my greatest resource."

With the confidence she gained from her mentor, Gaile has forged ahead to success. After getting employment authorization from the Immigration and Naturalization Service, she worked as a critical care nurse technician while finishing her nursing studies. She graduated in 2007 and started working as a registered nurse. She has also completed a baccalaureate degree in nursing from the University of Washington at Tacoma and will soon change her immigration status to permanent resident. She considers Dr. Clinton a resource for life and understands firsthand the value of reaching out to others.

THINK ABOUT GAILE AND THINK ABOUT YOURSELF

▶ **As the old saying goes, "No person is an island." What have you accomplished with a partner or team that you could not have done alone?**

▶ **How could reaching out to someone help you at school? Whom can you call? What help would you ask for?**

Source: Highline College Honors Scholar Program Success Stories (adapted with permission from original story, online at http://flightline .highline.edu/honors/success/gaile.htm).

You can reach out to others for help, or you can reach out to others to help *them*. **Salma Hayek** has done both. After coming to the U.S. from her native Mexico to pursue an acting career, Hayek got her first big break from director Roberto Rodriguez. Now an international star, Salma produces Latin-themed films and supports UNICEF in its drive to provide vaccinations to poor children.

HABIT FOR SUCCESS

Reach Out to Others

Below are examples of how you can put this habit into action in different situations. Use the three spaces to add your own ideas for actions you can accomplish now or in the future. Be specific, and be realistic.

Get advice from close friends or family about how not to overdo the alcohol when you need to relax on weekends.

Find writing and math help at your school's writing center or tutoring center.

When thinking about different majors, talk to students majoring in areas that interest you.

**Reach Out to Others
Habit for Success**

When you can't get to a chore or need support with family responsibilities, ask for help—or trade something you do for something you need done.

Post notes and questions to online communities that can provide advice as you work to lose weight.

BUILDING
SKILLS: For Successful Learning

NOTE THE IMPORTANT POINTS

Why are values the foundation of successful goal setting?

Describe three ways that identifying your values can help you achieve college and life goals.

_____

_____

_____

HOW DO YOU SET AND ACHIEVE GOALS?

Explain what short-term and long-term goals are and how they relate.

_____

_____

List the steps to take toward achieving a goal.

1. _____
2. _____
3. _____
4. _____
5. _____
6. _____

WHAT ARE WAYS TO MANAGE STRESS AS YOU PURSUE YOUR GOALS?

In your own words, define the word "stress" in the context of your life as a student.

_____

_____

Name three general categories of what to do to get stress under control, and include one strategy for each category.

1. _____
2. _____
3. _____

BUILDING
SKILLS: For Successful Learning (continued)

HOW WILL LEARNING TO WORK WITH OTHERS HELP
YOU TO REACH YOUR GOALS?

Describe what emotional intelligence is.

_____

_____

Give some ways to participate effectively in a group setting.

_____

_____

CRITICAL THINKING: Applying Learning to Life

USE SHORT-TERM GOALS TO EXPLORE MAJORS

Declaring a major is a long-term goal made up of short-term goal steps. Although many entering students don't yet know what they want to study, it's smart to explore possibilities now so that you can match your talents, skills, and dreams with an academic path. Use the following short-term goals to get moving.

Short-term goal #1: Identify interests and talents.

If you can choose a major that focuses on what interests you and what you do well, you are more likely to have a positive attitude and perform effectively. To pinpoint areas that may work for you, consider questions like the following:

▶ What are my favorite courses, topics to read about, activities?

▶ Am I a "natural" in any academic or skill area?

▶ How do I learn and work with others most effectively?

Based on your exploration, write down two majors that you think are worth considering.

▶ _____

▶ _____

Short-term goal #2: Explore general academic options.

Use the course catalog, the school Web site, or other resources to explore the following:

▶ When do you have to declare a major? _____

▶ What majors are offered at your school? (No need to write here; just read through the list.)

▶ What are the options in majoring? (double majors, minors, "interdisciplinary" majors that combine more than one academic area) _____

_____

▶ What is the process for changing a major once you have declared?

_____

_____

CRITICAL THINKING: Applying Learning to Life (continued)

Short-term goal #3: Explore details of selected majors.

Use the table to nail down specifics for each of the two majors that interest you. Check your course catalog and school Web site, talk to people currently majoring in this subject, and consult your academic advisor.

MAJORS	#1: _____	#2: _____
Minimum GPA for being accepted		
Minimum GPA required in coursework for the major		
Number of courses required		
Career areas that relate to this major		
Department head name		
Department secretary name and contact information		
How many students declare this major each year		
Where the department is located		
Courses you would have to take in the next year		

Finally, name the exact calendar date here when you will need to have declared your major:

_____ Put it in your planner and stick to it!

TEAM
BUILDING: Collaborative Solutions

ACTIVELY DEALING WITH STRESS

Working alone, look back at the college stress scale on page 117. Note the stressors you included in your "stress score" for the past year. As a class, identify four stressors most commonly experienced by students. Divide into four groups, and assign a stressor to each. With your group:

▶ Discuss your stressor and the effects it has on people

▶ Brainstorm solutions and strategies, making sure to include ones that relate to health and teamwork (eating, sleeping, exercise, substances, getting help)

▶ List best coping strategies

▶ Choose a group member to present strategies

Finally, each group makes a presentation to the rest of the class about ways to handle this stressor. Groups may want to make extra copies of their lists for every member of the class.

Test Prep: START IT NOW

WORK WITH OTHERS TO PREP FOR TESTS

Remember all of the advantages to studying in a group (see page 125)? Make them yours by setting up a study group now for your next big test. Check your syllabi and note here the topic, date, and course for your closest upcoming test:

Test topic _____

Test date and time _____

Course _____

Set up a study group with between one and four classmates. Write their names and contact information here:

_____   _____

_____   _____

_____   _____

_____   _____

How much time do you have from now until the test?_____

Plan at least two sessions during that time—one two days before the test and one a week or so earlier. For each, name the date, time, and location (put this information in your planner).

Session 1: _____

_____

Session 2: _____

_____

Finally, read over the strategies for group work success, and communicate with your group before you meet in order to set goals and decide who will serve as leader for both sessions.

UNIT 2

LEARN ABOUT LEARNING: SELF-REGULATED LEARNING AND OBJECTIVE TESTS

CHAPTER 6
LEARN

USING YOUR
DOMINANT
INTELLIGENCE,
PREFERRED
LEARNING
STYLE, AND
UNIQUE
PERSONALITY
TYPE TO
BECOME AN
ACTIVE
LEARNER

"We are led to truth by our weaknesses as well as our strengths."
—Parker Palmer

WHY READ THIS CHAPTER?

What's in it for me?

WHY is it important to understand what some old guy said about learning theory? *WHY* do I need to know my personality type? *WHY* will a chapter on discovering my learning style and dominant intelligence help me study better? *WHY* is it important to know the difference between my learning style and a learning strategy?

Why? Because discovering how "*TO* LEARN" and discovering how "*YOU* LEARN" are two of the most important things you will ever do for yourself as a college student. Learning **how TO learn** means that you know where to find information, how to store information in your brain so that it is easily retrievable, and how to make connections between one thing and another. Learning **how you learn** means that you know your own learning style, your primary intelligence, and your personality type and understand how to apply these characteristics to various learning situations. Knowing how you learn also affects the way you approach the task of mastering content. It is a dynamic discovery that will help you change your academic performance.

By carefully reading this chapter and taking the information provided seriously, you will be able to:

1. Define learning and discuss several historical learning theories.
2. Identify and discuss the steps in the learning process.
3. Identify and use your learning style to increase active and authentic learning.
4. Identify and use your primary intelligence to increase active and authentic learning.
5. Identify and use your personality type to increase active and authentic learning.

CHAPTER 6 / LEARN

"Learn everything you can, anytime you can, from anyone you can—there will always come a time when you will be grateful you did."

—Sarah Caldwell

There were times when I thought I might not make it. I struggled with some of my classes and had a few problems that almost sidetracked me, but I was determined to be a success and after my first term, I was determined to do whatever was necessary to learn how to study, how to process information, and how to make that information "stick." I had not had much success with this in the past and I quickly learned that it was because I did not know how I learned best.

I quickly found that learning **how I learn** was very important to every aspect of my academic life. When you're going to college, working, studying, and trying to have a life, your time is limited and valuable. Learning how to learn and learning how to use your memory correctly are two very important aspects of success. I found that I am a tactile and visual learner and this has helped me greatly. I know that classes where I do not have the opportunity to have a "hands-on approach" will require me to work harder. I learned that it also takes me longer to process information when the lecture is all I have to go on. The student success class I took showed me how to make the best of this situation by creating charts and pictures in my notes. I also found that using color is important to my retention as well.

I have found that for me, my classes in culinary arts are easiest—certainly because this is my major and I enjoy them, but also because these classes are very tactile. We don't just listen to a lecture, we actually "do" things. The more I can do and see, the better I learn. Whatever your learning style, discover it, use it to your best advantage, and work hard to develop skills to get you through the classes that do not match your learning or memory style. By keeping this in mind, I am constantly working hard to overcome any barriers where my learning style and the professor's teaching style do not match.

This chapter will give you the opportunity to discover your learning style, dominant intelligence, and personality type. When you discover which style and type you are, things will begin to change for you and you will have the tools necessary to make some important decisions about learning.

SCAN & QUESTION

In the preface of this book (page ix), you read about the **SQ3R Study Method**. Right now, take a few moments, **scan this chapter**, and on page 165 write **five questions** that you think will be important to your mastery of this material. In addition to the two questions below, you will find five questions from your authors. Use one of your **"On The Test"** stickers to flag this page for easy reference.

EXAMPLES:

▶ **What is the difference between a learning style and a learning strategy?** (from page 154)

▶ **What is the definition of tactile learning and how do you use it?** (from page 159)

WE HOPE YOU LEARNED YOUR LESSON!

What Is This Thing Called Learning, Anyway?

In its purest and simplest form, learning is a *cognitive mental action* in which new information is acquired or in which you learn to use old information in a new way. Learning can be *conscious* and/or *unconscious*. Do you remember the very day you learned how to walk or talk? Probably not. This learning was more of an unconscious nature. However, you probably do remember learning about the 50 states or subtraction or reading an Edgar Allan Poe poem for the first time. This learning was more conscious in nature. Learning can also be *formal* (schooling) or *informal* ("street knowledge"). Learning can happen in many ways such as through play, trial and error, mistakes, successes, repetition, environmental conditioning, parental discipline, social interactions, media, observation, and, yes, through formal study methods.

Learning is what you do *FOR* yourself; it is not done *TO* you. Parents may discipline you time and time and time again, but try as they might, until YOU learn the lesson trying to be taught, it will NOT be learned. Teachers can preach and talk until they are blue in the face about the 13 original colonies, but until you learn them and commit them to memory, they will NOT be learned. That is what this chapter is all about—helping you discover how you learn, why you learn, and assisting you in finding the best way to learn so that you can DO the learning for yourself on a more effective level.

Objective listening can be a difficult skill to learn. Have you encountered people with views radically different from your own? How do you respond?

What Do the Experts Say?

The question still begs: *HOW do we really learn?* By studying a textbook? By reading a newspaper? By looking at pictures? By interviewing someone about a topic? By watching a movie? By trying something to see if it works? Yes, but the process is much more complex than this. Around 300 BC, the great Greek philosopher Socrates introduced his theory of learning. He believed that we learn by asking questions. This is called the Socratic Method. His student, Plato, expanded on this theory, believing that we learn best by dialogue, called the Dialectic Method, which involves "the searcher" beginning a conversation on a topic and having a dialogue with "an expert" on the other side. He believed that through this back-and-forth conversation, knowledge could be acquired.

In the 5th century BC, the Chinese philosopher Lao-Tse wrote, "*If you tell me, I will listen. If you show me, I will see. But if you let me experience, I will learn.*" He was one of the first to proclaim that active, involved learning was a viable form of acquiring information. Kung Fu-tse (Confucius) first introduced the case study, which includes telling stories or parables and then having people discuss the issues or the case to learn and acquire knowledge. In 1690, the English philosopher John Locke introduced the theory of "the blank slate." He believed that all humans were born with empty minds and that we learn information about the world through what our senses bring to us (sensory learning). He felt that learning was like a pyramid—we learn the basics and then build on those simple principles until we can master complex ideas.

In the 1760s, the French philosopher Jean-Jacques Rousseau expanded on a theory that suggested that people learn best by experiencing rather

"*The mind is not a vessel to be filled, but rather a fire to be kindled.*"
—Plutarch

than by authority. In other words, we learn best by doing something rather than being told how someone else did it. He was the first to thoroughly introduce the concept of individual learning styles, believing that learning should be natural to us and follow our basic instincts and feelings. In the early 1900s, the American psychologist J. B. Watson developed the theory of behaviorism, believing that we learn best by conditioning. His theory was based on that of Pavlov (and his dog) and held the tenant that we act and learn in certain ways because we have been conditioned to do so. If a dog (or a person) is fed when it rings a bell, the dog (or the person) quickly learns to ring the bell when it *wants* to be fed.

In the mid 1900s, Swiss psychologist Jean Piaget introduced the groundbreaking theory of holistic learning. This theory is widely held today as one of the most important breakthroughs in educational psychology. Piaget believed that we learn best by experiencing a wide variety of stimuli such as reading, listening, experimenting, exploring, and questioning. In 1956, Benjamin Bloom introduced his taxonomy. Bloom believed in a mastery approach to learning. This theory suggests that we learn simple information and then transform that information into more complex ideas, solutions, and creations. His was an idea of learning how to process and actually use information in a meaningful way.

As you can see from these historical experts in the fields of learning, educational psychology, and philosophy, there are many theories on just HOW we learn best. Perhaps the most important thing to take from these examples is tied into Jean Piaget's theory of holistic learning—that as individuals with diverse and varied needs, backgrounds, and experiences, we require a variety of stimuli to help us learn and that we all learn differently at different stages in our lives.

> "Many things in life cannot be transmitted well by words, concepts, or books. Colors that we see cannot be described to a person born blind. Only a swimmer knows how swimming feels; the non-swimmer can get only the faintest idea of it with all the words and books in the world. And so it goes. Perhaps it is better to say that all of life must first be known experientially. There is no substitute for experience, none at all."
> —Abraham H. Maslow

GIVE YOUR BRAIN A WORKOUT
Can I Really Learn All This Stuff?

YES! YES! YES! YOU CAN LEARN! Think about all that you have already learned in your lifetime. You learned how to eat, walk, talk, play, make decisions, dress yourself, have a conversation, tie your shoes, make your bed, ride a bicycle, play a sport, drive a car, protect yourself, make associations based on observations, use a cell phone, play a video game, ask questions, and countless other simple and highly complex skills. The *proof* that you **CAN learn** is that you **HAVE learned** in the past. The old excuse of *"I can't learn this stuff"* is simply hogwash! You have the capacity to know more, do more, experience more, and acquire more knowledge. Your brain is a natural learning machine just as your heart is a natural pumping machine. It is in our nature to learn every single day. You just have to understand how this process works in order to make the most of your brain's natural learning power. And you have to **devote the time necessary to learn** the basics of something new and then build on that knowledge base. Time and effort are very important aspects of the learning process.

You also have to give your brain a "workout" to make sure it stays in shape. Just as your body needs exercise and activities to stay in shape, your brain does too. When you "work out" your brain and use it to learn new material, your brain releases a chemical called *cypin* (SIGH-pin). Cypin is found throughout the body, but in the brain, it helps build new branches, like a tree sprouting new growth. In a nutshell, when you exercise your brain, your brain rewards you with new learning patterns and new learning receptors. This is sometimes referred to as *neuroplasticity* (new-ro-plas-TIS-i-ty), or the brain's ability to change with new knowledge.

THE LEARNING PROCESS

What Are the Steps to Active, Authentic Learning?

"Human beings have an innate learning process, which includes a motivation to learn" (Smilkstein, 2003). You may be saying to yourself, *"If I have a natural, innate ability to learn, then why is chemistry so difficult for me to master?"* or *"Why is English such a crazy language with so many rules?"* The answer to both could rest in the notion that you are going AGAINST your natural, neurological learning pattern—that you are being taught, or are trying to learn by yourself, in a way that is unnatural to you, and your brain simply is having trouble adapting to this unnatural process.

If you learn best by doing and touching, **you need to do and touch**. If you learn best by listening and questioning, you need to **listen and question**. If you learn best by reading and studying in a quiet place, you need to **find a quiet place to read and study**. Basically, you must figure out your natural inclination for learning and build on it. You will also need to understand that learning takes time and that people need different amounts of time to master material. Janet may learn Concept X in a few hours, but it may take William three days of constant practice to learn the same concept. One thing is true for everyone: The more INVOLVED you are with the information you are trying to learn, the more you will retain.

In Figure 6.1 and the exercise shown in Figure 6.2, we have tried to simplify thousands of years of educational study on the topic of learning. Basically, learning something new can happen in the six steps outlined in Figure 6.1.

If you are trying to learn new facts, concepts, procedures, principles, systems, solutions, or processes, you could achieve this goal by using these six steps. Take a moment and carefully review them now.

As a practice activity, research one of the following topics (all of which we purposefully chose because of their uniqueness . . . OK, weirdness) using the six steps in the Learning Process chart (Figure 6.1). You can do this in your notebook or online journal. Remember, however, that you will need to devote some time to this activity. Learning new information does not happen instantaneously. You will also need to use a variety of sources. Do not depend solely on Wikipedia! Yes, there are other sources out there!

Possible topics:

▶ What was The Night of Long Knives?

▶ What is the mystery of the pyramid at Cheops?

▶ Why and how long can a cockroach live without a head?

▶ Who invented the electric chair and why?

▶ What is Sanskrit?

▶ How is paper made?

▶ Who invented the zero and what is its duel function?

▶ Who was Vlad the Impaler? What famous character did his life inspire?

UNDERSTANDING YOUR STRENGTHS

What Are the Advantages of Discovering and Polishing Your Talents?

On the next few pages, you will have the opportunity to complete three inventories: one to identify your **learning style**, one to identify your **personality type**, and one to identify your **dominant in-**

FIGURE

6.1 *The Learning Process*

1. Motivation to learn the material is the first step in the learning process. You have to possess the internal motivation and passion to WANT to learn what is being presented or what you are studying. You must also be motivated enough to devote the time to learning something new. Deep, purposeful learning does not happen in an instant; it takes work, patience and yes, motivation.

2. Understand the material through ambitious curiosity, keen observations, purposeful questioning, intense studying, eager determination, robust effort, and time devoted to task. You must answer questions such as: Who is involved? What happened? When did it happen? Where did it happen? How did it happen? How could it have happened? What does it all mean? Why is it important? What is the relationship between x and y? You should be able to describe it, discuss it, give examples, put the information into your own words, and tell others about it clearly.

3. Internalizie the material by asking: How can this information affect my life, my career, my studies, and my future? Why does this information matter? How can I control my emotions regarding the value of this information? If I think this information is useless, how can I change this perception?

4. Apply the material by asking: How can I use this information to improve? How can I use this information to work with others, to develop new ideas, or to build meaningful conclusions? Can I demonstrate it? Can I share this information with, or teach this information to, others intelligently? Is it possible to practice what I have learned?

5. Evaluate the material by determining the value of what I just learned. Do I trust my research and sources? Have I consulted others about their findings and knowledge? What did they learn? What can I learn from them? Have I asked for feedback? Can I debate this information with others?

6. Use the material to grow and change. How could I take this information (or the process of learning this information) and change my life, attitudes, or emotions? How could this information help me grow? What can I create out of this new information? How can I expand on this knowledge to learn more?

telligence. At the end of the chapter, you will have the opportunity to pull all of this information together to help you understand your learning patterns and to formulate a learning plan for the future.

These assessments are in no way intended to "label you." They are not a measure of how smart you are. They do not measure your worth or your capacities as a student or a citizen. The three assessments are included so that you might gain a better understanding of your dominant intelligence, identify your learning style, and discover your strongest personality type.

There are no right or wrong answers and there is no one best way to learn. We hope that by the end of this chapter, you will have experienced a "Wow" or "Ah-ha!" moment as you explore and discover new and exciting components of your education. We also hope that by the end of this chapter, you will have the skills you need to more effectively use your dominant traits and improve your less dominant characteristics.

FIGURE

6.2 *Take the MIS*

The Multiple Intelligences Survey
© *Robert M. Sherfield, Ph.D.*

Directions: Read each statement carefully and thoroughly. After reading the statement, rate your response using the scale below. There are no right or wrong answers. This is not a timed survey. The MIS is based, in part, on *Frames of Mind* by Howard Gardner, 1983.

3 = Often Applies

2 = Sometimes Applies

1 = Never or Almost Never Applies

____ 1. When someone gives me directions, I have to visualize them in my mind in order to understand them.

____ 2. I enjoy crossword puzzles and word games like Scrabble.

____ 3. I enjoy dancing and can keep up with the beat of music.

____ 4. I have little or no trouble conceptualizing information or facts.

____ 5. I like to repair things that are broken such as toasters, small engines, bicycles, and cars.

____ 6. I enjoy leadership activities on campus and in the community.

____ 7. I have the ability to get others to listen to me.

____ 8. I enjoy working with nature, animals, and plants.

____ 9. I know where everything is in my home such as supplies, gloves, flashlights, camera, and compact discs.

____10. I am a good speller.

____11. I often sing or hum to myself in the shower or car or while walking or just sitting.

____12. I am a very logical, orderly thinker.

____13. I use a lot of gestures when I talk to people.

____14. I can recognize and empathize with people's attitudes and emotions.

____15. I prefer to study alone.

____16. I can name many different things in the environment such as clouds, rocks, and plant types.

____17. I like to draw pictures, graphs, or charts to better understand information.

____18. I have a good memory for names and dates.

____19. When I hear music, I "get into it" by moving, humming, tapping, or even singing.

____20. I learn better by asking a lot of questions.

____21. I enjoy playing competitive sports.

____22. I communicate very well with other people.

____23. I know what I want and I set goals to accomplish it.

____24. I have some interest in herbal remedies and natural medicine.

____25. I enjoy working puzzles or mazes.

____26. I am a good storyteller.

____27. I can easily remember the words and melodies of songs.

____28. I enjoy solving problems in math and chemistry and working with computer programming problems.

____29. I usually touch people or pat them on the back when I talk to them.

____30. I understand my family and friends better than most other people do.

____31. I don't always talk about my accomplishments with others.

____32. I would rather work outside around nature than inside around people and equipment.

____33. I enjoy and learn more when seeing movies, slides, or videos in class.

____34. I am a very good listener and I enjoy listening to others' stories.

____35. I need to study with music.

____36. I enjoy games like Clue, Battleship, chess, and Rubik's Cube.

FIGURE 6.2   *Take the MIS (continued)*

____37. I enjoy physical activities such as bicycling, jogging, dancing, snowboarding, skateboarding, or swimming.

____38. I am good at solving people's problems and conflicts.

____39. I have to have time alone to think about new information in order to remember it.

____40. I enjoy sorting and organizing information, objects, and collectibles.

Refer to your score on each individual question. Place that score beside the appropriate question number below. Then, tally each line at the side.

Score					Total Across	Code
1____	9____	17____	25____	33____	____	Visual/Spatial
2____	10____	18____	26____	34____	____	Verbal/Linguistic
3____	11____	19____	27____	35____	____	Musical/Rhythm
4____	12____	20____	28____	36____	____	Logic/Math
5____	13____	21____	29____	37____	____	Body/Kinesthetic
6____	14____	22____	30____	38____	____	Interpersonal
7____	15____	23____	31____	39____	____	Intrapersonal
8____	16____	24____	32____	40____	____	Naturalistic

MIS Tally

Multiple Intelligences

Look at the scores on the MIS. What are your top three scores? Write them in the spaces below.

Top Score _____ Code _____
Second Score _____ Code _____
Third Score _____ Code _____

This tally can help you understand where some of your strengths may be. Again, this is not a measure of your worth or capacities, nor is it an indicator of your future successes. Read the following section to better understand multiple intelligences.

UNDERSTANDING MULTIPLE INTELLIGENCES

Why Is It Important to Discover New Ways of Looking at Yourself?

In 1983, Howard Gardner, a Harvard University professor, developed a theory called Multiple Intelligences. In his book *Frames of Mind,* he outlines seven intelligences that he feels are possessed by everyone: visual/spatial, verbal/linguistic, musical/rhythm, logic/math, body/kinesthetic, interpersonal, and intrapersonal. In 1996, he added an eighth intelligence: naturalistic. In short, if you have ever done things that came easily for you, you were probably drawing on one of your well-developed intelligences. On the other hand, if you have tried to do things that are very difficult to master or understand, you may be dealing with material that calls on one of your less developed intelligences. If playing the piano by ear comes easily to you, your musical/rhythm intelligence may be very strong. If you have trouble writing or understanding poetry, your verbal/linguistic intelligence may not be as well developed. This does not mean that you will never be able to write poetry; it simply means that this is not your dominant intelligence and you may need to spend more time on this activity.

DID YOU KNOW

PABLO PICASSO, the world-renowned, trend-setting artist, was born in Spain. He had a hard time in school and is said to have had a very difficult time with reading. He was diagnosed with a learning disability and his formal education never really benefited him. He left his college-level courses at the Academy of Arts in Madrid after less than a year of study. However, because of his immense artistic talent and his cubist interpretation of the universe, he changed the way the world looks at art. He is listed in the *Guinness Book of World Records* as THE most prolific painter in history, having completed nearly 14,000 paintings.

FIGURE

6.3 *The Eight Intelligences*

VISUAL/SPATIAL

- Picture Smart
- Thinks in pictures; knows where things are in the house; loves to create images and work with graphs, charts, pictures, and maps.

VERBAL/LINGUISTIC

- Word Smart
- Communicates well through language, likes to write, is good at spelling, great at telling stories, loves to read books.

MUSICAL/RHYTHM

- Music Smart
- Loves to sing, hum, and whistle; comprehends music; responds to music immediately; performs music.

LOGICAL/MATHEMATICAL

- Number Smart
- Can easily conceptualize and reason, uses logic, has good problem-solving skills, enjoys math and science.

BODY/KINESTHETIC

- Body Smart
- Learns through body sensation, moves around a lot, enjoys work involving the hands, is graced with some athletic ability.

INTERPERSONAL

- People Smart
- Loves to communicate with other people, possesses great leadership skills, has lots of friends, is involved in extracurricular activities.

INTRAPERSONAL

- Self Smart
- Has a deep awareness of own feelings, is very reflective, requires time to be alone, does not get involved with group activities.

NATURALISTIC

- Environment Smart
- Has interest in the environment and in nature; can easily recognize plants, animals, rocks, and cloud formations; may like hiking, camping, and fishing.

USING MULTIPLE INTELLIGENCES TO ENHANCE STUDYING AND LEARNING

Can You Make Them Work for You?

In Figure 6.4, you will find some helpful tips to assist you in creating a study environment and study habits using your multiple intelligences. Read each category because you may need to improve your less dominant intelligence in some of the classes you take. This list can help you build on your strengths and develop your less dominant areas.

FIGURE 6.4 *Using the Multiple Intelligences*

VISUAL/SPATIAL 	• Use visuals in your notes such as timelines, charts, graphs, and geometric shapes. • Work to create a mental or visual picture of the information at hand. • Use colored markers to make associations or to group items together. • Use mapping or webbing so that your main points are easily recognized. • When taking notes, draw pictures in the margins to illustrate the main points. • Visualize the information in your mind.
VERBAL/LINGUISTIC 	• Establish study groups so that you will have the opportunity to talk about the information. • Using the information you studied, create a story or a skit. • Read as much information about related areas as possible. • As you read chapters, outline them in your own words. • Summarize and recite your notes aloud.
MUSICAL/RHYTHM	• Listen to music while studying (if it does not distract you). • Write a song, jingle, or rap about the chapter or information. • Take short breaks from studying to listen to music. • Associate the information being studied to the music from your favorite song.
LOGICAL/ MATHEMATICAL	• Strive to make logical connections between subjects. • Don't just memorize the facts; apply them to real-life situations. • As you study the information, think of problems in society and how this information could solve those problems. • Create analyzing charts. Draw a line down the center of the page, put the information at hand in the left column and analyze, discuss, relate, and synthesize it in the right column. • Allow youself some time to reflect after studying.

(continued)

6.4 *Using the Multiple Intelligences (continued)*

BODY/KINESTHETIC	• Don't confine your study area to a desk or chair; move around, explore, go outside. • Act out the information. • Study in a group of people and change groups often. • Use charts, posters, flash cards, and chalkboards to study. • When appropriate or possible, build models using the information studied. • Verbalize the information to others. • Use games such as chess, Monopoly, Twister, or Clue when studying. • Trace words as you study them. • Use repetition to learn facts; write them many times. • Make study sheets.
INTERPERSONAL	• Study in groups. • Share the information with other people. • Teach the information to others. • Interview outside sources to learn more about the material at hand. • Have a debate with others about the information.
INTRAPERSONAL	• Study in a quiet area. • Study by youself. • Allow time for reflection and meditation about the subject matter. • Study in short time blocks and then spend some time absorbing the information. • Work at your own pace.
NATURALISTIC	• Study outside whenever possible. • Relate the information to the effect on the environment whenever possible. • When given the opportunity to choose your own topics or research projects, choose something related to nature. • Collect your own study data and resources. • Organize and label your information. • Keep separate notebooks on individual topics so that you can add new information to each topic as it becomes available to you.

UNDERSTANDING LEARNING STYLES THEORY

Why Is It Important to Know HOW I Learn?

A learning styles is "the way in which each learner begins to concentrate on, process, and retain new and difficult information" (Dunn and Griggs, 2000). There is a difference between a *learning style* and a *learning strategy*. A learning *style* is innate and involves your five senses. It is how you best process information that comes to you. A learning *strategy* is how you might choose to learn or study, such as by using note cards, flip charts, color slides, or cooperative learning groups. Your learning strategy also involves where you study (such as at a desk, in bed, at the library, in a quiet place, with music, etc.), how long you study, and what techniques you use to help you study (such as mnemonics, cooperative learning teams, or SQ3R).

If you learn best by *seeing* information, you have a more dominant *visual learning style*. If you learn best by *hearing* information, you have a more dominant *auditory learning style*. If you learn best by *touching or doing*, you have a more dominant *tactile learning style*. You may also hear the tactile learning style referred to as kinesthetic or hands-on.

FIGURE 6.5 *Take the Lead*

The Learning Evaluation and Assessment Directory

© *Robert M. Sherfield, Ph.D.*

Directions: Read each statement carefully and thoroughly. After reading the statement, rate your response using the scale below. There are no right or wrong answers. This is not a timed survey. The LEAD is based, in part, on research conducted by Rita Dunn.

3 = Often Applies

2 = Sometimes Applies

1 = Never or Almost Never Applies

_____ 1. I remember information better if I write it down or draw a picture of it.

_____ 2. I remember things better when I hear them instead of just reading or seeing them.

_____ 3. When I get something that has to be assembled, I just start doing it. I don't read the directions.

_____ 4. If I am taking a test, I can "see" the page of the text or lecture notes where the answer is located.

_____ 5. I would rather the professor explain a graph, chart, or diagram than just show it to me.

_____ 6. When learning new things, I want to "do it" rather than hear about it.

_____ 7. I would rather the instructor write the information on the board or overhead instead of just lecturing.

_____ 8. I would rather listen to a book on tape than read it.

_____ 9. I enjoy making things, putting things together, and working with my hands.

_____10. I am able to quickly conceptualize and visualize information.

_____11. I learn best by hearing words.

_____12. I have been called hyperactive by my parents, spouse, partner, or professor.

_____13. I have no trouble reading maps, charts, or diagrams.

_____14. I can usually pick up on small sounds like bells, crickets, or frogs, or distant sounds like train whistles.

_____15. I use my hands and gesture a lot when I speak to others.

Refer to your score on each individual question. Place that score beside the appropriate question number below. Then, tally each line at the side.

Score					Total Across	Code
1 _____	4 _____	7 _____	10 _____	13 _____	_____	Visual
2 _____	5 _____	8 _____	11 _____	14 _____	_____	Auditory
3 _____	6 _____	9 _____	12 _____	15 _____	_____	Tactile

LEAD (Learning Styles) SCORE

Look at the scores on the LEAD. What is your top score?

Top Score _____

Code _____

From Ordinary to Extraordinary

REAL PEOPLE | REAL LIVES | REAL CHANGE

CHEF ODETTE SMITH-RANSOME
Hospitality Instructor
The Art Institute of Pittsburgh, Pittsburgh, PA

At the age of 15, I found myself constantly in conflict with my mother, until one day I stood before her as she held a gun to my head. It was at that moment I knew I had to leave my parents' home, not just for my emotional well-being, but for my actual life and survival. My father was a good man, but he did not understand the entire situation with my mother's alcohol and diet pill addiction and he could do little to smooth out the situation between my mother and me. To complicate matters even more, my brother had just returned home from fighting in Vietnam and everyone was trying to adjust. It was a horrible time in the house where my ancestors had lived for over 100 years. So, I packed my clothes, dropped out of the 10th grade, and ran away over 1,000 miles to Charleston, South Carolina.

My first job was as a waitress. I worked in that job for over three years, realizing more every day that I was not using my talents and that without an education, I was doomed to work for minimum wage for the rest of my life. During this time, I met a friend in Charleston who was in the Navy. When he was re-leased, he offered to take me back to Pittsburgh. I agreed and upon my return, I went to work in the kitchen of a family-owned restaurant. They began to take an interest in me and made me feel proud of my work. I then decided to get my GED and determine what road to take that would allow me to use my culinary talents and help others at the same time.

I began my associate's degree, which required that students complete an apprenticeship. We worked 40 hours per week, Monday through Thursday, under the direction of a master chef and we were in class 8 hours a day on Friday. My apprenticeship was at the Hyatt Regency in Pittsburgh. In order to obtain your degree, you had to pass the apprenticeship, all of the classes, and a bank of tests that proved your profi-

> *So, I packed my clothes, dropped out of the 10th grade, and ran away over 1,000 miles to Charleston, South Carolina.*

152

From Ordinary to Extraordinary

REAL PEOPLE | REAL LIVES | REAL CHANGE

ciency in a variety of areas. If you failed one part of the tests, you could not get your degree. Proudly, I passed every test, every class, and my apprenticeship.

My first professional job came to me upon the recommendation of a friend. I interviewed for and was hired to become the Private Chef for the Chancellor of the University of Pittsburgh. I loved the job and it afforded me the opportunity to get my bachelor's degree. So, I juggled a full-time job, a two-year-old child, and a full load of classes. As I neared the end of my degree, I was offered a fellowship at the University of Pittsburgh that trained people to teach students with special needs. I graduated Cum Laude and began teaching and working with people who had cerebral palsy at Con-

nelley Academy. I loved the work, and the position solidified my desire to work with adults.

From there I taught at the Good Will Training Center and later at the Pittsburgh Job Corps, where my culinary team won a major national competition. Today, I am an Instructor at The Art Institute® of Pittsburgh, helping others reach their dreams of working in the hospitality industry. In 2005, I was named *Culinary Educator of the Year* by the American Culinary Federation®. I try to let my life and my struggles serve as a light for students who have faced adversity and may have felt that their past was going to determine their future. My advice to my students—and to you—is this: NEVER let anyone tell you that you can't do it, that you're not able to do it,

that you don't have the means to do it, or that you'll never succeed. YOU set your own course in life and you determine the direction of your future.

EXTRAORDINARY REFLECTION

Read the following statement and respond in your online journal or class notebook.

Chef Smith-Ransome had to literally leave her family to protect her life. Think about your family situation at the moment. Are your family members supportive of your efforts? Do they offer you support? Are they working with you to help you achieve your goals? If so, how does this make you stronger? Do they offer you guidance?

THINKING for CHANGE: An Activity for Critical Reflection

Kristin knew that her most powerful learning style was visual. She knew that she had always learned best when she could "see" the information in pictures, charts, graphs, PowerPoint® slides, videos, or other powerful visuals. Kristin also knew that when she was able to get involved with the information, she seemed to retain it better. She did not at first know what this was called, but later learned that she was also a tactile or "hands-on" learner.

When she discovered that different people have different ways of learning and instructors have different ways of teaching, things began to make more sense to her. She had wondered why she had always done poorly in classes that were all lecture—like her history class. This semester, she was becoming increasingly worried about her performance in her literature class. It, too, was all lecture—information about poems, plays, and sonnets. She decided to go to the Tutoring Center to find out what she could do to retain the information

more effectively. Her tutor showed her how to make the terms and ideas more "visual" by drawing pictures beside each one, using colors in her notes, creating small story boards, and creating a visual image of what was being discussed.

In your own words, what would you suggest that a classmate do if he or she is having trouble understanding, interpreting, or remembering information from a class where there is very little discussion or lecture and he or she is a very strong auditory learner? List at least three things that your classmate could do to strengthen his or her less dominant intelligence or learning style. Think about what services are offered on your campus and what people might be of assistance to him or her.

1. _____

2. _____

3. _____

Some of the most successful students master information and techniques by using all three styles. If you were learning how to skateboard, you might learn best by *hearing someone* talk about the different styles or techniques. Others might learn best by *watching a video* in which someone demonstrates the techniques. Still others would learn best by actually getting on the board and *trying it out.* Those who engage all of their senses gain the most.

After taking the LEAD and reading more about learning styles (Figure 6.6) list at least three concrete strategies that you can employ to enhance your learning strategies for each of the three areas.

WANTED: A VISUAL LEARNER WITH TACTILE SKILLS

Do You Know the Differences Between Your Primary Learning Style and Your Dominant Intelligence?

As discussed previously, a ***learning style*** and a ***learning strategy*** are different. A learning style and a ***dominant intelligence*** are also quite different. When you read over the descriptions of multiple intelligences theory and learning styles theory, you probably noticed several common elements. Both theories deal with the visual, auditory, and tactile (or kinesthetic). There are also similarities between the two theories, but the differences are great and important.

FIGURE 6.6   *Learning Styles*

VISUAL LEARNING STYLE

(Eye Smart). Thinks in pictures. Enjoys visual instructions, demonstrations, and descriptions; would rather read a text than listen to a lecture; avid note-taker; needs visual references; enjoys using charts, graphs, and pictures.

I can improve my visual learning style by …

1. _____
   _____
2. _____
   _____
3. _____
   _____

AUDITORY LEARNING STYLE

(Ear Smart). Prefers verbal instructions; would rather listen than read; often tapes lectures and listens to them in the car or at home; recites information out loud; enjoys talking, discussing issues, and verbal stimuli; talks out problems.

I can improve my auditory learning style by …

1. _____
   _____
2. _____
   _____
3. _____
   _____

TACTILE LEARNING STYLE

(Action Smart). Prefers hands-on approaches to learning; likes to take notes and uses a great deal of scratch paper; learns best by doing something, by touching it, or manipulating it; learns best while moving or while in action; often does not concentrate well when sitting and reading.

I can improve my tactile learning style by …

1. _____
   _____
2. _____
   _____
3. _____
   _____

Simply stated, you can have a visual learning style and yet **not have** visual/spatial as your dominant intelligence. *"How can this be possible?"* you may be asking. It may be that you **learn best** how to paint a picture by watching someone paint a picture—watching his or her brush-strokes, his or her method of mixing paints, and his or her spatial layout (this is your dominant visual learning style). However, you may not be as engaged or as talented at actually painting as the person you watched. Your painting may lack feeling, depth, and expression. You may find it hard to paint anything that is not copied from something else. You can't visualize a landscape in your mind because your visual/spatial intelligence is not very strong. In other words, you are not an innate artist at heart. This is an example of how your ***visual learning style*** can be a strong way for you to learn, but your visual/spatial intelligence may not be your dominant intelligence.

In your own words, compare and contrast YOUR primary learning style with your dominant intelligences. Give one example.

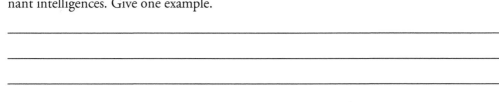

BLOOM LEVEL 2
QUESTION

6.7   *What Can You Learn about Personality?*

TAKE THE P.A.P.

The Personality Assessment Profile

© *Robert M. Sherfield, Ph.D.*

Directions: Read each statement carefully and thoroughly. After reading the statement, rate your response using the scale below. There are no right or wrong answers. This is not a timed survey. The PAP is based, in part, on the Myers-Briggs Type Indicator®(MBTI) by Katharine Briggs and Isabel Briggs-Myers.

3 = Often Applies

2 = Sometimes Applies

1 = Never or Almost Never Applies

____ 1a. I am a very talkative person.

____ 1b. I am a more reflective person than a verbal person.

____ 2a. I am a very factual and literal person.

____ 2b. I look to the future and I can see possibilities.

____ 3a. I value truth and justice over tact and emotion.

____ 3b. I find it easy to empathize with other people.

____ 4a. I am very ordered and efficient.

____ 4b. I enjoy having freedom from control.

____ 5a. I am a very friendly and social person.

____ 5b. I enjoy listening to others more than talking.

____ 6a. I enjoy being around and working with people who have a great deal of common sense.

____ 6b. I enjoy being around and working with people who are dreamers and have a great deal of imagination.

____ 7a. One of my motivating forces is to do a job very well.

____ 7b. I like to be recognized. I am motivated by my accomplishments and awards.

____ 8a. I like to plan out my day before I go to bed.

____ 8b. When I get up on a non-school or non-work day, I just like to let the day "plan itself."

____ 9a. I like to express my feelings and thoughts.

____ 9b. I enjoy a great deal of tranquility and quiet time to myself.

____10a. I am a very pragmatic and realistic person.

____10b. I like to create new ideas, methods, or ways of doing things.

____11a. I make decisions with my brain.

____11b. I make decisions with my heart.

____12a. I am a very disciplined and orderly person.

____12b. I don't make a lot of plans.

____13a. I like to work with a group of people.

____13b. I would rather work independently.

____14a. I learn best if I can see it, touch it, smell it, taste it, or hear it.

____14b. I learn best by relying on my gut feelings or intuition.

____15a. I am quick to criticize others.

____15b. I compliment others very easily and quickly.

____16a. My life is systematic and organized.

____16b. I don't really pay attention to deadlines.

____17a. I can be myself when I am around others.

____17b. I can be myself when I am alone.

____18a. I live in the here and now, in the present.

(continued)

FIGURE

6.7   *What Can You Learn about Personality? (continued)*

____18b. I live in the future, planning and dreaming.

____19a. I think that if someone breaks the rules, the person should be punished.

____19b. I think that if someone breaks the rules, we should look at the person who broke the rules, examine the rules, and look at the situation at hand before a decision is made.

____20a. I do my work, then I play.

____20b. I play, then do my work.

Refer to your score on each individual question. Place that score beside the appropriate question number below. Then, tally each line at the side.

Score					Total Across	Code
1a ____	5a ____	9a ____	13a ____	17a ____	____	E Extrovert
1b ____	5b ____	9b ____	13b ____	17b ____	____	I Introvert
2a ____	6a ____	10a ____	14a ____	18a ____	____	S Sensing
2b ____	6b ____	10b ____	14b ____	18b ____	____	N Intuition
3a ____	7a ____	11a ____	15a ____	19a ____	____	T Thinking
3b ____	7b ____	11b ____	15b ____	19b ____	____	F Feeling
4a ____	8a ____	12a ____	16a ____	20a ____	____	J Judging
4b ____	8b ____	12b ____	16b ____	20b ____	____	P Perceiving

PAP Scores

Personality Indicator

Look at the scores on your PAP. Is your score higher in the *E or the I* line? Is your score higher in the *S or the N* line? Is your score higher in the *T or the F* line? Is your score higher in the *J or the P* line? Write the code to the side of each section below.

Is your higher score   **E or I**   Code _____

Is your higher score   **S or N**   Code _____

Is your higher score   **T or F**   Code _____

Is your higher score   **J or P**   Code _____

UNDERSTANDING PERSONALITY TYPE

Are You ENFJ, ISTP, or ENTJ, and Why Does It Matter?

In 1921, Swiss psychologist **Carl Jung** (1875–1961) published his work *Psychological Types*. In this book, Jung suggested that human behavior is not random. He felt that behavior follows patterns and that these patterns are caused by differences in the way people use their minds. In 1942, Isabel Briggs-Myers and her mother, Katharine Briggs, began to put Jung's theory into practice. They developed the Myers-Briggs Type Indicator®, which after more than 50 years of research and refinement, has become the most widely used instrument for identifying and studying personality.

Personality typing can "help us discover what best motivates and energizes each of us as individuals" (Tieger and Barron-Tieger, 2007). The questions on the PAP helped you discover whether you are an **E** or an **I** (**E**xtroverted or **I**ntroverted), an **S** or an **N**

ESSENTIAL CORNERSTONE

Communication:

How can learning more about your personality, and the personalities of those around you, help you enhance your communication skills?

Social Networking Moment:

Share your response to this Essential Cornerstone with peers in your social network. Choose two responses from your peers and respond to their postings.

(**S**ensing or i**N**tuitive), a **T** or an **F** (**T**hinking or **F**eeling), and a **J** or a **P** (**J**udging or **P**erceiving). When all of the combinations of E/I, S/N, T/F, and J/P are combined, there are 16 personality types. Everyone will fit into **ONE** of the following categories:

ISTJ	ISFJ	INFJ	INTJ
ISTP	ISFP	INFP	INTP
ESTP	ESFP	ENFP	ENTP
ESTJ	ESFJ	ENFJ	ENTJ

Let's take a look at the four major categories of typing. Notice that the higher your score in one area, the stronger your personality type is for that area. For instance, if you scored 15 on the E (extroversion) questions, this means that you are a strong extrovert. If you scored 15 on the I (introversion) questions, this means that you are a strong introvert. However, if you scored 7 on the E questions and 8 on the I questions, your score indicates that you possess almost the same amount of extroverted and introverted qualities. The same is true for every other category of the PAP.

E versus I (Extroversion/Introversion)

This category deals with the way we *interact with others and the world around us; how we draw our energy*.

   Extroverts prefer to live in the outside world, drawing their strength from other people. They are outgoing and love interaction. They usually make decisions with others in mind. They enjoy being the center of attention. There are usually few secrets about extroverts.

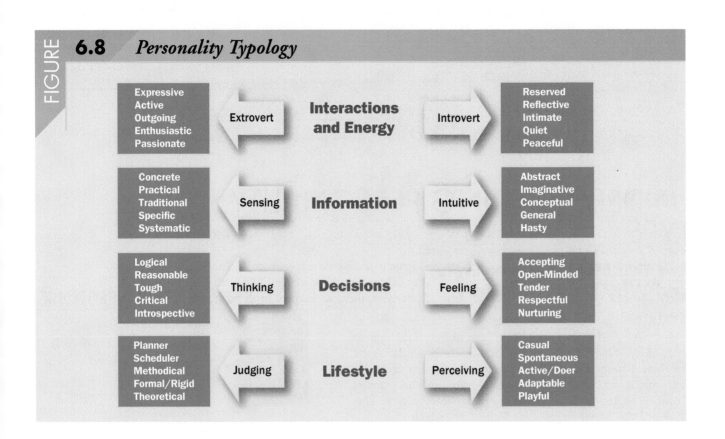

FIGURE 6.8   *Personality Typology*

Extrovert	Interactions and Energy	Introvert
Expressive / Active / Outgoing / Enthusiastic / Passionate		Reserved / Reflective / Intimate / Quiet / Peaceful

Sensing	Information	Intuitive
Concrete / Practical / Traditional / Specific / Systematic		Abstract / Imaginative / Conceptual / General / Hasty

Thinking	Decisions	Feeling
Logical / Reasonable / Tough / Critical / Introspective		Accepting / Open-Minded / Tender / Respectful / Nurturing

Judging	Lifestyle	Perceiving
Planner / Scheduler / Methodical / Formal/Rigid / Theoretical		Casual / Spontaneous / Active/Doer / Adaptable / Playful

Introverts draw their strength from the inner world. They need to spend time alone to think and ponder. They are usually quiet and reflective. They usually make decisions by themselves. They do not like being the center of attention. They are private.

S versus N (Sensing/iNtuition)

This category deals with the way we *learn and deal with information*.

Sensing types gather information through their five senses. They have a hard time believing something if it cannot be seen, touched, smelled, tasted, or heard. They like concrete facts and details. They do not rely on intuition or gut feelings. They usually have a great deal of common sense.

Intuitive types are not very detail-oriented. They can see possibilities, and they rely on their gut feelings. Usually, they are very innovative people. They tend to live in the future and often get bored once they have mastered a task.

T versus F (Thinking/Feeling)

This category deals with the way we *make decisions*.

Thinkers are very logical people. They do not make decisions based on feelings or emotions. They are analytical and sometimes do not take others' values into consideration when making decisions. They can easily identify the flaws of others. They can sometimes be seen as insensitive and lacking compassion.

Feelers make decisions based on what they feel is right and just. They like to have harmony, and they value others' opinions and feelings. They are usually very tactful people who like to please others. They are very warm people.

J versus P (Judging/Perceiving)

This category deals with the way we *live and our overall lifestyle*.

Judgers are very orderly people. They must have a great deal of structure in their lives. They are good at setting goals and sticking to them. They are the type of people who would seldom, if ever, play before their work was completed.

Perceivers are just the opposite. They are less structured and more spontaneous. They do not like timelines. Unlike the judgers, they will play before their work is done. They will take every chance to delay a decision or judgment. Sometimes, they can become involved in too many things at one time.

After you have studied the the Personality Type Chart (Figure 6.9) and other information in the chapter regarding your personality type, you can make some decisions about your study habits and even your career choices. For instance, if you scored very high in the extroversion section, it may not serve you well to pursue a career where you would be forced to work alone. It would probably also be unwise to try to spend all of your time studying alone. If you are a strong extrovert, you would want to work and study around people.

---

bring the CHANGE

Tips for Personal Success

Consider the following tips for making the most of your learning style, personality type, and dominant intelligence.

▶ Improve your weaker learning styles by incorporating at least one aspect of those learning styles into your daily study plans.

▶ If your personality type clashes with your professor's personality type, try to make adjustments that enable you to get through the class successfully.

▶ Adjust your learning style to match your professor's teaching style if possible.

▶ Use your primary intelligence to help you decide on your life's vocation.

Now, it is your turn. Create a list of at least three more tips that you would offer a fellow classmate to assist him or her in making the most of his or her learning style, intelligence, and personality type. Develop one strategy for each category.

1. Learning Style Tip _____
2. Multiple Intelligence Tip _____
3. Personality Type Tip _____

FIGURE **6.9** *A Closer Look at Your Personality Type*

ISTJ–THE DUTIFUL

(7–10% of Americans)

Have great power of concentration; very serious; dependable; logical and realistic; take responsibility for their own actions; they are not easily distracted.

ISTP–THE MECHANIC

(4–7% of Americans)

Very reserved; good at making things clear to others; interested in how and why things work; like to work with their hands; can sometimes be misunderstood as idle.

ESTP–THE DOER

(6–8% of Americans)

They are usually very happy; they don't let trivial things upset them; they have very good memories; very good at working with things and taking them apart.

ESTJ–THE GUARDIAN

(12–15% of Americans)

They are "take charge" people; they like to get things done; focus on results; very good at organizing; good at seeing what will not work; responsible; realists.

ISFJ–THE NURTURER

(7–10% of Americans)

Hard workers; detail-oriented; considerate of others' feelings; friendly and warm to others; very conscientious; they are down-to-earth and like to be around the same.

ISFP–THE ARTIST

(5–7% of Americans)

Very sensitive and modest; adapt easily to change; they are respectful of others' feelings and values; take criticism personally; don't enjoy leadership roles.

ESFP–THE PERFORMER

(8–10% of Americans)

Very good at sports and active exercises; good common sense; easygoing; good at communication; can be impulsive; do not enjoy working alone; have fun and enjoy living and life.

ESFJ–THE CAREGIVER

(11–14% of Americans)

Enjoy many friendly relationships; popular; love to help others; do not take criticism very well; need praise; need to work with people; organized; talkative; active.

INFJ–THE PROTECTOR

(2–3% of Americans)

Enjoy an atmosphere where all get along; they do what is needed of them; they have strong beliefs and principles; enjoy helping others achieve their goals.

INFP–THE IDEALIST

(3–4% of Americans)

They work well alone; must know others well to interact; faithful to others and their jobs; excellent at communication; open-minded; dreamers; tend to do too much.

ENFP–THE INSPIRERS

(6–7% of Americans)

Creative and industrious; can easily find success in activities and projects that interest them; good at motivating others; organized; do not like routine.

ENFJ–THE GIVER

(3–5% of Americans)

Very concerned about others' feelings; respect others; good leaders; usually popular; good at public speaking; can make decisions too quickly; trust easily.

INTJ–THE SCIENTIST

(2–3% of Americans)

They are very independent; enjoy challenges; inventors; can be skeptical; they are perfectionists; they believe in their own work, sometimes to a fault.

INTP–THE THINKER

(3–4% of Americans)

Extremely logical; very analytical; good at planning; love to learn; excellent problem solvers; they don't enjoy needless conversation; hard to understand at times.

ENTP–THE VISIONARY

(4–6% of Americans)

Great problem solvers; love to argue either side; can do almost anything; good at speaking/motivating; love challenges; very creative; do not like routine; over-confident.

ENTJ–THE EXECUTIVE

(3–5% of Americans)

Excellent leaders; speak very well; hard-working; may be workaholics; may not give enough praise; like to learn; great planners; enjoy helping others reach their goals.

Adapted from Tieger and Barron-Tieger, Do What You Are, 2007, and The Personality Type Portraits at www.personalitypage.com.

CHANGING IDEAS TO *Reality*

REFLECTIONS ON LEARNING HOW TO LEARN

Unlike an IQ test, learning style, multiple intelligence, and personality type assessments do not pretend to determine if you are "smart" or not. These assessments simply allow you to look more closely at how you learn, what innate strengths you possess, and what your dominant intelligence may be.

Discovering your learning style can greatly enhance your classroom performance. For example, finally understanding that your learning style is visual and that your professor's teaching style is totally verbal (oral) can answer many questions about why you may have performed poorly in the past in a "strictly lecture" class. Now that you have discovered that you are a feeling extrovert, you can better understand why you love associating with others and learn a great deal by working in groups. And now that you have discovered that your primary intelligence is logical/mathematical, you know why math and science are easier for you than history or literature.

Possessing this knowledge and developing the tools to make your learning style, dominant intelligence, and personality type work for you, not against you, will be paramount to your success. As you continue to use your learning style, dominant intelligence, and personality type to enhance your learning, consider the following:

▶ Get involved in a *variety* of learning and social situations.

▶ Use your less dominant areas more often to *strengthen* them.

▶ *Read more* about personality typing and learning styles.

▶ *Surround yourself* with people who learn differently from the way you do.

▶ Try *different ways* of learning and studying.

▶ Remember that inventories *do not* measure your worth.

By understanding how you process information, learning can become an entirely new and exciting venture for you. Good luck to you on this new journey.

> *"Education is learning what you did not know you did not know."*
> —Daniel Boorstin

KNOWLEDGE *in* BLOOM

CREATING Your Personal Life Profile

Each chapter-end assessment is based on *Bloom's Taxonomy of Learning*. See the inside front cover for a quick review.

UTILIZES LEVELS 4 AND 5 OF THE TAXONOMY

Throughout the chapter, you have discovered three things about the way you learn best: your multiple intelligence, your learning style, and your personality type. Write them down in the spaces below:

My **dominant intelligence** is _____

My **primary learning style** is _____

My **strongest personality type** is _____

Now that you see them all together, think of them as a puzzle for which you need to "connect the dots." In other words, put them all together and what do they look like? What do they mean? How do they affect your studies, your relationships, your communication skills, and your career choices?

EXAMPLE: If Mike's dominant intelligence is **interpersonal**, his learning style is **verbal**, and his personality type is **ENFJ**, *connecting the dots* may suggest that he is the type of person who loves to be around other people and is an extrovert who learns best by listening to other people or explaining how something is done. He is a person who would probably speak up in class, be more of a leader than a follower, and start a study group if one did not exist because he is outgoing, organized, and very much a goal setter. Mike is the type of person who values relationships and listens to what others are saying. He is a person who shares and does not mind taking the time to explain things to others. He could easily become a good friend.

Some of the challenges that Mike could encounter might involve taking a class where discussions are rare, having to sit and never being able to share ideas or views, or having a professor who is not very organized and skips around. He would not deal very well with peers who are disrespectful and do not pull their own weight in the study group. He might also have a hard time with group members or classmates who are very quiet and prefer to observe rather than contribute. He would have trouble being around people who have no goals or direction in life. He might also run into some trouble because he is a very social person and loves to be around others in social settings. He may thus overcommit himself to groups and clubs and, on occasion, socialize more than study.

As you can see, by connecting the dots, Mike's **Personal Life Profile** tells us a great deal about his strengths and challenges. It also gives him an understanding of how to approach many different situations, capitalize on his strengths, and work to improve his weaker areas.

Now, it is your turn.

Take your time and refer to the chapter for any information you may need. Examine your assessments and create your own profile in the four areas listed below. Discuss your strengths and challenges for each area.

THE PERSONAL LIFE PROFILE OF _____

Academic Strengths: I found that I . . .

_____
_____
_____
_____
_____
_____
_____
_____
_____
_____
_____

Academic Challenges: I found that I . . .

_____
_____
_____
_____
_____
_____
_____
_____
_____
_____
_____
_____
_____

Communication Strengths: I found that I . . .

_____

_____

_____

_____

_____

_____

_____

_____

_____

_____

_____

_____

Communication Challenges: I found that I . . .

_____

_____

_____

_____

_____

_____

_____

_____

_____

_____

_____

_____

_____

Relationship Strengths: I found that I . . .

_____

_____

_____

_____

_____

_____

_____

_____

_____

_____

_____

Relationship Challenges: I found that I . . .

_____
_____
_____
_____
_____
_____
_____
_____

Career Strengths: I found that I . . .

_____
_____
_____
_____
_____
_____
_____
_____

Career Challenges: I found that I . . .

_____
_____
_____
_____
_____
_____
_____
_____

Looking at all of this together, write an extensive paragraph about what all of this means about you. Include thoughts on your learning style, your personality, your study habits, your communication skills, and your overall success strategy.

_____
_____
_____
_____
_____
_____

SQ3R *Mastery* Study Sheet

EXAMPLE QUESTION: *(from page 154)* What is the difference between a learning style and a learning strategy?		**ANSWER:**
EXAMPLE QUESTION: *(from page 158)* What is the definition of tactile and how do you use it?		**ANSWER:**
AUTHOR QUESTION: *(from page 147)* Discuss at least three theories of learning from the historical figures discussed.		**ANSWER:**
AUTHOR QUESTION: *(from page 151)* Who is Howard Gardner and why is his work important?		**ANSWER:**
AUTHOR QUESTION: *(from page 154)* Explain the difference between your learning style and your dominant intelligence.		**ANSWER:**
AUTHOR QUESTION: *(from page 155)* What is the difference between a visual learning style and visual intelligence?		**ANSWER:**
AUTHOR QUESTION: *(from page 157)* How can your personality type affect your study time?		**ANSWER:**
YOUR QUESTION: *(from page ____)*		**ANSWER:**
YOUR QUESTION: *(from page ____)*		**ANSWER:**
YOUR QUESTION: *(from page ____)*		**ANSWER:**
YOUR QUESTION: *(from page ____)*		**ANSWER:**
YOUR QUESTION: *(from page ____)*		**ANSWER:**

Finally, after answering these questions, recite this chapter's major points in your mind. Consider the following general questions to help you master this material.

- ▶ What was it about?
- ▶ What does it mean?
- ▶ What was the most important thing I learned? Why?
- ▶ What were the key points to remember?

CHAPTER 7
RECORD: LISTENING & NOTE TAKING

CULTIVATING
YOUR
LISTENING
SKILLS AND
DEVELOPING
A NOTE-TAKING
SYSTEM
THAT WORKS
FOR YOU

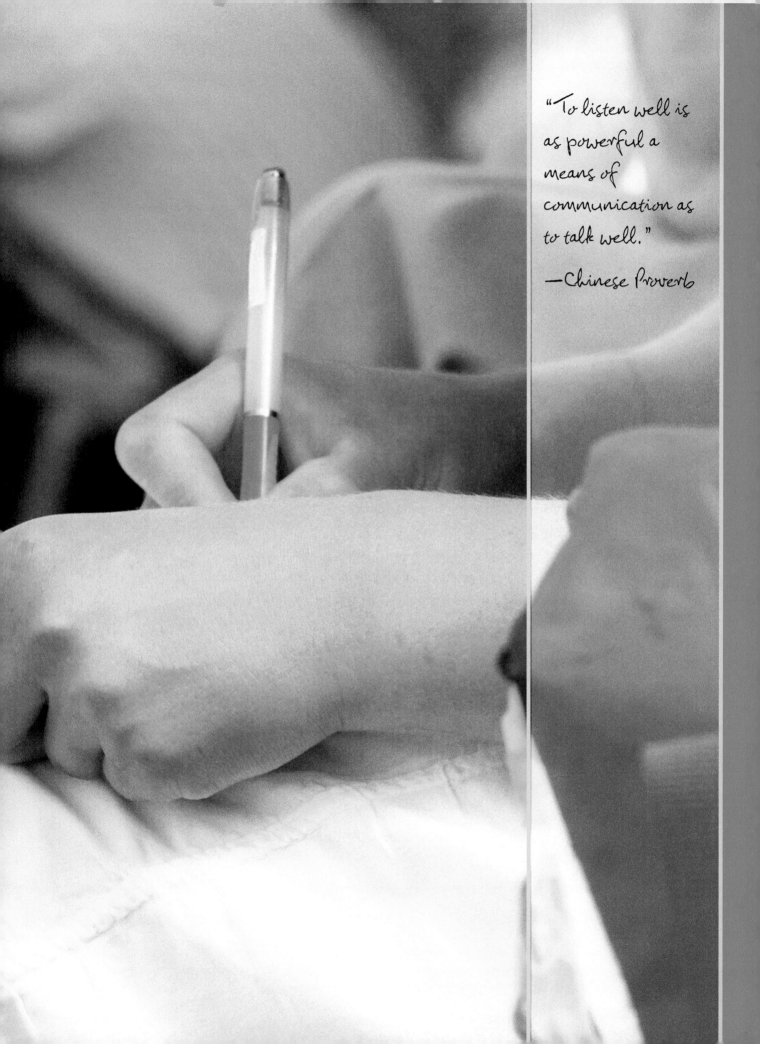

"To listen well is as powerful a means of communication as to talk well."

—Chinese Proverb

WHY READ THIS CHAPTER?

What's in it for me?

WHY do I need to become a better listener? WHY will a chapter on listening and note taking help me become a better student? WHY do instructors make such a big deal about note taking anyway? WHY is listening so important to my overall quality of life?

Why? Because listening is considered by many communication experts to be one of the, if not THE, most essential skills for building healthy relationships, solving problems, becoming open-minded, learning new information, and getting along in life. Listening will help you in terms of note taking, retaining information, and becoming actively involved in the learning process. The ability to listen in a variety of situations will also help you become a more efficient note-taker. Listening and note taking are important because well-designed notes create a history of your time in class, what you have read in your text and various articles, and what you might have studied with a group. You will find that there are different listening styles and note-taking styles and you will have to experiment to find which work best for you.

By carefully reading this chapter and taking the information provided seriously, you will be able to:

1. Understand the difference between listening and hearing.
2. Define the four listening styles.
3. Overcome the obstacles to listening and how to listen in different situations.
4. Discuss the importance of note taking and list specific tips to increase effectiveness.
5. Identify, discuss, and use the three types of note-taking systems: Cornell, outline, and mapping.

CHAPTER 7 / RECORD

"You cannot truly listen to anyone and do anything else at the same time."

—M. Scott Peck

WHY READ THIS CHAPTER?

. . . FROM MY PERSPECTIVE

NAME: Griffin Jones
INSTITUTION: Point Park University, Pittsburgh, PA
MAJOR: Cinema
AGE: 20

When you're making big decisions in your life, you will always have people who are older and more experienced than you bursting at the seams to give you "life lessons" and other advice. There is no point in your life where this will be more prevalent than when you first begin college. You will be bombarded with advice on sex, classes, drinking, relationships, and so on. A lot of it is just a rehash of all of the stuff you heard going into high school. However, many of the things we're asked to listen to can be helpful. Figuring out which ones are helpful is the hardest part. This is where listening comes in handy.

For most college students, listening to others is a ludicrous concept. We tend to want to try everything for ourselves. As someone who is quite stubborn, I completely understand, but over the past couple of years since enrolling in college, I've found that it's good to find a middle ground with these things. First, many people do actually know what they are talking about because they have "lived it," and we're just better off listening to their hard-earned advice and taking their word on it. On the other hand, trying something new for yourself isn't always a bad idea either. There are those people who don't know what they're talking about, either because they're completely oblivious to the real world or because they're trying to tell you stuff that doesn't necessarily apply to you. Again, this is where critical listening can

come in very handy. Sometimes, you have to listen for what is not said. Also, trying something for yourself and failing is a great way of learning. Trial and error shouldn't be a forbidden activity.

What I have discovered is this: Find people who you know to be level-headed and in touch with the present and listen to them. Really listen to them. And even if you determine that they're not level-headed, take their advice and consider what they have to say anyway . . . store it away for another time; you never know when you will need their guidance. They may know what they're talking about but just don't know how to present it rationally. Just don't be afraid to step out of your boundaries and listen to others' viewpoints, listen to their lives, and use others' advice to live for yourself. This chapter on listening and note taking can help you become a much more active listener.

SCAN & QUESTION

In the preface of this book (page ix), you read about the **SQ3R Study Method.** Right now, take a few moments, **scan this chapter**, and on page 189, write **five questions** that you think will be important to your mastery of this material. In addition to the two questions below, you will find five questions from your authors. Use one of your **"On The Test"** stickers to flag this page for easy reference.

EXAMPLES:

▶ **What are the four components of the Chinese verb "to listen"?** (from page 171)

▶ **Why is it important to identify key words during a lecture?** (from page 175)

THE IMPORTANCE OF LISTENING

Why Does Listening Really Matter in Classes and Relationships?

Listening is a survival skill. Period! It is that simple! *"I know listening is important,"* you might say, but few ever think of the paramount significance listening has in our everyday lives. It is necessary for:

How can becoming a critical listener help you in and out of the classroom?

▶ establishing and improving relationships,

▶ personal growth,

▶ showing respect to others,

▶ professional rapport,

▶ showing empathy and compassion,

▶ learning new information,

▶ understanding others' opinions and views,

▶ basic survival,

▶ entertainment, and

▶ health.

How much time do you think you spend listening every day? Research suggests that we spend almost 70% of our waking time communicating, and **53% of that time is spent in listening situations** (Adler et al., 2006). Effective listening skills can mean the difference between A's and F's, relationships and loneliness, and in some cases and careers, success and failure.

LISTENING DEFINED

Is There Really a Difference Between Listening and Hearing?

No doubt you've been in a communication situation in which a misunderstanding takes place. Either you hear something incorrectly or someone hears you incorrectly OR it could be that someone hears your message but misinterprets it. These communication blunders arise because we tend to view listening (and communicating in general) as an automatic response, when in fact it is not. **Listening is a learned, voluntary activity. You must choose to do it.** It is a skill just like driving a car, painting a picture, or playing the piano. Becoming an active listener requires practice, time, mistakes, guidance, and active participation. **Hearing, however, is not learned; it is automatic and involuntary.** If you are within range of a sound, you will probably hear it even though you may not be listening to it. Hearing a sound does not guarantee that you know from where the sound comes. Listening actively, though, means making a conscious effort to focus on the sound you heard and to determine what it is.

According to Ronald Adler (Adler et al., 2006), the drawing of the Chinese verb "to listen" provides a comprehensive and practical definition of listening. (See Figure 7.1.)

In this figure, listening involves the ears, the eyes, undivided attention, and the heart. Do you make it a habit to listen with more than your ears? The Chinese view listening as a whole-body experience. At its core, listening is "the ability to hear, understand, analyze, respect, and appropriately respond to the meaning of another person's spoken and nonverbal messages" (Daly and Engleberg, 2006). Although this definition involves the word "hear," listening goes far beyond just the physical ability to catch sound waves.

FIGURE 7.1 *Chinese Verb "To Listen"*

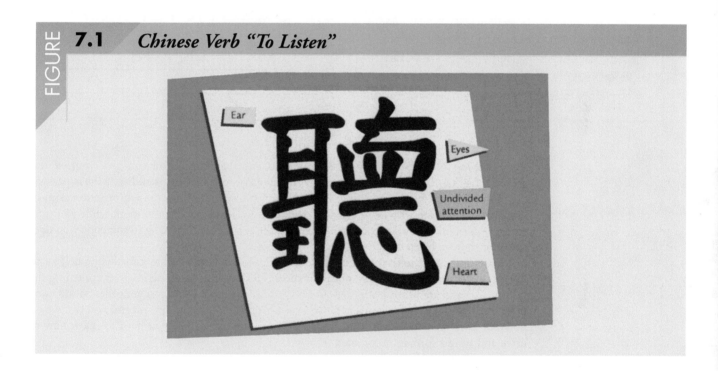

Categories of Listening

The first step of listening *is* hearing, but true listening involves one's full attention and the ability to filter out distractions, emotional barriers, cultural differences, and religious biases. Listening means that you are making a conscious decision to understand and show reverence for the other person's communication efforts. Listening involves being open-minded as well. To understand listening as a whole-body experience, we can divide it into three different categories:

1. Listening with a **purpose**

2. Listening **objectively**

3. Listening **constructively**

Listening with a purpose suggests a need to recognize different types of listening situations— for example, class, worship, entertainment, and relationships. People do not listen the same way in every situation.

Jennifer greatly disliked her biology instructor. She could not put her finger on exactly WHY she disliked her; she just knew that Dr. Lipmon rubbed her the wrong way. This had been the case since the first day of class. Other students seemed to like her and were able to carry on conversations with her—but Jennifer could not. "Why?" she thought. "Why do I dislike her so much? She's not a bad teacher," she reasoned, "but I just can't stand to listen to her."

Jennifer decided to sit in class for the next week and really try to figure out what the main problem was. As she sat in class and listened, she finally put her finger on the problem: She and Dr. Lipmon had completely different views on many things including evolution and women's reproductive rights. Every time Dr. Lipmon made a statement contrary to Jennifer's core beliefs, Jennifer cringed.

She "shut down" and refused to listen any further. She then transferred her dislike of Dr. Lipmon's lectures and opinions onto her as a person. She knew this was affecting her grade and her knowledge base in class, but did not know how to manage or change the situation.

In your own words, what would you suggest that Jennifer do at this point? Pretend that she is enrolled at your institution. List at least three things that she could do to ensure her success in her biology class. Think about what services are offered and what people might be of assistance to her.

1. _____

2. _____

3. _____

Listening objectively means listening with an open mind. You can give yourself few greater gifts than the gift of knowing how to listen without bias or prejudice. This is perhaps the most difficult aspect of listening. If you have ever been cut off in mid-conversation or mid-sentence by someone who disagreed with you, or if someone has left the room while you were giving your opinion of a situation, you have had the experience of talking to someone who does not know how to listen objectively.

Listening constructively means listening with the attitude: "How can this be helpful to my life, my education, my career, or my finances?" This type of listening involves evaluating the information you are hearing and determining whether it has meaning to your life. Sound easy? It is more difficult than it sounds because, again, we all tend to shut out information that we do not view as immediately helpful or useful. To listen constructively, you need to know how to listen and store information for later.

THE FOUR LISTENING STYLES

What Is Your Orientation?

According to Steven McCornack (2007), interpersonal communication expert, author, and educator, there are *four different listening styles*: action-oriented, time-oriented, people-oriented, and content-oriented. Study Figure 7.2 to determine which style best describes you as a listener.

Which style best describes you? _____

What are the "pros" of being this type of listener? _____

_____

_____

_____

FIGURE **7.2**   *Four Listening Styles*

ACTION-ORIENTED LISTENERS	**TIME-ORIENTED LISTENERS**
✓ want to get their messages quickly and to-the-point. ✓ do not like fluff and grow impatient when they perceive people to be "wasting their time." ✓ become frustrated when information is not orderly. ✓ are quick to dismiss people who "ramble" and falter when they speak.	✓ want their information in brief, concise meetings ✓ are consumed with how much time is taken to convey a message ✓ set time limits for listening (and communicating in general) ✓ will ask people to "move the message along" if they feel it is taking too long
PEOPLE-ORIENTED LISTENERS	**CONTENT-ORIENTED LISTENERS**
✓ are in contrast to time- and action-oriented listeners ✓ view listening as a chance to connect with other people ✓ enjoy listening to people so that relationships can be built ✓ become emotionally involved with the person communicating	✓ enjoy an intellectual challenge ✓ like to listen to technical information, facts, and evidence ✓ enjoy complex information that must be deciphered and filtered ✓ carefully evaluate information and facts before forming an opinion ✓ enjoy asking questions

What are the "cons" of being this type of listener? _____

_____

_____

_____

LISTENING CAN BE SO HARD

Can You Really Overcome the Obstacles to Listening?

Several major obstacles stand in the way of becoming an effective listener. To begin building active listening skills, you first have to remove some barriers.

Obstacle One: Prejudging

Prejudging, the act of automatically shutting out what is being said, is one of the biggest obstacles to active listening. You may prejudge because you don't like or agree with the information or the person communicating it. You may also have prejudging problems because of your environment, culture, religion, social status, or attitude.

DO YOU PREJUDGE INFORMATION OR ITS SOURCE?

Answer yes or no to the following questions:

1. I tune out when something is boring.	YES	NO
2. I tune out when I do not agree with the information.	YES	NO
3. I argue mentally with the speaker about information.	YES	NO
4. I do not listen to people I do not like.	YES	NO
5. I make decisions about information before I understand all of its implications or consequences.	YES	NO

If you answered yes to two or more of these questions, you tend to prejudge in a listening situation.

TIPS FOR OVERCOMING PREJUDGING

▶ Listen for information that may be valuable to you as a student. Some material may not be pleasant to hear but may be useful to you later on.

▶ Listen to the message, not the messenger. If you do not like the speaker, try to go beyond personality and listen to what is being said, without regard to the person saying it. Conversely, you may like the speaker so much that you automatically accept the material or answers without listening objectively to what is being said.

▶ Try to remove cultural, racial, gender, social, and environmental barriers. Just because a person is different from you or holds a different point of view does not make that person wrong; and just because a person is like you or holds a similar point of view does not make that person right. Sometimes, you have to cross cultural and environmental barriers to learn new material and see with brighter eyes.

Obstacle Two: Talking

Not even the best listener in the world can listen while he or she is talking. The next time you are in a conversation with a friend, try speaking while your friend is speaking—then see if you know what your friend said. To become an effective listener, you need to learn the power of silence. Silence gives you the opportunity to think about what is being said before you respond. The first rule of listening is: Stop talking. The second rule of listening is: Stop talking. And, you guessed it, the third rule of listening is: Stop talking.

ARE YOU A TALKER RATHER THAN A LISTENER?

Answer yes or no to the following questions:

1. I often interrupt the speaker so that I can say what I want.	YES	NO
2. I am thinking of my next statement while others are talking.	YES	NO
3. My mind wanders when others talk.	YES	NO
4. I answer my own questions.	YES	NO
5. I answer questions that are asked of other people.	YES	NO

If you answered yes to two or more questions, you tend to talk too much in a listening situation.

TIPS FOR OVERCOMING THE URGE TO TALK TOO MUCH

▶ Avoid interrupting the speaker. Force yourself to be silent at parties, family gatherings, and friendly get-togethers. You should not be unsociable, but force yourself to be silent for 10 minutes. You'll be surprised at what you hear. You may also be surprised how hard it is to do this. Test yourself.

▶ Ask someone a question and then allow that person to answer the question.

▶ Too often we ask questions and answer them ourselves. Force yourself to wait until the person has formulated a response. If you ask questions and wait for answers, you will force yourself to listen.

▶ Concentrate on what is being said at the moment, not on what you want to say next.

Obstacle Three: Becoming Too Emotional

Emotions can form a strong barrier to active listening. Worries, problems, fears, and anger can keep you from listening to the greatest advantage. Have you ever sat in a lecture and before you knew what was happening, your mind was a million miles away because you were angry or worried about something? If you have, you know what it's like to bring your emotions to the table.

DO YOU BRING YOUR EMOTIONS TO THE LISTENING SITUATION?

Answer yes or no to the following questions:

1. I get angry before I hear the whole story.   YES   NO
2. I look for underlying or hidden messages in information.   YES   NO
3. Sometimes, I begin listening on a negative note.   YES   NO
4. I base my opinions of information on what others are saying or doing.   YES   NO
5. I readily accept information as correct from people whom I like or respect.   YES   NO

If you answered yes to two or more of these questions, you tend to bring your emotions to a listening situation.

TIPS FOR OVERCOMING EMOTIONS

▶ Know how you feel before you begin the listening experience. Take stock of your emotions and feelings ahead of time.

▶ Focus on the message; determine how to use the information.

▶ Create a positive image about the message you are hearing.

▶ Avoid overreacting and jumping to conclusions.

LISTENING FOR KEY WORDS, PHRASES, AND HINTS

Do Professors Really Offer Test Clues in Their Lectures?

Do you find it easy or hard to pick up on a professor's clues in class that may indicate important test information?

Learning how to listen for key words, phrases, and hints can help you become an active listener and an effective note-taker. For example, if your English instructor begins a lecture by saying, "There are 10 basic elements to writing poetry," jot down the number 10 under the heading "Poetry" or write the numbers 1 through 10 on your notebook page, leaving space for notes. If at the end of class you find that you listed only six elements to writing poetry, you know that you missed part of the lecture. At this point, you need to ask the instructor some questions.

ESSENTIAL CORNERSTONE

Knowledge:
How can learning to take more effective notes help you master knowledge and learn more?

Social Networking Moment:
Share your response to this Essential Cornerstone with peers in your social network. Choose two responses from your peers and respond to their postings.

Here are some key phrases and words to listen for:

in addition to	another way	above all
most important	such as	specifically
you'll see this again	therefore	finally
for example	to illustrate	as stated previously
in contrast	in comparison	nevertheless
the characteristics of	the main issue is	moreover
on the other hand	as a result of	because

Picking up on *transition words* such as these will help you filter out less important information and thus listen more carefully to what is most important.

LISTENING IN DIFFICULT SITUATIONS

What Do You Do When English Is Your Second Language?

For students whose first language is not English, the college classroom can present some uniquely challenging situations. One of the most pressing and important challenges is the ability to listen, translate, understand, and capture the message on paper in a quick and continuous manner. According to Lynn Forkos, professor and coordinator of the Conversation Center for International Students at the College of Southern Nevada, the following tips can be beneficial:

▶ Don't be afraid to stop the instructor to ask for clarification. Asking questions allows you to take an active part in the listening process. If the instructor doesn't answer your questions sufficiently, make an appointment to speak with him or her during office hours.

▶ If you are in a situation where the instructor can't stop or you're watching a movie or video in class, listen for words that you do understand and try to figure out unfamiliar words in the context of the sentence. Jot down questions to ask later.

▶ Enhance your vocabulary by watching and listening to TV programs such as *Dateline, 20/20, Primetime Live, 60 Minutes,* and the evening news. You might also try listening to radio stations such as National Public Radio as you walk or drive.

▶ Write down everything that the instructor puts on the board, overhead, or PowerPoint slide. You may not need every piece of this information, but this technique gives you (and hopefully your study group) the ability to sift through the information outside of class. It also gives you a visual history of what the instructor said.

▶ Join a study group with people who speak English well and have the patience to assist you.

▶ Finally, if there is a conversation group or club that meets on campus, take the opportunity to join. **By practicing language**, you become more attuned to common words and phrases. If a conversation group is not available, consider starting one of your own.

TAKING EFFECTIVE NOTES

Is It Just a Big, Crazy Chore?

Go to class, take notes. Listen, take notes. Read a text, take notes. Watch a film, take notes. Jeez! Is it really that important? Actually, knowing how to take useful, accurate notes can dramatically improve your academic life. If you are an effective listener and note-taker, you have two of the most valuable skills any student could ever use. There are several reasons why it is important to take notes:

- ▶ You become an active part of the listening process.
- ▶ You create a history of your course's content when you take notes.
- ▶ You have written criteria to follow when studying.
- ▶ You create a visual aid for your material.
- ▶ Studying becomes much easier.
- ▶ You retain information at a greater rate than non-note-takers.
- ▶ Effective note-takers average higher grades than non-note-takers (Kiewra and Fletcher, 1984).

TIPS FOR EFFECTIVE NOTE TAKING

How Can I Write It Right?

You have already learned several skills that you will need to take notes, such as cultivating your active listening skills, overcoming obstacles to effective listening, and familiarizing yourself with key phrases used by instructors. Next, prepare yourself mentally and physically to take notes that are going to be helpful to you. Consider the following ideas as you think about expanding your note-taking abilities.

- ▶ **Physically AND mentally attend class.** This may sound like stating the obvious, but it is surprising how many college students feel they do not need to go to class. Not only do you have to physically show up, you also have to be there mentally and emotionally—ready to listen, take notes, question, scrutinize, and interpret.

- ▶ **Come to class prepared.**   Scan, read, and use your textbook to establish a basic understanding of the material before coming to class It is always easier to take notes when you have a preliminary understanding of what is being said. Coming to class prepared also means bringing the proper materials for taking notes: lab manuals, pens, a notebook, and a highlighter.

- ▶ **Bring your textbook to class.**   Although many students think they do not need to bring their textbooks to class if they have read the homework assignment, you will find that many instructors repeatedly refer to the text while lecturing. The instructor may ask you to highlight, underline, or refer to the text in class, and following along in the text as the instructor lectures may also help you organize your notes.

- ▶ **Ask questions and participate in class.**   Two of the most critical actions you can perform in class are to ask questions and to participate in the class discussion. If you do not understand a concept or theory, ask questions. Don't leave class without understanding what has happened and assume you'll pick it up on your own.

Good note-taking skills help you do more than simply record what you learn in class or read in a book so that you can recall it. These skills can also help reinforce that information so that you actually know it.

YOU'LL BE SEEING STARS

What Is the L-STAR System and How Can I Use It?

One of the most effective ways to take notes begins with the **L-STAR system**.

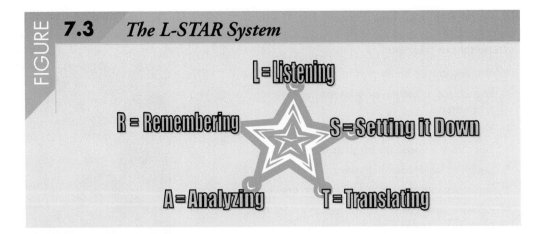

FIGURE 7.3   *The L-STAR System*

This five-step program will enable you to compile complete, accurate, and visual notes for future reference. Along with improving your note-taking skills, using this system will enhance your ability to participate in class, help other students, study more effectively, and perform well on exams and quizzes.

L—Listening

One of the best ways to become an effective note-taker is to become an active listener. A concrete step you can take toward becoming an active listener in class is to sit near the front of the room, where you can hear the instructor and see the board and overheads. Choose a spot that allows you to see the instructor's mouth and facial expressions. If you see that the instructor's face has become animated or expressive, you can bet that you are hearing important information. Write it down! If you sit in the back of the room, you may miss out on these important clues.

S—Setting It Down

The actual writing of notes can be a difficult task. Some instructors are organized in their delivery of information; others are not. Some stick to an easy-to-follow outline and others ramble around, making it more difficult to follow them and take notes. Your listening skills, once again, are going to play an important role in determining what needs to be written down. In most cases, you will not have time to take notes verbatim. Some instructors talk very fast. You will thus have to be selective about the information you choose to set down. One of the best ways to keep up with the information being presented is to develop a shorthand system of your own. Many of the symbols you use will be universal, but you may use some symbols, pictures, and markings that are uniquely your own. Some of the more common symbols are:

w/	with	w/o	without
=	equals	≠	does not equal
<	less than	>	greater than
%	percentage	#	number
&	and	∧	increase
+	plus or addition	–	minus
*	important	etc.	and so on
e.g.	for example	vs.	against
esp	especially	"	quote
?	question	. . .	and so on

These symbols can save you valuable time when taking notes. Because you will use them frequently, it might be a good idea to memorize them.

T—Translating

Translating can save you hours of work as you begin to study for exams. Many students feel that this step is not important, or is too time consuming, and leave it out. Don't. Often, students take notes so quickly that they make mistakes or use abbreviations that they may not be able to decipher later.

After each class, go to the library or some other quiet place and review your notes. You don't have to do this immediately after class, but before the end of the day, you will need to rewrite and translate your classroom notes. This process gives you the opportunity to put the notes in your own words and to incorporate your text notes into your classroom notes. This practice also provides a first opportunity to commit this information to memory.

Translating your notes helps you make connections among previous material discussed, your own personal experiences, readings, and new material presented. Translating aids in recalling and applying new information. Few things are more difficult than trying to reconstruct your notes the night before a test, especially when they were made several weeks previously.

A—Analyzing

This step takes place while you translate your notes from class. When you analyze your notes, you are asking two basic questions: (1) What does this mean? and (2) Why is it important? If you can answer these two questions about your material, you have almost mastered the information. Though some instructors will want you to spit back the exact same information you were given, others will ask you for a more detailed understanding and a synthesis of the material. When you are translating your notes, begin to answer these two questions using your notes, textbook, supplemental materials, and information gathered from outside research. Once again, this process is not simple or quick, but testing your understanding of the material is important. Remember that many lectures are built on past lectures. If you do not understand what happened in class on September 17, you may not be able to understand what happens on September 19. Analyzing your notes while translating them will give you a more complete understanding of the material.

R—Remembering

Once you have listened to the lecture, set your notes on paper, and translated and analyzed the material, it is time to study, or remember, the information. Some effective ways to remember information include creating a visual picture, speaking the notes out loud, using mnemonic devices, and finding a study partner.

bring the CHANGE

Tips for Personal Success

Consider the following tips for improving your listening skills and taking notes more effectively:

▶ Sit near the front of the room and establish eye contact with the instructor.

▶ Read the text or handouts beforehand to familiarize yourself with the upcoming information.

▶ Come to class with an open mind and positive attitude about learning. Listen purposefully, objectively, and constructively.

Now, it is your turn. Create a list of at least three more tips that you would offer a fellow classmate to assist him or her with bringing about positive change in his or her listening and note-taking skills.

1. _____

2. _____

3. _____

THREE COMMON NOTE-TAKING SYSTEMS

Why Doesn't Everyone Take Notes the Same Way?

There are three common note-taking systems: (1) the **outline** technique; (2) the **Cornell**, or split-page, technique (also called the T system); and (3) the **mapping** technique. You may find each technique useful or you may find that one is more effective for you than the others.

IT'S AS SIMPLE AS A, B, C—1, 2, 3

The Outline Technique

The outline system uses a series of major headings and multiple subheadings formatted in hierarchical order (Figure 7.4). The outline technique is one of the most commonly used note-taking systems, yet it is also one of the most misused systems. It can be difficult to outline notes in class, especially if your instructor does not follow an outline format while lecturing.

When using the outline system, it is best to get all the information from the lecture and, afterward, combine your lecture notes and text notes to create an outline. Most instructors would advise against using the outline system of note taking during class, although you may be able to use a modified version. The most important thing to remember is not to get bogged down in a

FIGURE 7.4   *The Outline Technique*

October 20

Topic: Maslow's Hierarchy of Basic Needs

I. Abraham Maslow (1908–1970)
- American psychologist
- Born - Raised Brooklyn, N.Y.
- Parents = Uneducated Jewish immigrants
- Lonely - unhappy childhood
- 1st studied law @ city coll. of N.Y.
- Grad school - Univ of Wisconsin
- Studied human behavior & experience
- Leader of humanistic school of psy.

II. H of B. Needs (Theory)
- Written in A Theory of Human Motivation in 1943
- Needs of human arranged like a ladder
- Basic needs of food, air, water at bottom
- Higher needs "up" the ladder
- Lower needs must be met to experience the higher needs

III. H of B. Needs (Features)
- Physiological needs
  - Breathing
  - Food
  - Air & water
  - Sleep
- Safety needs
  - Security of body
  - Employment

system during class; what is critical is getting the ideas down on paper. You can always go back after class and rearrange your notes as needed.

If you are going to use a modified or informal outline while taking notes in class, you may want to consider grouping information together under a heading as a means of outlining. It is easier to remember information that is logically grouped than information that is scattered across several pages. If your study skills lecture is on listening, you might outline your notes using the headings "The Process of Listening" and "Definitions of Listening."

After you have rewritten your notes using class lecture information and material from your textbook, your notes may look like those in Figure 7.4

IT'S A SPLIT DECISION

The Cornell (Modified Cornell, Split-Page, or T) System

The basic principle of the Cornell system, developed by Dr. Walter Pauk of Cornell University, is to split the page into two sections, each to be used for different information (see Figure 7.5). Section B (the larger section) is used for the actual notes from class or your text. Section A (the smaller section) should be used for headings OR questions. Review Figure 7.5 to see an example of Cornell note taking. An example of outline notes using the Cornell system appears in Figure 7.6.

FIGURE 7.5 *Cornell Note-Taking System Example*

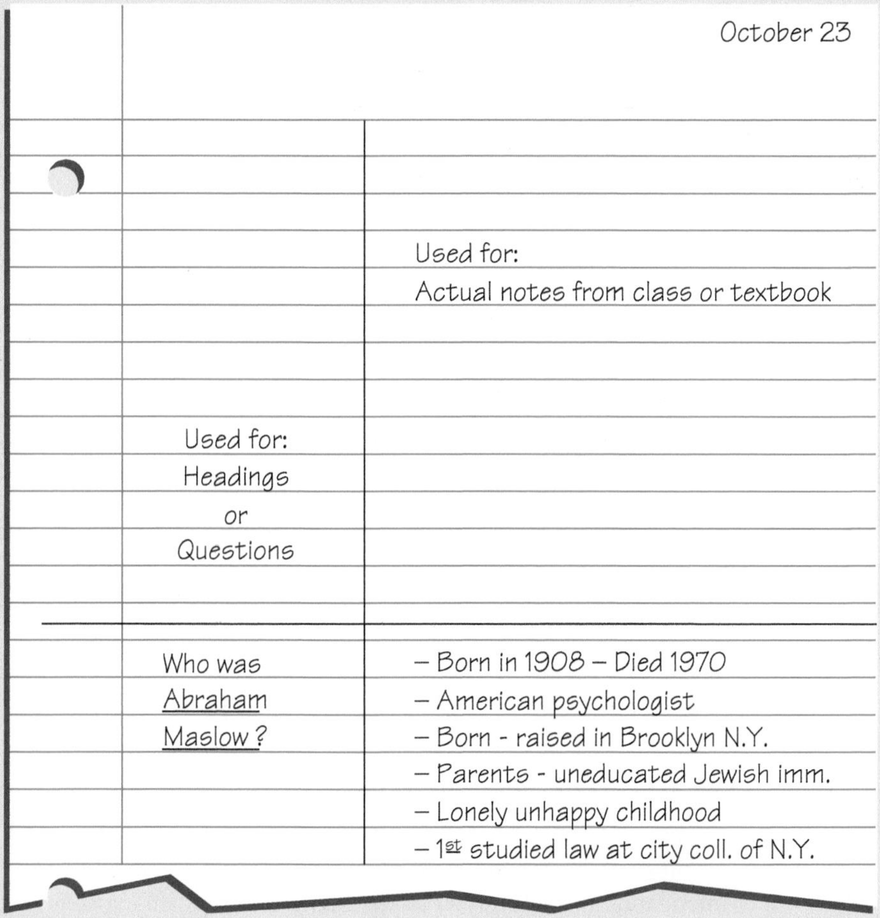

October 23

Used for:
Actual notes from class or textbook

Used for:
Headings
or
Questions

Who was Abraham Maslow ?	– Born in 1908 – Died 1970
	– American psychologist
	– Born - raised in Brooklyn N.Y.
	– Parents - uneducated Jewish imm.
	– Lonely unhappy childhood
	– 1st studied law at city coll. of N.Y.

FIGURE 7.6 *Outline Using a Cornell Frame*

> October 30
>
> Topic: Maslow's Hierarchy of Basic Needs
>
> | | |
> |---|---|
> | What is the theory of basic needs? | I. Published in 1943 in
— "A Theory of human motivation"
— Study of human motivation
— Observation of innate curiosity
— Studied exemplary people |
> | | II. Needs arranged like ladder
— Basic needs at the bottom
— Basic needs = deficiency needs
— Highest need = aesthetic need |
> | What are the Steps in the Hierarchy? | I. Physiological needs
— Breathing
— Food, water
— Sex
— Sleep |
> | | II. Safety needs
— Security of body
— Security of employment
— Resources of
    — Family
    — Health |
> | | III. Love - Belonging needs
— Friendships
— Family
— Sexual intimacy |

GOING AROUND IN CIRCLES

The Mapping System

If you are a visual learner, the mapping system may be especially useful for you. The mapping system of note taking generates a picture of information (Figure 7.7) by creating a map, or web, of information that allows you to see the relationships among facts or ideas. Figure 7.8 shows how to use the mapping system in a Cornell frame.

FIGURE **7.7**   *The Mapping System*

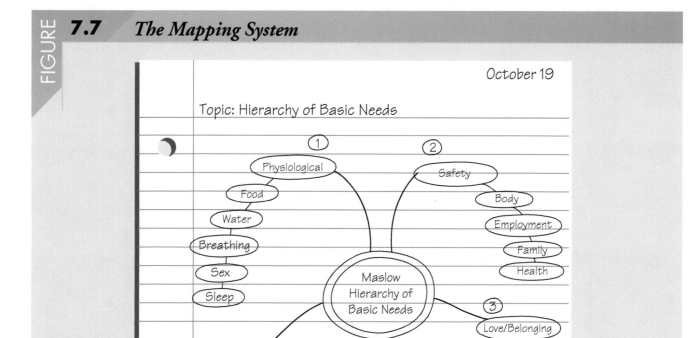

A note-taking system *must work for you.* Do not use a system because your friends use it or because you feel that you should use it. Experiment with each system or combination to determine which is best for you.

Always remember to keep your notes organized, dated, and neat. Notes that cannot be read are no good to you or to anyone else.

TMI! TMI! (TOO MUCH INFORMATION)

What Do I Do if I Get Lost While Taking Notes During the Lecture?

Have you ever been in a classroom trying to take notes, but the instructor is speaking so rapidly that you cannot possibly get all of the information? And just when you think you're caught up, you realize that he or she has made an important statement and you missed it. What do you do? How can you handle, or avoid, this difficult note-taking situation? Here are several hints:

ESSENTIAL CORNERSTONE

Adaptability:
How can the skill of adaptability help you if you get lost while taking notes during a lecture?

Social Networking Moment:
Share your response to this Essential Cornerstone with peers in your social network. Choose two responses from your peers and respond to their postings.

FIGURE **7.8** *The Mapping System in a Cornell Frame*

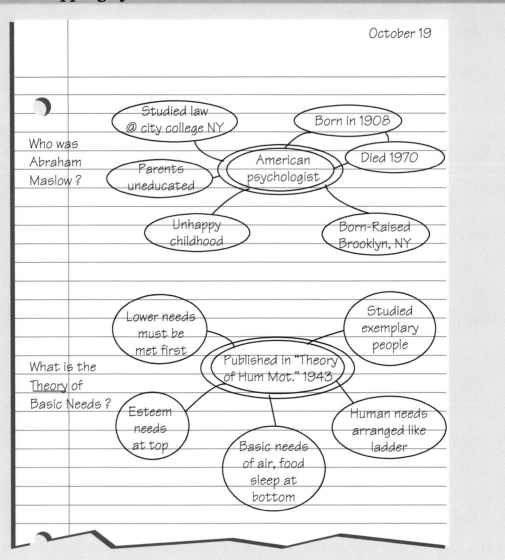

- ▶ Raise your hand and ask the instructor to repeat the information.
- ▶ Ask your instructor to slow down.
- ▶ If he or she will do neither, leave a blank space with a question mark in the side margin (Figure 7.9). You can get this information after class from your instructor, a classmate, or your study buddy. This can be a difficult task to master. The key is to focus on the information at hand. Focus on what is being said at the exact moment. Don't give up!
- ▶ Meet with your instructor immediately after class or at the earliest time convenient for both of you.
- ▶ Form a note-taking group that meets after each class. This serves two purposes: (1) you can discuss and review the lecture, and (2) you will be able to get the notes from one of your note-taking buddies.

FIGURE 7.9   *What To Do if You Get Lost*

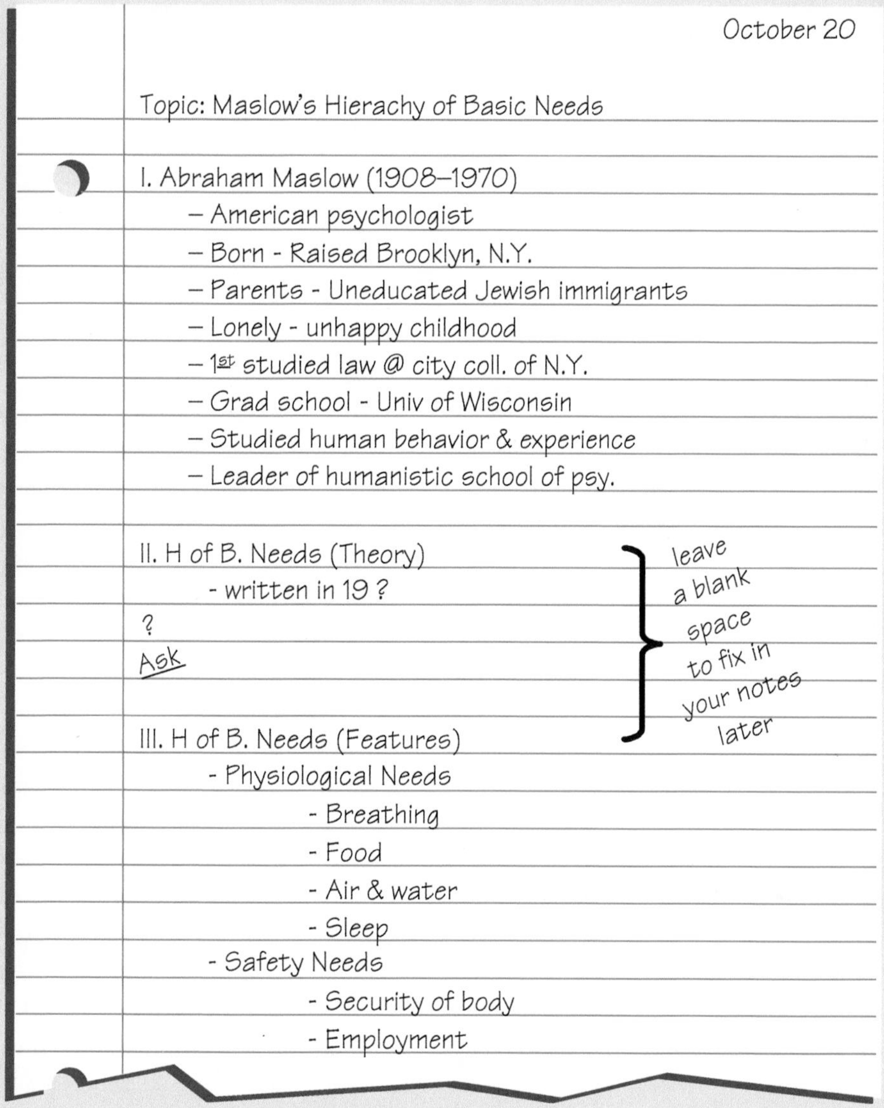

October 20

Topic: Maslow's Hierachy of Basic Needs

I. Abraham Maslow (1908–1970)
- American psychologist
- Born - Raised Brooklyn, N.Y.
- Parents - Uneducated Jewish immigrants
- Lonely - unhappy childhood
- 1st studied law @ city coll. of N.Y.
- Grad school - Univ of Wisconsin
- Studied human behavior & experience
- Leader of humanistic school of psy.

II. H of B. Needs (Theory)
- written in 19 ?
?
Ask

leave a blank space to fix in your notes later

III. H of B. Needs (Features)
- Physiological Needs
- Breathing
- Food
- Air & water
- Sleep
- Safety Needs
- Security of body
- Employment

▶ Never lean over and ask questions of another student during the lecture. This will cause that person to miss information as well. It will probably also annoy your peers and the instructor.

▶ Rehearse your note-taking skills at home by taking notes from TV news magazines or channels like the History Channel.

▶ Ask the instructor's permission to use a tape recorder during the lecture. Do not record a lecture without permission. We suggest that you try to use other avenues, such as the ones listed above, instead of taping your notes. It is a time-consuming task to listen to the lecture for a second time. However, if this system works for you, use it.

From Ordinary to Extraordinary

REAL PEOPLE | REAL LIVES | REAL CHANGE

CATHERINE SCHLEIGH
Customer Service Coordinator, Kinkos-FedEx, Inc.
Philadelphia, PA

I don't like to speculate, but I would say that few college students in America have to take a bus two and a half hours each way, five days a week, to attend classes. I did. I would also speculate that few college students became the primary caregiver for his or her mother at the age of seven. I did. I might also speculate that few people feel lucky, proud, and honored to simply be able to hold his or her head high and say, "I made it." I do. My name is Catherine Schleigh and despite my past family history and personal struggles, I am a first-generation college graduate and hold a professional position with a major corporation in one of the most wonderful cities in America.

Growing up, I had no real family to speak of. My dad left my mom and me when I was young, and from the age of seven, I was left to care for my mother, who is a diagnosed paranoid schizophrenic. Growing up, I received no help, no support, and no encouragement from her or any other members of my family. Often, she would not take her

> I was left to care for my mother, who is a diagnosed paranoid schizophrenic.

medications (or the medications had been improperly prescribed) and would thus be physically, emotionally, and verbally abusive to me. It was hard to watch her talk to herself or invisible people. We lived in a very poor, drug-infested, gang-populated area of Philly and many times, I could not see how I would ever survive.

I managed to complete high school and I began attending Job Corps, studying business. From there, I began my college studies and majored in business administration. I had to work very hard, and the adjustment from high school to college was massive. I had to learn how to motivate myself, but the most important thing I learned was that there are people in this world who will help you if you let them.

From Ordinary to Extraordinary

REAL PEOPLE | REAL LIVES | REAL CHANGE

Some of my instructors did not understand my situation at first. I cried a lot in class, did not have my projects completed from time to time, and basically lived the life of an introvert. Once everyone learned that I was caring for my mother, traveling five hours a day to class, and struggling just to eat, they became my family. They taught me that I had to put my education first. They taught me that without an education, I would most likely have to work in dead-end jobs for the rest of my life. I began to really look at all of the people in my neighborhood, and I made a committed decision that I was not going to fall prey to the temptations of alcohol, sex, unemployment, and drugs.

As I began to succeed in my classes, my self-esteem became healthier. I began to understand how to support myself, take pride in my successes, and help others in any way possible. I still struggle with my mother as she seeks therapy and better medical care, but I also know that I must take care of my own life and keep working toward my own goals. My life is my first priority.

Today, I am an honors graduate. I completed my Bachelor of Arts in business administration with a GPA of 3.50. At the graduation ceremony, I was presented an award by the faculty and staff for my dedication, hard work, and overcoming all odds to obtain my degree. I hope in some small way that my story can help you "hold on" and

reach your dreams. Happiness and success are possible for you.

EXTRAORDINARY REFLECTION

Read the following statement and respond in your online journal or class notebook.

Ms. Schleigh had no family support in college. As a matter of fact, because her father was gone, she was the primary caregiver for her mother. How has your family support (or lack of support) affected your college studies? Do you think it is important to have your family's support to succeed?

REFLECTIONS ON LISTENING AND NOTE TAKING

Yes, listening is a learned skill, but it is more than that. It is a gift that you give to yourself. It is a gift that promotes knowledge, understanding, stronger relationships, and open-mindedness. Good listening skills can help you manage conflicts, avoid misunderstandings, and establish trusting relationships. Perhaps most importantly at this point in your life, listening can help you become a more successful student. Once you learn how to listen with your whole body and mind, you will begin to see how your notes, your grades, your attitude, your relationships, and your learning processes change. As you work toward improving your listening skills and developing your note-taking system, consider the following:

▶ When listening, evaluate the content before you judge the messenger.

▶ Keep your emotions and preconceived notions in check while listening.

▶ Sit where you can see and hear the instructor.

▶ Listen for "how" something is said.

▶ Listen to the "entire story" before making a judgment call.

▶ Listen for major ideas and key words.

▶ Use a separate notebook for every class.

▶ Use abbreviations whenever possible.

▶ Write down what the instructor puts on the board or PowerPoint slide.

Becoming adept at listening and developing your own note-taking system are two essential skills that can help you become a more active learner.

> *"Listening is an attitude of the heart, a genuine desire to be with another person."*
>
> —S. Isham

KNOWLEDGE *in* BLOOM

Listening with an Open Mind

Each chapter-end assessment is based on *Bloom's Taxonomy of Learning.* See the inside front cover for a quick review.

UTILIZES LEVELS 4 AND 5 ON THE TAXONOMY

EXPLANATION: Seldom (if ever) would you pop in a CD, click a song on your iPod, or tune your radio to a station that you strongly disliked. It just does not seem like a good use of time, and it is not something that you would probably enjoy doing on a daily basis. However, for this exercise, we are going to ask that you do precisely what we've described above and then apply what you've experienced and learned to several questions and four **ESSENTIAL CORNERSTONES** from Chapter 1.

PROCESS: Over the course of the next few days, find a song from your *least favorite* genre. If you are a huge fan of R&B, move away from that genre and choose something from a genre of which you are not particularly fond. You might choose an old country song or a song from rap or bluegrass. If you enjoy listening to "Easy Love Songs," try something different such as metal or swing. The only stipulation is that the **song must have lyrics**.

You will have to listen to the song several times to answer the questions. HOWEVER, it is important that you read the questions BEFORE you listen to the song—particularly question #2. The key to this exercise is to practice listening with an open mind, listening for content, and listening to words when barriers are in the way (the barrier in this case would be the music itself).

1. What is the song's title and artist? _____

_____

2. What emotional and mental responses did you have to the song the first time you listened to it? Why do you think you had this response? _____

_____

_____

_____

_____

3. While listening to the song, what happened to your appreciation level? Did it increase or decrease? Why?

_____

_____

_____

_____

4. In your opinion, what was the message (theme) of the song? _____

_____

_____

_____

_____

5. What about the song most surprised you? The lyrics? The actual music? Your like or dislike of the song? The artist's voice? Etc. . . . _____

_____

_____

_____

_____

6. If you HAD to say that you gained or learned one positive thing from this song, what would it be? _____

_____

_____

7. From memory, list at least two statements, comments, or quotes from the song. _____

_____

_____

_____

Now, using the following **ESSENTIAL CORNERSTONES from page 8 of Chapter 1** consider how becoming a more effective listener can help you with each.

By enhancing my listening skills, I can become more **OPEN-MINDED** by

_____

_____

_____

_____

_____

By enhancing my listening skills, I can become more **CREATIVE** by _____
_____
_____
_____
_____

By enhancing my listening skills, I can become more **KNOWLEDGEABLE** by _____
_____
_____
_____
_____

By enhancing my listening skills, I can increase my **RESOURCEFULNESS** level by
_____
_____
_____
_____

SQ3R *Mastery* STUDY SHEET

EXAMPLE QUESTION: *(from page 171)* What are the four components of the Chinese verb "to listen"?		**ANSWER:**
EXAMPLE QUESTION: *(from page 175)* Why is it important to identify key words during a lecture?		**ANSWER:**
AUTHOR QUESTION: *(from page 172)* What is objective listening?		**ANSWER:**
AUTHOR QUESTION: *(from page 173)* List and define the four listening styles.		**ANSWER:**
AUTHOR QUESTION: *(from page 178)* Discuss the five steps in the L-STAR note-taking system.		**ANSWER:**
AUTHOR QUESTION: *(from page 180)* Discuss the benefits and drawbacks of using outline technique to take notes during class.		**ANSWER:**
AUTHOR QUESTION: *(from page 182)* When would be the best time to use the mapping system of note taking? Justify your answer.		**ANSWER:**
YOUR QUESTION: *(from page ____)*		**ANSWER:**
YOUR QUESTION: *(from page ____)*		**ANSWER:**
YOUR QUESTION: *(from page ____)*		**ANSWER:**
YOUR QUESTION: *(from page ____)*		**ANSWER:**
YOUR QUESTION: *(from page ____)*		**ANSWER:**

Finally, after answering these questions, recite this chapter's major points in your mind. Consider the following general questions to help you master this material.

- ▶ What was it about?
- ▶ What does it mean?
- ▶ What was the most important thing I learned? Why?
- ▶ What were the key points to remember?

CHAPTER 8
MEMORY

MAXIMIZING RECALL FOR TEST SUCCESS

Tammy is studying hard—in six-hour stretches if she can keep her eyes open—for mid-terms coming at the end of the month. She reads her textbook and class notes over and over again and, to be sure the material is fresh in her mind, she studies until four in the morning before each test. When she gets back her grades, she is shocked: a C+ in two courses, a C in a third, and a C– in a fourth. "How could this have happened?" she groans to a friend. "I studied so hard. I really thought this stuff was in my brain."

IN THIS CHAPTER . . .

You explore answers to the following questions:

Put Your Senses to Work

Note—and then look beyond—what you see and hear. Open your sensory pathways up to all kinds of information. Using all five senses as you learn can help you lock information into long-term memory in a meaningful way.

HOW DOES MEMORY WORK?

Memory forms the foundation for both learning and test success. Doing well on exams requires that you understand and memorize key information. Memorization puts concepts, facts, processes, formulas, and so on at your fingertips so you can answer knowledge-based questions.

Memorization also gives you the tools to tackle higher level thinking questions. Moving from lower thinking levels (knowledge and understanding) to higher ones (application, analysis, synthesis, and evaluation) requires that you have good recall of information. You will study this concept, known as Bloom's Taxonomy.

To avoid Tammy's struggle, you need to retain what you learn. This chapter provides a host of memory-improvement techniques that you can make your own with a positive attitude and active involvement. Your first step is to explore how memory works.

The Information Processing Model of Memory

Memory refers to the way the brain stores and recalls information or experiences that are acquired through the five senses. While you take in thousands of pieces of information every second—everything from the shape and color of your chair to how your history text describes Abraham Lincoln's presidency—you remember few. Unconsciously, your brain sorts through stimuli and stores only what it considers important.

Look at Key 8.1 as you read how the brain forms lasting memories:

1. Raw information, gathered through the five senses, reaches the brain.

2. This information enters **sensory registers**, where it stays for only seconds.

Repetition can reinforce memory. This student is comparing classroom notes to her text, strengthening her memory of the information by reading it again in the chapter.

© Patrick White/
Merrill Education

The more mental gymnastics you do, the more agile and the quicker your brain becomes.
—Nathan Tublitz, University of Oregon neurobiologist!

KEY 8.1 *Information Processing Model of Memory*

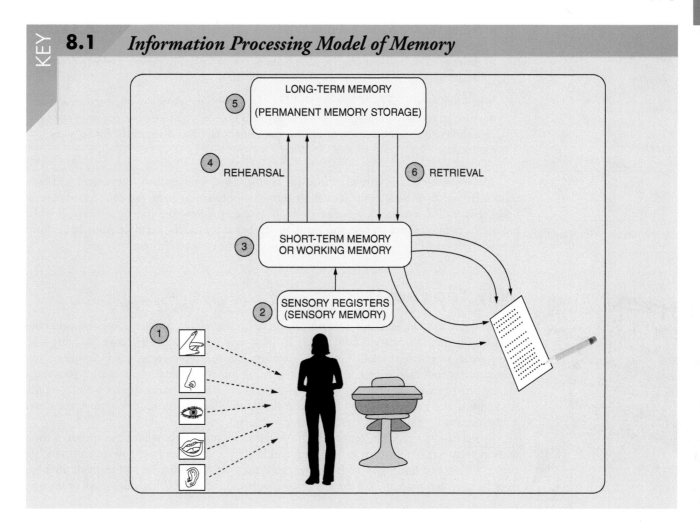

3. You then choose to pay attention to some information in the sensory register. When you selectively look, listen, smell, taste, or feel the information, you move it into **short-term memory**, also known as working memory, which contains what you are thinking at any moment and makes information available for further processing. Short-term memory lasts no more than about 30 seconds and has limited storage.

4. Through *rote rehearsal*—the process of repeating information to yourself or even out loud—you keep information in short-term memory. (You use rote rehearsal when dialing a phone number you just learned.) This is only temporary learning unless you move the information into long-term memory.

5. You keep information in **long-term memory** through diligent, active rehearsal over time. Long-term memory is the storage house for everything you know from Civil War battle dates to the lyrics of a favorite song. There are no limits to how much information long-term memory can hold or how long it can hold it.

Long-term memory has three separate storage houses:

▶ **Storage of procedural memory.** This area stores information about *procedures*, or, in other words, how to do things—ride a bike, drive a car, blow into the mouthpiece of a trombone. It takes awhile to develop these memories, but they are difficult to lose.

Sensory registers
brain filters through which sensory information enters the brain and is sent to short-term memory.

Short-term Memory
the brain's temporary information storehouse in which information remains for a few seconds.

▶ **Storage of declarative memory.** Memories of facts, concepts, formulas, etc. are stored here. These are relatively easy to learn but are easy to forget without continual review.
▶ **Storage of episodic memory.** Memories of events linked to personal experiences are stored here.

6. When you need a piece of information from long-term memory, the brain retrieves it and places it in short-term memory. On test day, this enables you to choose the right answer on a multiple-choice question or lay out a reasoned, fact-based argument for an essay question.

The movement of information into the sensory register, then into short-term and long-term memory, then back again into short-term memory strengthens the connections among brain cells, called *neurons*. Memories are built at the *synapses*—the junctions through which brain cells communicate. When you learn an algebra formula, for example, your brain forms new connections. Every time you review the formula, the connections get stronger.

Why You Forget

Long-term Memory
the brain's permanent information storehouse from which information can be retrieved.

Problems like head injuries and poor nutrition can cause memory problems, but the most common reason that information fails to stay in long-term memory is ineffective studying—not doing what is needed to retain what you learn. As Key 8.2 shows, retaining information over time requires continual review. You are still learning information 10 minutes after you hear it for the first time. If you review the material over time—after 24 hours, after a week, a month, six months, and more—you will hold onto the knowledge. If you do not review, the neural connections will weaken, and eventually you will forget.

In a classic study conducted in 1885, researcher Herman Ebbinghaus memorized a list of meaningless three-letter words such as CEF and LAZ. He then examined how quickly he forgot them. Within one hour, he had forgotten more than 50% of what he had learned; after two days, he knew less than 30% of the memorized words. Although Ebbinghaus's recall of the non-

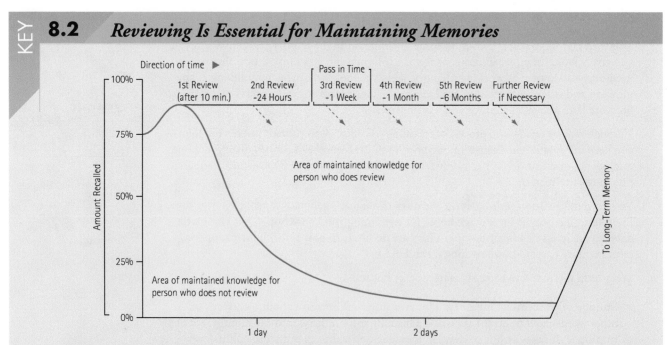

KEY **8.2** *Reviewing Is Essential for Maintaining Memories*

Source: From *Use Both Sides of Your Brain* by Tony Buzan, © 1974, 1983 by Tony Buzan. Used by permission of Dutton, a division of Penguin Group (USA) Inc.

sense syllables remained fairly stable after that, his experiment shows how fragile memory can be—even when you take the time and expend the energy to memorize information.[3]

If forgetting is so common, why do some people have better memories than others? Some may have an inborn talent. More often, though, they succeed because they actively and consistently use techniques for improving recall.

HOW CAN YOU IMPROVE YOUR MEMORY?

As you learn new material, your goal is to anchor information in long-term memory. Memory strategies will help you succeed.

Have Purpose, Intention, and Emotional Connection

Why can you remember the lyrics to dozens of popular songs but not the functions of the pancreas? Why can you remember where you were on September 11, 2001, the day the World Trade Center towers were attacked, but not how to record business transactions for your accounting course? Perhaps this is because you have an emotional tie to the lyrics and what happened on 9-11. When you care about something, your brain responds differently, and you learn and remember more easily.

To achieve the same results in school, try to create a purpose and will to remember by becoming emotionally involved with what you are studying. For example, an accounting student might think of a friend who is running a small business and needs to keep his records in order—to pay bills on time, to record income, to meet tax payments. Without proper accounting, the business cannot operate. Putting himself in the position of his friend's accountant, the student connects learning accounting principles with making a difference in a friend's life.

Understand What You Memorize

Something that has meaning is easier to recall than something that makes little sense. This basic principle applies to everything you study. Figure out logical connections, and use these connections to help you learn. For example, in a plant biology course, memorize plant families; in a history course, memorize events by linking them in a cause-and-effect chain.

When you are having trouble remembering something new, think about how the new idea fits into what you already know. A simple example: If you can't remember what a word means, look at the word's root, prefix, or suffix. Knowing that the root *bellum* means "war" and the prefix *ante* means "before" will help you recognize that *antebellum* means "before the war."

Use Critical Thinking

Critical thinking encourages you to associate new information with what you already know. Imagine you have to remember information about the signing of the Treaty of Versailles, which ended World War I. How can critical thinking help?

▶ Recall everything that you know about the topic.

▶ Think about how this event is similar to other events in history.

▶ Consider what is different and unique about this treaty in comparison with other treaties.

▶ Explore the causes that led up to this event, and look at the event's effects.

▶ Evaluate how successful you think the treaty was.

This critical exploration makes it easier to remember the material you are studying.

Real People
Put Their Senses to Work through the Power of Memory

A MAN WITHOUT A MEMORY[4]

© Tyrone Turner/The New York Times/Redux
Henry Gustav Molaison

In 1935, when he was 9 years old, Henry Gustav Molaison was run down by a bicycle. He fell and hit his head hard on the pavement. Soon after, he began suffering severe seizures, which worsened over the years.

By the time Henry was 27, he endured as many as 10 seizures a day. Blacking out, convulsing, and unable to work, he was desperate for help and agreed to undergo experimental surgery.

His surgeon inserted a metal tube into his brain and removed two finger-sized pieces of tissue from a portion of the brain called the hippocampus. The operation reduced Henry's seizures but robbed him of the ability to form *current* memories. His only lasting memories were of his early life.

Brain researcher David Amaral explained how this changed Henry's life. When Henry was in his 70s, "I asked him to describe what he looked like. He said without hesitation that he had dark curly hair. He was recalling what he looked like before the surgery. He didn't have the ability to remember that he had aged. Think about it. Every time Henry looked in the mirror, he saw a stranger."

STOP AND THINK

Imagine living without the ability to form memories.

Would you be the same person? Would you be able to fulfill your goals and dreams?

From the time of his surgery in 1953 to his death in 2008, Henry was the most studied individual in medical science. "Before Henry, scientists had no idea how memory was organized," said brain researcher Larry Squire. From their work with Henry, they learned that two separate brain systems controlled memory formation. The first, known as declarative memory and located in the hippocampus, is responsible for the ability to remember names, faces, and new experiences; store them in long-term memory; and retrieve them when needed. The second memory system, located in another brain region, controls procedural memory (how to perform physical actions like walking). This part of Henry's brain was unaffected.

STOP AND THINK

Thinking about the separate declarative and procedural memory systems, consider your own ability to form memories. Do you have an easier time with one form of memory than the other?

Remarkably, Henry's short-term memory was strong—he could hold onto thoughts for about 20 seconds—but

without a hippocampus, he couldn't move them into long-term memory. So each time he met one of his long-time researchers, it was like he was meeting him for the first time.

For many years after his surgery, Henry lived with his parents. He was able to do the ordinary tasks of life—making lunch, watching television, mowing the lawn—by relying on what he remembered from his pre-surgery years. He seemed to sense that he was part of a major breakthrough, although he was not sure what it was. One thing that he never forgot was his own name.

THINK ABOUT HENRY AND THINK ABOUT YOURSELF

What does Henry's story tell you about the conn-ection between who you are and what you know and remember? Respond to this statement: *Knowing how memories are formed convinces me that my bra-in has enormous power to gather and remember sensory information and that I can use that power to succeed.*

Knowing that he was dying of pancreatic cancer, Professor *Randy Pausch* gave a "last lecture" about what mattered most to him and about the preciousness of every experience and sensation. His book, titled *The Last Lecture*, is read on college campuses all over the country, and videos of his lecture are available on YouTube.

Limit and Organize the Items You Are Processing

This involves three activities:

SEPARATE MAIN POINTS FROM UNIMPORTANT DETAILS. Ask yourself, "What is the most important information?" Highlight only the key points in your texts, and write notes in the margins about central ideas (see Key 8.6).

DIVIDE MATERIAL INTO MANAGEABLE SECTIONS. Generally, when material is short and easy to understand, studying it from start to finish improves recall. With longer material, however, you may benefit from dividing it into logical sections, mastering each section, putting all the sections together, and then testing your memory of all the material. **Chunking** increases the capacity of short-term and long-term memory. For example, while it is hard to remember these 10 digits—4808371557—it is easier to remember them in three chunks—480 837 1557. In general, try to limit groups to 10 items or fewer.

The eight-day study plan in Key 8.3 relies on chunking as it links test success to memorization.[5] The plan starts eight days before a big exam and ends on test day.

USE ORGANIZATIONAL TOOLS. Rely on an outline, a think link, or another organizational tool to record material and the logical connections among the elements. These tools expose gaps in your understanding as they help you study and learn.

> **Chunking**
> placing disconnected information into smaller units that are easier to remember.

Recite, Rehearse, and Write

When you *recite* material, you repeat key concepts aloud, in your own words, to aid memorization. You also summarize these concepts. *Rehearsing* is similar to reciting but is done silently. *Writing* is reciting on paper. All three processes actively involve you in learning and remembering material. Use these steps to get the greatest benefit:

▶ Focus as you read on *main ideas*, which are usually found in the topic sentences of paragraphs. Then recite, rehearse, or write the ideas down.

▶ Convert each main idea into a key word, phrase, or visual image—something that is easy to recall and that will set off a chain of memories that will bring you back to the original material. Write each key word or phrase on an index card.

▶ One by one, look at the key words on your cards and recite, rehearse, or write all the associated information you can recall. Check your recall against the original material.

These steps are part of the process of consolidating and summarizing lecture and text notes as you study.

Reciting, rehearsing, and writing involve more than rereading material and then parroting words out loud, in your head, or on paper. Because rereading does not necessarily require involvement, you can reread without learning, which Tammy may have done in her marathon study sessions. However, you cannot help but think and learn when you convert text concepts into key points, rewrite main ideas as key words and phrases, and assess what you know and what you still need to learn.

TAKE ACTION: Linking Memorization and Critical Thinking

Identify the course that interests you the most this term. Engaging your intrapersonal intelligence, think about the roles that memorization and critical thinking are likely to play in your studying. Then complete the following:

Describe some material you have to memorize:

_____

_____

_____

Describe specific ways in which you will use critical thinking to learn and retain the material:

_____

_____

_____

Evaluate how the material you have to remember will be important to your working and/or personal life after college. Describe the connection:

_____

_____

_____

Study During Short, Frequent Sessions

By the way…

shortchanging your sleep during the week impairs your ability to remember and learn, even if you try to make up for it by sleeping all weekend.[6]

You can improve your chances of remembering material if you learn it more than once. A pattern of short sessions, say three 20-minute study sessions, followed by brief periods of rest is more effective than continual studying with little or no rest. (Tammy would probably have retained more had she followed this advice.)

Try studying on your own or with a classmate during breaks in your schedule. Although studying between classes isn't for everyone, you may find that it can help you remember more. If you study in bed—even for short periods—try to sit up straight to avoid dozing.

When you finish studying for an exam the next day, try to go to sleep. Sleep improves memory as it reduces interference from new information. When you can't go to sleep right away, put off studying other subjects until your exam is over. When studying for several tests at once, avoid studying two similar subjects back to back. Your memory may be more accurate when you study history after biology rather than chemistry after biology.

KEY 8.3   *Study Plan Success Depends on a Good Memory*

Day 8 (in eight days, you'll be taking a test)

Planning Day

- List everything that may be on the exam. (Check your syllabus and class notes; talk with your instructor.)
- Divide the material into four learning chunks.
- Decide on a study schedule for the next seven days—when you will study, with whom you will study, the materials you need, etc.

Day 7 (Countdown: seven days to go)

Study Chunk A

- Use the techniques described earlier to study Chunk A.
- Memorize key concepts, facts, formulas, etc. that may be on the test.
- Take an active approach to learning: take practice tests, summarize what you read in your own words, use critical thinking to connect ideas, etc.

Day 6 (Countdown: six days to go)

- *Use the same techniques to study chunk B.*

Day 5 (Countdown: five days to go)

- *Use the same techniques to study chunk C.*

Day 4 (Countdown: four days to go)

- *Use the same techniques to study chunk D.*

Day 3 (Countdown: three days to go)

- *Combine and review chunks A and B.*

Day 2 (Countdown: two days to go)

- *Combine and review chunks C and D.*

Day 1 (Countdown: one day to go)

Put it all together: Review chunks A, B, C, and D.
- Take an active approach to review all four chunks.
- Make sure you have committed every concept, fact, formula, process, etc. to memory.
- Take a timed practice test. Write out complete answers so that concepts and words stick in your memory.
- Create a sheet with important information to memorize (again) on test day.

Test Day—Do Your Best Work

- Look at your last-minute study sheet right before you enter the test room so that difficult information sticks.
- As soon as you get your test, write down critical facts on the back of the paper.

Practice the Middle

When you are trying to learn something, you usually study some material first, attack other material in the middle of the session, and approach still other topics at the end. The weak link is likely to be what you study midway. Knowing this, try to give this material special attention.

Use Flash Cards

Flash cards give you short, repeated review sessions that provide immediate feedback. Use the front of a 3-by-5-inch index card to write a word, idea, or phrase you want to remember. Use the back for a definition, explanation, and other key facts. Key 8.4 shows two flash cards used to study for a psychology exam.

KEY **8.4** *Flash Cards Help You Memorize Important Facts*

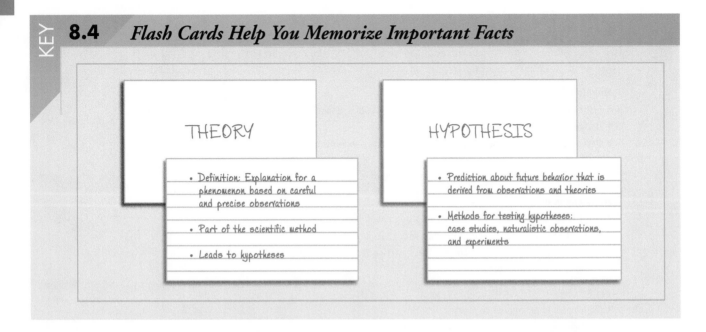

THEORY

- Definition: Explanation for a phenomenon based on careful and precise observations
- Part of the scientific method
- Leads to hypotheses

HYPOTHESIS

- Prediction about future behavior that is derived from observations and theories
- Methods for testing hypotheses: case studies, naturalistic observations, and experiments

Technology has made many audio learning and study strategies possible. These students are using MP3 players and other electronic devices to study in the library.

© Najlah Feanny/Corbis

Here are some suggestions for making the most of your flash cards:

► **Use the cards as a self-test.** As you go through them, divide them into two piles—the material you know and the material you are learning.

► **Carry the cards with you and review them frequently.** You'll learn the most if you start using cards early in the course, well ahead of exam time.

► **Shuffle the cards and learn the information in various orders.** This will help you avoid putting too much focus on some items and not enough on others.

► **Test yourself in both directions.** First, look at the terms and provide the definitions or explanations. Then turn the cards over and reverse the process.

► **Reduce the stack as you learn.** Eliminate cards when you are sure of your knowledge. As you watch the pile shrink, your motivation will grow. As test time approaches, put all the cards together again for a final review.

Use Audio Strategies

Although all students can benefit from these strategies, they are especially useful if you learn best through hearing.

CREATE AUDIO FLASH CARDS. Record short-answer study questions and leave 10 to 15 seconds between questions, so you can answer out loud. Record the correct answer after the pause for immediate feedback. For example, part of a recording for a writing class might say, "Three elements that require analysis before writing are . . . (*10- to 15- second pause*) . . . topic, audience, and purpose."

USE PODCASTS. Audio segments that are downloadable to your computer or MP3 player, podcasts are especially helpful to students who learn best through listening. Ask your instructors if they intend to make any of their lectures available in podcast format. Podcasts with coaching tips are available on MyStudentSuccessLab.

Use the Information

In the days after you learn something new, try to use the information in every way you can. Apply it to new situations, and link it to problems. Explain the material to a classmate. Test your knowledge to make sure the material is in long-term memory. "Don't confuse recognizing information with being able to recall it," says learning expert Adam Robinson. "Be sure you can recall the information without looking at your notes for clues. And don't move on until you have created some sort of sense-memory hook for calling it back up when you need it."[7] As you will see next, mnemonic devices create sense-memory hooks that are difficult to forget.

INSIDE TIPS

FROM JOYCE, TECHNOLOGY COACH
Several technology tools exist to support your memory. Electronic flash cards enable to you copy and paste articles from the Web and organize them as you would a stack of 3-by-5 cards (example: www.flashcardexchange.com). Another useful tool is mind-mapping software, which enables you to outline your information in a visual way and then turn the visual diagram into a formal outline at the click of a button (example: www.gliffy.com).

Activity

On a scale of 1 to 10, with 1 being the lowest and 10 being the highest, rate yourself on your memory skills. Then indicate where you want to be at the end of this course.

MEMORY SKILL	RATING NOW	RATING GOAL
Making emotional connections with material	_____	_____
Understanding what you memorize	_____	_____
Using critical thinking	_____	_____
Using rehearsal techniques	_____	_____
Chunking and organizing material	_____	_____
Getting enough sleep	_____	_____
Making a smart study schedule	_____	_____
Practicing material in the middle	_____	_____
Using flash cards	_____	_____
Using digital recordings and podcasts	_____	_____
Using what you just learned	_____	_____
Using different mnemonic devices	_____	_____

HOW CAN MNEMONICS BOOST RECALL?

Mnemonic Devices
memory techniques that use vivid associations and acronyms to link new information to what you already know.

Certain performers entertain audiences by remembering the names of 100 strangers or flawlessly repeating 30 ten-digit numbers. Although these performers probably have superior memories, they also rely on memory techniques, known as **mnemonic devices** (pronounced neh-MAHN-ick), for assistance. Mnemonics include visual images, associations, and acronyms.

Mnemonics depend on vivid associations (relating new information to other information) that engage your emotions. Instead of learning new facts by *rote* (repetitive practice), associations give you a "hook" on which to hang these facts and retrieve them later. Mnemonics make information unforgettable through unusual mental associations and visual pictures.

Mnemonics take time and effort to create, and you'll have to be motivated to remember them. Because of this, use them only when necessary—for instance, to distinguish confusing concepts that consistently trip you up. Also know that no matter how clever they are and how easy they are to remember, *mnemonics have nothing to do with understanding*. Their sole objective is to help you memorize.

Create Visual Images and Associations

Turning information into mental pictures helps improve memory, especially for visual learners. To remember that the Spanish artist Picasso painted *The Three Women*, you might imagine the women in a circle dancing to a Spanish song with a pig and a donkey (pig-asso). The best images involve bright colors, three dimensions, action scenes, inanimate objects with human traits, and humor.

Here is another example: Say you are trying to learn some Spanish vocabulary, including the words *carta, río,* and *dinero*. Instead of relying on rote learning, you might come up with mental images such as those in Key 8.5.

Use Visual Images to Remember Items in a List

Using the *mental walk* strategy, you imagine storing new ideas in familiar locations. Say, for example, that on your next biology test you have to remember the body's major endocrine glands. To do this, think of your route to the library. You pass the college theater, the science center, the bookstore, the cafeteria, the athletic center, and the social science building before reaching the library. At

KEY 8.5 *Visual Images Aid Recall*

SPANISH WORD	DEFINITION	MENTAL IMAGE
carta	letter	A person pushing a shopping cart filled with letters into a post office.
río	river	A school of sharks rioting in the river. One of the sharks is pulling a banner inscribed with the word *riot*. A killer shark bites off the *t* in riot as he takes charge of the group. "I'm the king of this river," he says.
dinero	money	A man eating lasagna at a dinner. The lasagna is made of layers of money.

each spot along the way, you "place" a concept you want to learn. You then link the concept with a similar-sounding word that brings to mind a vivid image (see Key 8.6):

▶ At the campus theater, you imagine bumping into the actor Brad **Pitt** (pituitary gland).

▶ At the science center, you visualize a body builder with bulging **thighs** (thyroid gland).

▶ At the campus bookstore, you envision a second body builder with his **thighs** covered in **mus**tard (thymus gland).

▶ In the cafeteria, you bump into **Dean Al** (adrenal gland).

KEY **8.6** *A Mental Walk Helps You Remember Items in a List*

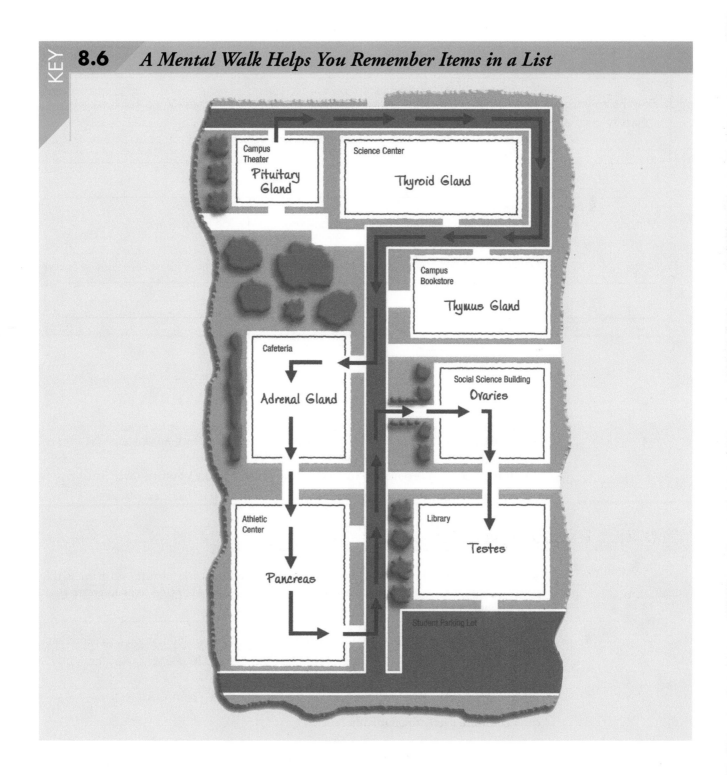

TAKE ACTION: Create Your Own Mnemonic

Identify material you have to memorize for a course. Then complete the following:

Create a mnemonic to help you memorize the details. (If you need more space, use separate paper.)

_____

_____

Describe the images you used in the mnemonic. Were they visual images? Were they sounds? Were they humorous, ridiculous, or colorful?

_____

_____

Why do you think these types of images help you retain information? How did they tap into your visual or your musical intelligence?

_____

_____

➤ At the athletic center, you think of the school team, the Panthers—nicknamed the Pans— and remember the sound of the cheer "**Pans-R-Us**" (pancreas).

➤ At the social science building, you imagine receiving a standing **ova**tion (ovaries).

➤ And at the library, you visualize sitting at a table taking a **test** that is **easy** (testes).

Create a Vocabulary Cartoon

Visual cartoons use the *DAP method*—definition, association, and picture—to harness the power of humor to remember challenging vocabulary. Use the following steps to create your own vocabulary cartoons:

STEP 1. Write down the new vocabulary word followed by its pronunciation and definition. For example:

> **word: histrionic**
> **pronunciation: (his tree AHN ik)**
> **definition: overly dramatic, theatrical**

STEP 2. Think of a link word—an *association*—that rhymes with your word or sounds like it:

association: history

STEP 3. Create a *picture* or simple cartoon with the main word and the link word, to serve as a visual mnemonic. Then write a caption that connects the word you are trying to learn with the link word and visually illustrates its meaning:

"Professor Bradley liked his history on the histrionic side—with a lot of theatrics."

STEP 4. Use the word in sentences of your own:

The histrionic child threw herself on her bed when she didn't get her way. The histrionic actor's portrayal of the calm professor did not ring true.

HISTRIONIC
(his tree AHN ik)
overly dramatic, theatrical
<u>Link:</u>   <u>HIST</u>ORY

Source: Sam Burchers, Vocabulary Cartoons: Building an Educated Vocabulary with Visual Mnemonics, Punta Gorda, FL: New Monic Books, 1997, p.40. Reprinted with permission.

Create Acronyms

Another helpful association method involves **acronyms**. In history class, you can remember the Allies during World War II—Britain, America, and Russia—with the acronym BAR. This is an example of a *word acronym*, because the first letters of the items you want to remember spell a word. The word (or words) spelled don't necessarily have to be real words. See Key 8.7 for an acronym—the name Roy G. Biv—that will help you remember the colors of the spectrum.

Other acronyms take the form of an entire sentence, in which the first letter of each word in each sentence stands for the first letter of the memorized term. This is called a *list order acronym*. When astronomy students want to remember the list of planets in order of their distance from the sun (Mercury, Venus, Earth, Mars, Jupiter, Saturn, Uranus, and Neptune), they might learn this sentence: *My very elegant mother just served us nectarines.*

Suppose you want to remember the names of the first six U.S. presidents. You notice that the first letters of their last names—Washington, Adams, Jefferson, Madison, Monroe, and Adams—together read W A J M M A. To remember them, first you might insert an e after the J and create a short nonsense word—*wajemma*. Then, to make sure you don't forget the nonsense word, you might picture the six presidents sitting in a row and wearing pajamas.

Acronym
a word formed from the first letters of a series of words created to help you remember the series.

Use Songs or Rhymes

Some of the classic mnemonics involve rhymes. This one helps you remember a spelling rule:

I before E, except after C, or when sounded like A as in "neighbor" and "weigh." Four exceptions if you please: either, neither, seizure, seize.

Make up your own poems or songs, linking familiar tunes or rhymes with information you want to remember. Thinking back to the "wajemma" example, imagine that you want to

KEY **8.7**   *Use This Acronym to Remember the Colors of the Spectrum*

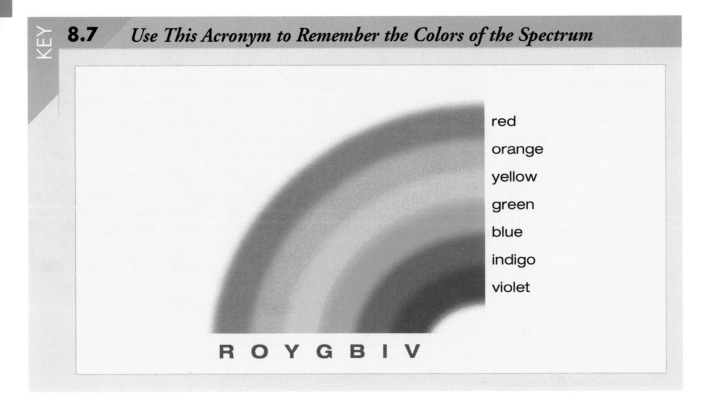

red

orange

yellow

green

blue

indigo

violet

R O Y G B I V

POWERFUL QUESTIONS

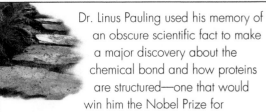

Dr. Linus Pauling used his memory of an obscure scientific fact to make a major discovery about the chemical bond and how proteins are structured—one that would win him the Nobel Prize for Chemistry. He made this breakthrough while doodling during a long train ride, which created the environment for an "aha" moment that would change modern medicine.[8]

Have you ever put important ideas together during unexpected times—during a morning shower or an afternoon run, while cooking dinner or looking through a digital photo album? Why do you think unrelated sensory experiences lead to new ideas?

remember the presidents' first names as well. You might set those first names—George, John, Thomas, James, James, and John—to the tune of "Happy Birthday." Or, to extend the history theme, you might use the first musical phrase of the national anthem.

WHY DO YOU NEED A GOOD MEMORY WHEN YOU HAVE THE INTERNET?

With computers, smartphones, and wireless connections bringing the Internet to you whenever you need it, it is reasonable to ask why memorization skills are important when you can look almost everything up. The best answer is because the reservoir of facts in your long-term memory powers your intellectual potential. With a well-stocked reservoir that is constantly being replenished, you can put new ideas together and think of unique approaches to problems. With one that is nearly empty, you are a blank slate.

A final thought: The facts that you store in your memory help define who you are as a person and can lead to fulfilling academic, career, and life choices. If you love baseball and memorize World Series statistics, for example, your passion will make an impression on everyone you meet and will communicate something meaningful about you to friends, teachers, and prospective employers.

Multiple Intelligence Strategies to Boost Your Memory

Briefly describe a memory problem that you're having in one of your courses.

_____

_____

Now brainstorm potential solutions to your problem, linking each solution to an intelligence. Use the right-hand column to record your ideas.

INTELLIGENCE	SUGGESTED STRATEGIES	USE MI STRATEGIES TO COME UP WITH SOLUTIONS
Verbal-Linguistic	■ Develop a story line for a mnemonic first, then work on the visual images. ■ Write out answers to practice essay questions.	
Logical-Mathematical	■ Create logical groupings that help you memorize knowledge chunks. ■ When you study material in the middle, link it to what comes before and after.	
Bodily-Kinesthetic	■ Create a mnemonic story board on a poster board. Tape the board to a wall and walk back and forth as you memorize. ■ Record information onto a digital recorder and listen as you walk between classes.	
Visual-Spatial	■ Focus on visual mnemonics such as mental walks or vocabulary cartoons. ■ Use markers to add color to the images.	
Interpersonal	■ Do flash-card drills with a study partner. ■ Recite critical material to a study partner.	
Intrapersonal	■ Listen to an audio podcast that reviews test material. ■ Create vocabulary cartoons and test yourself on the material.	
Musical	■ Play music while you brainstorm ideas. ■ Create a mnemonic in the form of a musical rhyme.	
Naturalistic	■ Organize what you have to learn so that you know how everything fits together. ■ Sit outside and go through your flash cards.	

Put Your Senses to Work

Below are examples of how you can put this habit into action in different situations. Use the three spaces to add your own ideas for actions you can accomplish now or in the future. Be specific, and be realistic.

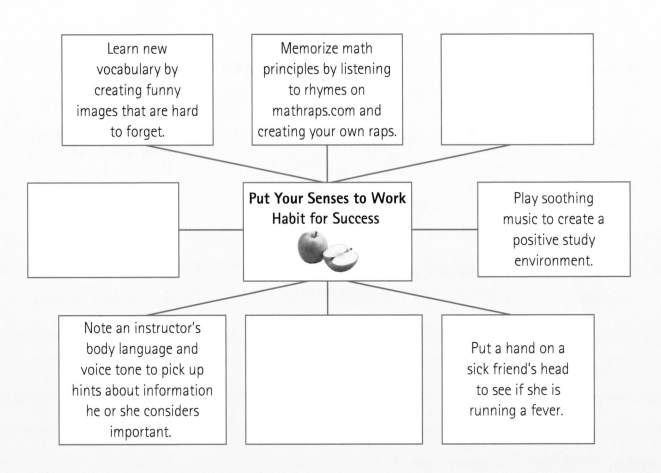

Learn new vocabulary by creating funny images that are hard to forget.

Memorize math principles by listening to rhymes on mathraps.com and creating your own raps.

Put Your Senses to Work Habit for Success

Play soothing music to create a positive study environment.

Note an instructor's body language and voice tone to pick up hints about information he or she considers important.

Put a hand on a sick friend's head to see if she is running a fever.

As an airline pilot, "good memorization skills helped me to quickly become familiar with thousands of pages of flight manuals, aircraft limitations, procedures, terminology, etc. I'm sure 'good memorizers' in other professions feel the same way."
—Sim Erdos, from a letter in response to a newspaper article on why memorizing sports trivia is good for the brain[9]

BUILDING
SKILLS: **For Successful Learning**

NOTE THE IMPORTANT POINTS

How does memory work?

Describe two reasons why memory is the basis for learning.

_____

_____

Describe what each of the following does in the information processing model of memory:

sensory registers _____

short-term memory _____

long-term memory _____

How can you improve your memory?

Describe three memory strategies you learned in this chapter that you are likely to start using.

1. _____

2. _____

3. _____

How can mnemonics boost recall?

Explain how mnemonic devices help you remember material._____

_____

Describe two different types of mnemonics you learned about in the chapter that you are likely to use.

1. _____

2. _____

Why do you need a good memory when you have the Internet?

Explain why it is important to "know something" even when you can easily look it up._____

_____

CRITICAL THINKING: Applying Learning to Life

EVALUATE YOUR MEMORY IN THREE DIFFERENT AREAS

Next to these classifications of information in long-term memory, write down two examples from your personal experience:

Episodic memory (events)

Sample: I remember the first time I conducted an experiment in chemistry class.

Example #1: _____

Example #2: _____

Declarative memory (facts)

Sample: I know that the electoral college must vote before a new U.S. president is officially elected.

Example #1: _____

Example #2: _____

Procedural memory (motion)

Sample: I know how to type without looking at the keyboard.

Example #1: _____

Example #2: _____

Which type of memory is easiest for you to remember over a long period of time?

_____

Which type of memory is hardest for you to remember over a long period of time?

_____

Most exams test declarative memory. List three actions you can take when you study for your next exam to improve your declarative memory.

1. _____

2. _____

3. _____

TEAM
BUILDING: Collaborative Solutions

ASSESS YOUR MEMORY AND THEN BOOST ITS POWER

Gather as a class if there are fewer than 20 people, or divide into two groups if it is larger. Then do the following. (You'll need a timer or a stopwatch.)

▶ Each person in your group should place at least one item on a table (try to avoid repeats). When all the items are laid out, allow one minute to look at them.

▶ Then cover the items and have each person list as many items as possible.

▶ Compare the lists to the actual items to see how you did.

▶ Talk as a group about the results, what you didn't remember and why, and what helped you remember. List your observations here and on a separate sheet, if necessary.

_____

_____

_____

Now repeat the exercise using a mnemonic device. For example, create a new group of items, and then allow five minutes to look at them and to develop a mnemonic in that time. Then cover the items and make lists again. Finally, talk about whether this helped you remember more items. Write your findings here.

_____

_____

_____

_____

Test Prep: START IT NOW

IMPROVE YOUR MEMORY FOR TEST SUCCESS

Nearly every student has memory challenges that affect test grades. But nearly every student also has the ability to improve. Start here:

Describe your biggest memory challenge that limits your ability to remember test material.

_____

_____

Describe two strategies you learned in this chapter that you will use to get better test results. Focus on engaging your senses.

1. _____

_____

2. _____

_____

Now use these techniques to improve your grade on an upcoming test:

Course and date of test: _____

Date when you will use each technique. (Place a checkmark in the box after you use it.)

Technique #1: _____

Technique #2: _____

Evaluate the results: How do you think these techniques improved your test performance?

_____

_____

_____

_____

TIME *for a* CHANGE

Take Steps to Improve a Habit for Success

FIRST: Write the second of your three *strongest* Habits for Success here. _____

_____

_____

Why does it work for you? Name a result of this habit that helps you solve problems and move toward important goals. _____

_____

_____

NOW: Write the second of your three *least developed* Habits for Success here. _____

_____

_____

Why do you want to develop this habit—in other words, what positive effect do you think it will have on your ability to solve problems and achieve goals? _____

_____

_____

FOCUS ON THIS CHALLENGING HABIT MORE CAREFULLY. Name two specific, short-term actions you can take to power up this habit.

1. _____

2. _____

Name a support person, and briefly describe your plan for communicating your progress and getting encouragement (for example, have your person call, e-mail, or text you on a regular basis).

_____

_____

Remember, the way to make a habit stick is to do it over and over again over a period of at least 21 days. *Right now,* commit to checking your progress on a regular basis over the next three weeks, using whatever method you prefer.

Describe the Method You Will Use to Track Your Habit Development.

What will you use? (example: date book, electronic planner, cell phone alarm, e-mail alert)

_____

_____

When and how often will you use it? (example: every day at bedtime, every other day when I get up, twice a week after a particular class)

_____

_____

It's time for a change—put your plan in motion *today*.

Revisit Your Progress

Look back at the Time for a Change exercise at the end of Chapter 4 on page 105. Take a moment to describe how you have developed this habit, including how consistently you perform your chosen actions, how well you document your progress, the helpfulness of your support system, and whether you are satisfied with your progress. If you are not satisfied, describe how you will adjust your actions in order to move ahead.

_____

_____

_____

_____

_____

_____

_____

_____

_____

_____

_____

_____

_____

_____

_____

_____

_____

_____

_____

_____

_____

_____

_____

_____

_____

_____

_____

FIGURE

8.8   *A Quick Reference Guide to Studying Math and Science*

© **Robert M. Sherfield, Ph.D.**

Before Class

▶ **NEVER** take a math or science course (or any course for that matter) for which you are not prepared. If you think you need, or test into a basic, remedial, or transitional class *take it*!!! Look at it as a chance to start over with new hope and knowledge.

▶ **UNDERSTAND** that most math and science classes build on previous knowledge. If you begin the class with a weak background, you must work very hard to learn missed information.

▶ **AVOID** taking math or science classes during "short" terms if possible. The more time you spend with the material, the better, especially if math and/or science are not your strong suits.

▶ **KNOW** your own learning style. If you're visual, use colors, charts, and photos. If you're auditory, practice your listening skills. If you're tactile, work to create situations where you can "act out" or touch the material.

▶ **PREPARE** yourself *before class* by reading the chapter. EVEN if you don't understand all of it, read through the material and write down questions about material you did not understand.

▶ **SCAN** all of the introductory and summation materials provided in the text or study guides.

▶ **JOIN** a study group. If there is not one, start one. Cooperative learning teams can be life savers.

▶ **SEEK** tutorial assistance on campus from the first day. Go visit the center and get familiar with how it operates. Get to know the people who work there. Don't wait until you get behind to seek assistance.

During Class

▶ **COME to EVERY** class, study group, or lab.

▶ **CONTROL** your own anger and frustration. The past is the past and you can't change any part of it—but you can change YOUR future. Learn to make your negative self-talker "be quiet!"

▶ **ASK** questions. **ASK** questions. **ASK** questions. **ASK** questions. . . . and be specific in your questioning. Don't just say, "I don't understand that." Ask detailed and specific questions such as, *"I don't understand why $f(x + h)$ doesn't equal $f(x) + f(h)$."* Or, *"I don't understand the difference between 'algia' and 'dynia.' Why are two different words used for pain?"*

▶ **SLOW DOWN** and read the material carefully.

▶ **FIND** the formulas and write them down on note cards.

▶ **WRITE** down the explanatory remarks made by the instructor such as:

   ▶ How do you get from one step to the next?

   ▶ How does this problem differ from other problems?

   ▶ Why do you need to use formula "x" instead of formula "y"?

   ▶ Were any steps combined—why or why not?

▶ **TRY** to learn from a *general to specific* end. That is, try to get a feeling of the overall goal of the material before you hone in on smaller problems.

▶ **WRITE** down any theorem, formula, or technique that the instructor puts on the board, overhead, or PowerPoint.

▶ **LEAVE** a space in your notes for any material you missed or did not understand. This will help you keep your notes organized when you go back after class and add the explanation.

▶ **BRING** Post-it® Notes, strips of paper, or bookmarks to class with you so that you can "tag" pages with important information and concepts. Use the tabs included with your text to help you mark important information.

After Class

▶ **VISIT** your instructor's office (make an appointment to visit during office hours).

▶ **FILL** in the missing information in your notes by reviewing the text, going to your study group, or getting clarification from your instructor.

(continued)

FIGURE

8.8 *A Quick Reference Guide to Studying Math and Science (continued)*

▶ **PRACTICE** the problems in your text or study guide and then practice them again, and again, and again until they become second nature. Much of Math and Science is learned by DOING . . . so DO . . . and then DO again.

▶ **APPLY** what you learned in class or lab. Find a way to make it "speak" to your life in a practical way.

▶ **CONTINUALLY** review all of the theorems, formulas, concepts, and terms from each chapter so they become second nature to you.

▶ When doing practice tests, **PRETEND** that you are in an actual test and adhere to the timelines, rules, and policies of your instructor. This helps replicate the actual testing situation.

Before the Test

▶ **ASK** questions that will reduce your anxiety such as:

  ▶ What is the point value of each question?

  ▶ How many questions will be on the test?

  ▶ Will the questions be multiple choice, etc. . . . ?

  ▶ What materials do I need to bring to class?

  ▶ Will I be allowed to use a calculator or any other technology?

  ▶ Is there a time limit on the test?

  ▶ What is the overall grade value of the test?

▶ **MAKE** every effort to attend any study or review sessions offered by the instructor or peers.

During Tests

▶ **READ** the directions carefully.

▶ **QUICKLY** glance over the test to determine the number of questions and the degree of difficulty as related to the time you have to complete the test.

▶ **WORK** by the clock. If you have 60 minutes to take a test that has 120 questions, this means you have about 30 seconds per question.

▶ **BEGIN** by solving the problems that are easiest or most familiar to you.

▶ **READ** the questions on the test carefully and MORE than once and don't jump to conclusions.

▶ **DETERMINE** which formulas you will need to use.

▶ **DECIDE** how you want to solve the problem.

▶ **CHECK** your work by using multiple solving techniques. (If the problem is division, can it be rechecked with multiplication? This is called Opposite Operations).

▶ **DRAW** pictures if you encounter word problems. Visualization is very important.

▶ **SHOW** all of your work, even if it is not required. This will help the instructor (and you) see what you did correctly and/or incorrectly.

▶ **RECHECK** every answer if you have time.

▶ **WORK** backward if at all possible. This may help answer the question and catch mistakes.

▶ After you've completed the answer, **reread** the question to determine if you did everything the question asked you do to.

▶ **NEVER** erase your margin work or mistakes. This wastes time and you may erase something that you need (or worse, something that was correct).

After Tests

▶ **IMMEDIATELY** after the test, try to determine if the majority of test questions came from classroom notes, your textbook, your study guide, or from your homework. This will help you prepare for the next test.

▶ **THINK** about the way you studied for this test and how you could improve your techniques for the next time. Consider the amount of time spent studying for this test.

▶ Once the test is graded, **DETERMINE** what caused you to lose the most points: Simple errors? Applying incorrect formulas or theorems? Misunderstanding of the questions asked? Intensified test anxiety? Poor study habits in general?

HAKUNA MATATA

How in the World Can I Study with Small Children in the House?

For many college students, finding a place or time to study is the hardest part of studying. Some students live at home with younger siblings; some students have children of their own. If you have young children in the home, you may find the following hints helpful when it comes time to study.

STUDY AT SCHOOL. Your schedule may have you running from work to school directly to home. Try to squeeze in even as little as half an hour at school for studying, perhaps immediately before or after class. A half hour of pure study time can prove more valuable than five hours at home with constant interruptions.

CREATE CRAFTS AND HOBBIES. Your children need to be occupied while you study. Choose projects your children can do by themselves, without your help. Explain to your children that you are studying and that they can use this time to be creative; when everyone is finished, you'll share with each other what you've done. Give them little rewards for their work and for helping you have quiet time to study.

STUDY WITH YOUR CHILDREN. One of the best ways to instill the value of education in your children is to let them see you participating in your own education. Set aside one or two hours per night when you and your children study. You may be able to study in one place, or you may have separate study areas.

RENT MOVIES OR LET YOUR CHILDREN WATCH TV. Research has shown that viewing a limited amount of educational television, such as *Sesame Street, Reading Rainbow,* or *Barney and Friends,* can be beneficial for children. If you do not like what is on television, you might consider renting or purchasing age-appropriate educational videos for your children.

INVITE YOUR CHILDREN'S FRIENDS OVER. What?! That's right. A child who has a friend to play or study with may create less of a distraction for you. Chances are your children would rather be occupied with someone their own age, and you will gain valuable study time.

HIRE A SITTER OR EXCHANGE SITTING SERVICES with another student. Arrange to have a sitter come to your house a couple of times a week if you can afford it. If you have a classmate who also has children at home, you might take turns watching the children for each other. You could each take the children for one day a week, or devise any other schedule that suits you both best.

FIND OUT IF YOUR COLLEGE HAS AN ON-SITE DAY-CARE center such as the Boys and Girls Club. Some colleges provide day-care facilities at a reduced cost, and some provide day care at no charge. It is certainly worth checking out.

TALK TO THE FINANCIAL AID OFFICE on your campus. In some instances, there will be grants or aid to assist you in finding affordable day care for your child.

Do you think it is a good idea to involve your children (or younger siblings) in your education? Why or why not?

ESSENTIAL CORNERSTONE

Adaptability:
How can learning to be more adaptable help you study with your children or with distractions all around you?

Social Networking Moment:
Share your response to this Essential Cornerstone with peers in your social network. Choose two responses from your peers and respond to their postings.

STUDYING IN A CRUNCH

TOMORROW? What Do You Mean the Test Is Tomorrow?

ESSENTIAL CORNERSTONE

Knowledge:
How can procrastinating and not studying effectively affect your knowledge base negatively?

Social Networking Moment:
Share your response to this Essential Cornerstone with peers in your social network. Choose two responses from your peers and respond to their postings.

Let's be straight up front. No study skills textbook will ever advise you to cram. It is simply a dangerous and often futile exercise in desperation. You will ***never read the words***, "Don't waste your time studying, just CRAM the night before so you can party harder and longer!" in a study skills textbook. Cramming is the complete opposite of what this whole chapter is about—knowing versus memorizing. Cramming will not help you own the material; it can only help you memorize a few things for storage in short-term memory. You may spend several hours cramming, and shortly after the test, the information is gone, evaporated, vanished! If you find yourself in this spot, consider the following tips and suggestions for cramming. These probably won't get you an A, but they may help you with a few questions.

DEPRESSURIZE. Just tell yourself up front what you are doing. Don't pretend that cramming is going to save you. Let yourself realize that you are memorizing material for short-term gain and that you won't be able to keep it all. With this admission, your stress will diminish.

KNOW THE SCORE. When cramming, it is important to know what you're cramming for. If you're cramming for a multiple-choice test, you'll need different types of information than for an essay test. Know what type of test it is for which you are studying.

READ IT QUICKLY. Think about **H2 FLIB**. This is a mnemonic for: read the **h**eadings, **h**ighlight the important words, read the **f**irst sentence of every paragraph, read the **l**ast sentence of every paragraph, read the **i**ndented and **b**oxed material. This can help you get through a chapter when pinched for time.

> "Don't just learn something from every experience, learn something positive."
> —Al Neuharth

MAKE CONNECTIONS. As you are reading, quickly determine if any of the information has a connection with something else you know. Is there a relationship of any kind? Is there a cause and effect in motion? Can you pinpoint an example to clarify the information? Is there a mnemonic that can help you with this information? These questions can help you with retention and long-term memory commitment.

USE YOUR SYLLABUS OR STUDY GUIDE. If your instructor lists questions in the syllabus that you should know the answers to (mastery questions), or if he or she gave you a study sheet (or you developed your own study sheet, like the one you have created at the end of each *Cornerstone* chapter), this is the place to start. Answer those questions. If you don't have either, look to see if the text gives study questions at the end of the chapter.

SEE IT. Visualizing the information through mapping, diagrams, photos, drawings, and outlines can help you commit this information to short-term memory.

CHECK YOUR NOTES. Did the professor indicate that certain things are important to know for the test?

CHOOSE WISELY. If you're cramming, you can't do it all. Make wise choices about which material you plan to study. This can be driven by your study sheet, your lecture notes, or questions in your syllabus (if they are listed).

Information you've crammed is going to leave you after the test. Don't rely on it for the next test or the final. You will need to go back and relearn (truly understand) the information you "crammed" in order to commit it to long-term memory.

THINKING ABOUT TESTING

Can Changing My Attitude and Reducing Stress Really Help?

Yes, both are necessary to help you get through tests. A positive or negative attitude can truly mean the difference between success and failure. With an attitude adjustment from negative to positive and some basic preparation, you can overcome a good deal of your anxiety about tests and do well. You can reduce anxiety when you are in control of the situation, and you can gain control by convincing yourself that you **can be** and **will be** successful. If you think positively and can honestly say that you have done everything possible to prepare for a test, then the results will most likely be positive.

Silencing *your negative self-talk* is one of the most powerful things you can do for yourself. Consider the following tips for reducing test anxiety during your next test. You will not be able to employ them all, but if you learn and use a few new ones each time, before you know it, you'll be a testing pro!

- ▶ Prepare yourself emotionally for the test, control your self-talk, and be positive.
- ▶ Study and learn the material—NO! You can't study too much.
- ▶ Ask peers who have had a certain professor what type of tests he or she gives.
- ▶ Arrive early for the test (at least 15 minutes early).
- ▶ Go to the test with everything you need: pencils, calculator, and other supplies.
- ▶ Listen to the instructor before the test begins, know his or her rules about testing, and READ the instructions.
- ▶ Keep an eye on the clock during the test so that you can finish on time. However, don't let time cause you undue stress or anxiety.
- ▶ Answer what you know first, the questions that are easiest for you.
- ▶ Check your answers, but remember, your first response is usually correct.
- ▶ Find out ahead of time exactly what the test will cover.
- ▶ Ask the instructor for a study sheet; you may not get one, but it does not hurt to ask!
- ▶ When you get the test, jot down on the back or at the top of a page any mnemonics you might have developed.

QUIZZING YOUR INSTRUCTOR AND KNOWING YOUR RESPONSE TYPE

What Are Some Techniques I Can Use to Help Me During Tests?

Several classes before the test is scheduled to be given, **quiz your instructor** about the logistics and specifics of the test. This information can help you

---

bring the CHANGE

Tips for Personal Success

Consider the following tips for making time for studying and committing information to long-term memory:

- ▶ Study daily to avoid having to "cram" the night before your test.
- ▶ Form a study group with people who are motivated and keep you on track.
- ▶ Keep up with your daily readings and homework.

Now, it is your turn. Create a list of at least three more tips that you would offer a fellow classmate to assist him or her in making time in his/her life to study.

1. _____

2. _____

3. _____

What techniques have you found help you reduce your anxiety and negative self-talk during quizzes and exams?

study more effectively and eliminate the anxiety that comes with uncertainty. If you don't know whether the test is going to be true-false or essay or both, it is much more difficult to study. Some questions you need to ask are:

1. What types of questions will be on the test?

2. How many questions will be on the test?

3. Is there a time limit on the test?

4. Will there be any special instructions, such as "use pen only" or "use a number 2 pencil"?

5. Is there a study sheet?

6. Will there be a review session?

7. What is the grade value of the test?

8. What chapters or sections will the test cover?

Asking these simple questions will help you know what type of test will be administered, how you should prepare for it, and what supplies you will need.

What Do I Do When I Can't Remember the Answer?

Almost every test question will elicit one of three types of responses from you as the test taker:

▶ Quick-time response

▶ Lag-time response

▶ No response

Your response is a *quick-time response* when you read a question and know the answer immediately. You may need to read only one key word in the test question to know the correct response. Even if you have a quick-time response, however, always read the entire question before answering it. The question may be worded in such a way that the correct response is not the one you originally thought of.

You have a *lag-time response* when you read a question and the answer does not come to you immediately. You may have to read the question several times or even move on to another question before you think of the correct response. Information in another question will sometimes trigger the response you need. Once you've begun to answer other questions, you usually begin to remember more, and the response may come to you.

No response is the least desirable situation when you are taking a test. You may read a question two or three times and still have no response. At this point, you should move on to another question to try to find some related information. When this happens, you have some options:

1. Leave this question until the very end of the test.

2. Make an intelligent guess.

3. Try to eliminate all unreasonable answers by association.

4. Watch for modifiers within the question.

It is very difficult to use intelligent guessing with essay or fill-in-the-blank questions. Remember these important tips about the three types of responses:

1. Don't be overly anxious if your *response is quick*; read the entire question and be careful not to make a mistake.

2. Don't get nervous if you have a *lag-time response*; the answer may come to you later, so just relax and move on.

3. Don't put down just anything if you have *no response*; take the remaining time and use intelligent guessing.

THINKING FOR CHANGE: An Activity for Critical Reflection

After the second week of classes, Jose was devastated by his first test score. The instructor put the range of grades on the board, and he was shocked to see that many people passed the test and that his score was in the bottom 10%.

He began asking classmates if they did well or not and found some who had made A's and others who had made D's. When he spoke with one classmate, Letty, she told him that he should just chill and take a "cheat sheet" to class. "The instructor never looks, man, and she left the classroom twice. She'll never know. That's how I got my A."

"Cheat," Jose thought, "I don't think I can do that." He knew that others had made better grades than he over the years, but he also knew that he had never once cheated on an exam. Never.

Jose went to the Tutoring Center and worked with a tutor on content and on how to take a test more effectively. On the next test, Jose scored a C. "It may not be the best grade in the class," he thought, "but it is all mine. I did it."

In your own words, what two suggestions would you give Jose to improve his grades without cheating?

1. _____

2. _____

TEST-TAKING STRATEGIES AND HINTS FOR SUCCESS

What Are Some Tips for Taking Tests?

Before you read about the strategies for answering these different types of questions, think about this: ***There is no substitute for studying!*** You can know all the tips, ways to reduce anxiety, mnemonics, and strategies on earth, but if you have not studied, they will be of little help to you.

Strategies for Matching Questions

Matching questions frequently involve knowledge of people, dates, places, or vocabulary. When answering matching questions, you should:

- ▶ Read the directions carefully.
- ▶ Read each column before you answer.
- ▶ Determine whether there is an equal number of items in each column.
- ▶ Match what you know first.
- ▶ Cross off information that is already used.
- ▶ Use the process of elimination for answers you might not know.
- ▶ Look for logical clues.
- ▶ Use the longer statement as a question; use the shorter statement as an answer.

Strategies for True-False Questions

True-false questions ask whether a statement is true or not. True-false questions can be some of the trickiest questions ever developed. Some students like them; some hate

Sample Test #1 MATCHING

DIRECTIONS: Match the information in column A with the correct information in column B. Use uppercase letters.

GOALS, MOTIVATION, & SELF-ESTEEM

A		B
_____	They can be long or short, social, academic, religious, or financial	A. Child within
_____	They bring out the worst in you	B. Objectivity
_____	I CAN'T Syndrome	C. Contaminated people
_____	Your "true self"	D. Negative thoughts
_____	Listening with an open mind	E. Goals

them. There is a 50/50 chance of answering correctly, but you can use the following strategies to increase your odds with true-false questions:

▶ Read each statement carefully and watch for key words in each statement.

▶ Read each statement for double negatives such as "not untruthful."

▶ Pay attention to words that may indicate that a statement is true, such as "some," "few," "many," and "often."

▶ Pay attention to words that may indicate that a statement is false, such as "never," "all," "every," and "only."

▶ Remember that if any part of a statement is false, the entire statement is false.

▶ Answer every question unless there is a penalty for guessing.

Sample Test #2 TRUE/FALSE

Place "T" for true or "F" for false beside each statement.

NOTE-TAKING SKILLS

1. _____ Note taking creates a history of your course content.
2. _____ "Most importantly" is not a key phrase.
3. _____ You should always write down everything the instructor says.
4. _____ You should never ask questions in class.
5. _____ The L-STAR system is a way of studying.

Strategies for Multiple-Choice Questions

Many college instructors give multiple-choice tests because they are easy to grade and provide quick, precise responses. A multiple-choice question asks you to choose from among, usually, two to five answers to complete a sentence. Some strategies for increasing your success when answering multiple-choice questions are the following:

▶ Read the question and try to answer it before you read the answers provided.

▶ Look for similar answers; one of them is usually the correct response.

► Recognize that answers containing extreme modifiers, such as *always, every,* and *never,* are usually wrong.

► Cross off answers that you know are incorrect.

► Read all the options before selecting your answer. Even if you believe that A is the correct response, read them all.

► Recognize that when the answers are all numbers, the highest and lowest numbers are usually incorrect.

► Understand that the most inclusive and longest answers are often correct.

► If you cannot answer a question, move on to the next one and continue through the test; another question may trigger the answer you couldn't come up with previously.

► Answer every question unless there is a penalty for guessing.

Sample Test #3 MULTIPLE CHOICE

DIRECTIONS: Read each statement and select the best response from the answers given below.

STUDY SKILLS

1. Which statement is true according to the 2007 Labor Statistics, Bureau of Census?
   A. Men earn more than women.
   B. Women earn more than men.
   C. People with a professional degree earn the most money of any education level.
   D. Unemployment is greatest among those with a doctorate degree.

2. To calculate a GPA, you would:
   A. Divide quality points by the number of semester hours.
   B. Multiply total points by quality points.
   C. Divide total points by the number of semester hours.
   D. Multiply the quality points by the total points.

3. To be an effective priority manager, you have to:
   A. Be very structured, organized, and self-disciplined.
   B. Be very unstructured and disorganized.
   C. Be mildly structured and organized.
   D. Know what type of person you are and avoid working from that perspective.

Strategies for Short-Answer Questions

Short-answer questions, also called fill-in-the-blanks, ask you to supply the answer yourself, not select it from a list. Although "short answer" sounds easy, these questions are often very difficult. Short-answer questions require you to draw from your long-term memory. The following hints can help you answer this type of question successfully:

► Read each question and be sure that you know what is being asked.

► Be brief in your response.

► Give the same number of answers as there are blanks; for example, _____ and _____ would require two answers.

► Never assume that the length of the blank has anything to do with the length of the answer.

► Remember that your initial response is usually correct.

▶ Pay close attention to the word immediately preceding the blank; if the word is "an," give a response that begins with a vowel (a, e, i, o, u).

▶ Look for key words in the sentence that may trigger a response.

Sample Test #4 SHORT ANSWER

DIRECTIONS: Fill in the blanks with the correct response. Write clearly.

LISTENING SKILLS

1. Listening is a _____ act. We choose to do it.
2. The three elements of listening involve listening objectively, _____, and _____.
3. _____ is the same as listening with an open mind.
4. Prejudging is an _____ to listening.
5. Leaning forward, making eye contact, being patient, and leaving your emotions at home are characteristics of _____ listeners.

Strategies for Essay Questions

Most students look at essay questions with dismay because they take more time. Yet essay tests can be one of the easiest tests to take because they give you a chance to show what you really know. An essay question requires you to supply the information. If you have studied, you will find that once you begin to answer an essay question, your answer will flow more easily. Some tips for answering essay questions are the following:

▶ More is not always better; sometimes more is just more. Try to be as concise and informative as possible. An instructor would rather see one page of excellent material than five pages of fluff.

▶ Pay close attention to the action word used in the question and respond with the appropriate type of answer. Key words used in essay questions include the following:

discuss	illustrate	enumerate	describe
compare	define	relate	list
contrast	summarize	analyze	explain
trace	evaluate	critique	interpret
diagram	argue	justify	prove

▶ Write a thesis statement for each answer.

▶ Outline your thoughts before you begin to write.

▶ Watch your spelling, grammar, and punctuation.

▶ Use details, such as times, dates, places, and proper names, where appropriate.

▶ Be sure to answer all parts of the question; some essay questions have more than one part.

▶ Summarize your main ideas toward the end of your answer.

▶ Write neatly.

▶ Proofread your answer.

Learning how to take a test and learning how to reduce your anxiety are two of the most important gifts you can give yourself as a student. Although tips and hints may help you, don't forget that there is no substitute for studying and knowing the material.

Sample Test #5 ESSAY

DIRECTIONS: Answer each question completely. Use a separate paper if you wish.

STUDY SKILLS

1. Identify and discuss two examples of mnemonics.
2. Justify why it is important to use the SQ3R method when reading.
3. Compare an effective study environment with an ineffective study environment.

CHANGING IDEAS TO *Reality*

REFLECTIONS ON
NOTE TAKING AND
TESTING

Just as reading is a learned skill, so are memory development, studying, and learning how to take assessments. You can improve your memory, but it will take practice, patience, and persistence. You can improve your study skills, but it will take time and work. And you can increase your ability to do well on tests, but it will take a commitment on your part to study smarter and put in the time and dedication required. By making the decision "I CAN DO THIS," you've won the battle, for when you make that decision, your studying and learning become easier.

Your challenge is to focus on developing excellent memory techniques, study patterns, and test-taking abilities while earning the best grades you can. When you have done this, you can look in the mirror and be proud of the person you see without having to be ashamed of your character or having to worry about being caught cheating or wondering if you really did your best. When studying for your next class or taking your next test, consider the following:

▶ Study the hardest material first.
▶ Review your classroom and textbook notes frequently.
▶ Use mnemonics to help you remember lists.
▶ Learn the material from many different angles.
▶ *Ask* questions of the instructor before the test.
▶ Glance at the entire test *before* beginning.
▶ *Ignore* the pace of your classmates.
▶ Watch *time* limits.
▶ Use academic integrity.

As you study and learn to enter your chosen profession, remember this: "You are building your character for the long haul—not just a few short years."

"Change occurs, progress is made, and difficulties are resolved if people merely do the right thing—and rarely do people NOT KNOW what the right thing is."
—Father Hessburg

KNOWLEDGE in BLOOM

Using and Evaluating your GUIDING STATEMENT

Each chapter-end assessment is based on *Bloom's Taxonomy of Learning.* See the inside front cover for a quick review.

UTILIZES LEVELS 3 AND 6 OF THE TAXONOMY

EXPLANATION: Now that you have read and studied this chapter and, no doubt, taken a few tests this semester, you have a better understanding of what happens to you physically and mentally during an exam.

Below, you will find listed six of the common physical or mental symptoms of anxiety reported by students while testing.

PROCESS: Beside each symptom, **create a list** of at least three concrete, doable, realistic strategies to overcome this physical or emotional anxiety symptom before or during a testing situation.

SYMPTOM	HOW TO REDUCE IT
Fatigue	1. 2. 3.
Frustration	1. 2. 3.
Fear	1. 2. 3.
Anger	1. 2. 3.
Nervousness/Nausea	1. 2. 3.
Uncertainty/Doubt	1. 2. 3.

SQ3R *Mastery* STUDY SHEET

EXAMPLE QUESTION: *(from page 217)* Discuss three strategies for studying math.	**ANSWER:**
EXAMPLE QUESTION: Why are mnemonics important?	**ANSWER:**
AUTHOR QUESTION: What is the difference between short-term and long-term memory?	**ANSWER:**
AUTHOR QUESTION: Discuss the five steps in VCR3.	**ANSWER:**
AUTHOR QUESTION: *(from page 220)* What is H2 FLIB and how can it help you?	**ANSWER:**
AUTHOR QUESTION: *(from page 221)* Discuss five ways to reduce test anxiety.	**ANSWER:**
AUTHOR QUESTION: *(from page 223)* Discuss one strategy for each type of testing situation.	**ANSWER:**
YOUR QUESTION: *(from page ____)*	**ANSWER:**
YOUR QUESTION: *(from page ____)*	**ANSWER:**
YOUR QUESTION: *(from page ____)*	**ANSWER:**
YOUR QUESTION: *(from page ____)*	**ANSWER:**
YOUR QUESTION: *(from page ____)*	**ANSWER:**

Finally, after answering these questions, recite this chapter's major points in your mind. Consider the following general questions to help you master this material.

- ▶ What was it about?
- ▶ What does it mean?
- ▶ What was the most important thing I learned? Why?
- ▶ What were the key points to remember?

UNIT 3

DEVELOP CRITICAL THINKING AND RESEARCH SKILLS FOR ESSAY TESTS AND RESEARCH PROJECTS

Chapter 9: Think

CHAPTER 9
THINK

EXPANDING
YOUR APTITUDE
FOR CRITICAL
THINKING,
EMOTIONAL
INTELLIGENCE,
AND
INFORMATION
LITERACY SKILLS

"Many people think they are thinking when they are merely rearranging their prejudices."

—William James

WHY READ THIS CHAPTER?

What's in it for me?

WHY do I need to understand my emotions and know about emotional intelligence? WHY will a chapter on problem solving help me with my studies? WHY is information literacy important? WHY do I need to read a chapter on critical thinking when I'm thinking all the time?

Why? Because critical thinking affects your life positively or negatively every day. You use it when you go to the grocery store, you use it when you purchase gasoline, you use it when you choose what TV program to watch, you use it when you select classes for your degree, and you use it when you discuss important issues with your friends. Critical thinking is a major aspect of your daily life, affecting the very nature of the way you live and function in society. It helps you make decisions that will enhance your quality of life. Learning how to think more critically means that you are going to be able to look at situations differently, evaluate research sources more effectively, manage your emotions more closely, and solve problems more effectively than ever before. Your ability to think critically, solve problems, and become information literate is going to help you greatly in all of your classes and well into your career.

By carefully reading this chapter and taking the information provided seriously, you will be able to:

1. Define the eight steps in critical thinking, recognize their uses, and understand their importance.

2. Use emotional restraint, emotional intelligence, and emotional guidelines to aid in logical, rational thinking.

3. Manage information and become more information literate.

4. Learn to identify, narrow, and solve problems.

5. Learn to use creative thinking to become more resourceful.

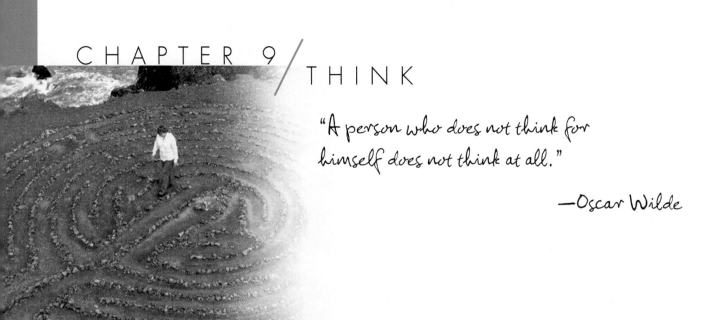

CHAPTER 9 / THINK

"A person who does not think for himself does not think at all."

—Oscar Wilde

NAME: Martin Cram
INSTITUTION: Butler Community College, El Dorado, KS
MAJOR: Music Education
AGE: 19

For years, I thought that my life was everyone's life. I was raised and educated in a rather rural part of Kansas where everybody was basically "the same." Little did I know that in a few short weeks of college, my life, my attitude, and my views would be tested and changed.

I soon learned that everyone had a different story, a different life, a different background, and a different perspective on world events. Learning how to be a more open-minded person through critical thinking helped me grow and change in ways I had never imagined. I was in class with people who are African American, Latino, Native American, and yes, Caucasians who were not from Kansas. I quickly learned that my life was not everyone's life and that my views were not everyone's views. This was a great gift that I received from learning more about critical thinking.

Critical thinking has also helped me become a much more effective manager of my time. I work on campus in the office of financial aid and with this job, my choral activities, classes, and other obligations, I quickly learned that I had to think about my schedule and learn how to plan and plot a course to success. Critical thinking taught me how to look down the road, plan ahead, and get things done. It taught me how to ask for help, how to ask the right questions, and how to apply what I was learning to everyday life, my major, and my future.

Perhaps one of the most important areas where critical thinking helped me was my major. I sat down and made a list of all of the things I liked and what I was good at. I began to analyze my abilities and look for patterns. Critical thinking helped me decide that music was the one thing that I could not live without. It was then that I changed my major to music education.

I know that in the future, my critical thinking skills will help me become a better show choir director and educator. I also know that it will help me be more adept at thinking on my feet during job interviews and when things get rough in my profession. I learned that critical thinking affects my life every day. This chapter will help you learn how to look at the world with an open mind, embrace change, plan your activities, and plot a course to your future.

SCAN & QUESTION

In the preface of this book (page ix), you read about the **SQ3R Study Method.** Right now, take a few moments, **scan this chapter**, and on page 260, write **five questions** that you think will be important to your mastery of this material. In addition to the two questions below, you will find five questions from your authors. Use one of your **"On The Test"** stickers to flag this page for easy reference.

EXAMPLES:

▶ **Why is emotional intelligence important to critical thinking?** (from page 237)

▶ **What is information literacy?** (from page 244)

THINKING ABOUT THINKING

Do You Know *Why* You Think *What* You Think?

Same-sex couples should be able to marry and adopt children. Think about that statement for a moment. You may be saying to yourself, *"I don't have to think about it—I know what my opinions on same-sex marriage and adoption are."* However, do you know WHY you have these opinions? Can you trace your decisions back to certain events or moments in your life? Do you think that your emotions cloud your thoughts on this issue? Is there a right or wrong side to this debate? Does your religion or culture come into play when thinking about this issue? Did someone else influence your thoughts or are they your very own, developed through research and conversations regarding this issue?

What are you thinking right now? More importantly, why are you thinking the way you are right now? What is causing you to believe, feel, or think one way or the other regarding this issue? What are the facts and/or opinions that have led you to your conclusion? At this moment, what are the origins on which you are basing your thoughts about this issue—emotions or facts, fallacies or truths, data or opinions, interviews or hearsay, reason or misjudgment, fear or empathy?

We purposefully chose a "hot topic" issue to open this chapter because understanding why and how we formulate thoughts and ideas is the main objective of this chapter and critical thinking in general. This chapter is about believing and disbelieving, seeking, uncovering, debunking myths, uncovering biases, identifying and solving problems, using information correctly, and proving the impossible possible. It is about proof, logic, evidence, and developing ideas and opinions based on hard-core facts and credible research. This chapter is about seeking truth and expanding your mind to unimaginable limits. This chapter is about the fundamental hallmarks of becoming an educated citizen; it is about human thought and reasoning.

THE IMPORTANCE OF CRITICAL THINKING

When Will I Ever Use it?

Have you ever made a decision that turned out to be a mistake? Have you ever said to yourself, *"If only I could go back and . . . "*? Have you ever regretted actions you took toward a person or situation? Have you ever planned a paper or speech that was flawless? Have you ever had to make a hard, painful decision that turned out to be "the best decision of your life"? If the answer to any of these questions is yes, you might be able to trace the consequences back to your *thought process* at the time of the decision. Let's face it, sometimes good and bad things just happen out of luck or circumstance. More often than not, however, many events in our lives are driven by the thought processes involved when we made the initial decision and chose to act on that decision.

Critical thinking can serve us in many areas as students and citizens in a free society. As a student, ***critical thinking can help you***:

▶ focus on relevant issues/problems and avoid wasting time on trivia.

▶ gather relevant, accurate information regarding finances, goals, decision making, relationships, civic responsibility, and environmental issues, to name a few.

▶ understand and remember facts and organize thoughts logically.

▶ look more deeply at problems, analyze their causes, and solve them more accurately.

▶ develop appropriate and meaningful study plans and manage your priorities.

▶ improve your problem-solving skills.

▶ control your emotions so that you can make rational judgments and become more open-minded.

▶ produce new knowledge through research and analysis.

▶ determine the accuracy of printed and spoken words.

▶ detect bias and determine the relevance of arguments and persuasion.

Can you think of a professional career where critical thinking will not be required?

AN EIGHT-POINT PLAN FOR CRITICAL THINKING

Can You Really Make Critical Thinking Work for You in Everyday Life?

Does critical thinking really matter? Seriously? Can it do anything to improve the quality of your life? The answer is yes. Critical thinking has daily, practical uses, from making sound financial decisions to improving personal relationships to helping you become a better student. You can improve your critical thinking skills by watching your emotional reactions, using solid research and facts to build your examples and thoughts, and practicing open-mindedness.

Conversely, can the lack of critical thinking skills cause real problems? The answer, once again, is yes. Poor critical thinking skills can impair your judgment, lead you to make rash decisions, and even cause you to let your emotions rule (and sometimes ruin) your life. Critical thinking can be hampered by a number of factors including closed-mindedness, unflappable opinions based on rumor instead of facts, cultural and/or religious bias, lack of accurate information, faulty arguments, and negativity.

As you begin to build and expand your critical thinking skills, consider the eight steps in Figure 9.1.

Step One: Understanding and Using Emotional Intelligence

Emotions play a vital role in our lives. They help us feel compassion, help us help others, help us reach out in times of need, and help us relate to others. On the other hand, emotions can also cause some problems in your critical thinking process. You do not—and should not have to—eliminate emotions from your thoughts, but it is crucial that you know when your emotions are clouding an issue and causing you to act and speak before thinking.

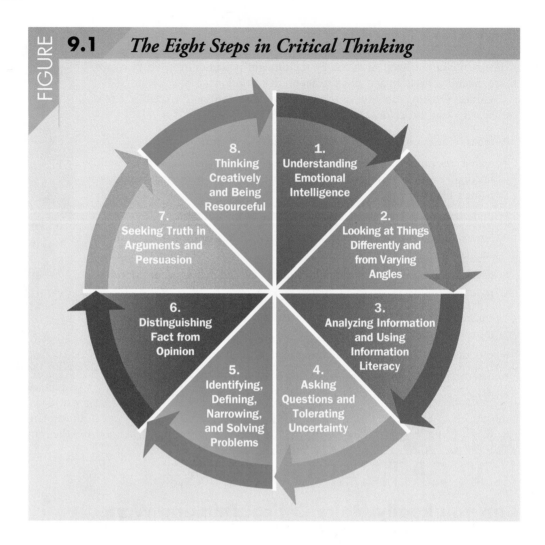

FIGURE 9.1 *The Eight Steps in Critical Thinking*

1. Understanding Emotional Intelligence
2. Looking at Things Differently and from Varying Angles
3. Analyzing Information and Using Information Literacy
4. Asking Questions and Tolerating Uncertainty
5. Identifying, Defining, Narrowing, and Solving Problems
6. Distinguishing Fact from Opinion
7. Seeking Truth in Arguments and Persuasion
8. Thinking Creatively and Being Resourceful

Consider the following topics:

▶ Should drugs and prostitution be totally legalized in the United States?

▶ Can the theories of evolution and creationism coexist?

▶ Can affirmative action reverse discrimination?

▶ Should illegal aliens be given amnesty and made U.S. citizens?

▶ Should the legal drinking age be lowered to 18?

▶ Should terminally ill patients have the right to assisted suicide?

▶ Should prayer be allowed in public schools?

As you read these topics, did you immediately form an opinion? Did old arguments surface? Did you feel your emotions coming into play as you thought about the questions? If you had an immediate answer, it is likely that you allowed some past judgments, opinions, and emotions to enter the decision-making process, unless you have just done a comprehensive, unbiased study of one of these issues. If you had to discuss these issues in class or with your friends and had to defend your position, how would you react? Do you think you would get angry? Would you find yourself groping for words? Would you find it hard to explain why you hold the opinion that you voiced? If so, these are warning signs that you are allowing your emotions to drive your decisions. If you allow your emotions to run rampant (not restrain them) and fail to use research, logic, and evidence, you may not be able to examine the issues critically or have a logical discussion regarding the statements.

> "Simply stated, people who are emotionally intelligent harness emotions and work with them to improve problem solving and boost creativity."
>
> —Snyder and Lopez

SHARPENING YOUR EMOTIONAL INTELLIGENCE (EI) SKILLS

How Does EI Affect Critical Thinking and Problem Solving?

If you have ever heard the old saying, "THINK before you act," you were actually being told to use *emotional intelligence EI*. Everyone knows that intelligence quotient is important to success in college, work, and life, but many experts believe that **EI** is just as important to being successful. EI helps people cope with the social and emotional demands in daily life. "Emotional intelligence is the single most influencing variable in personal achievement, career success, leadership, and life satisfaction" (Nelson and Low, 2003). "The data that exist suggest it can be *as powerful*, and at times *more powerful*, than IQ" (Goleman, 2006).

Exactly what is EI? EI includes all the skills and knowledge necessary for building strong, effective relationships through managing and understanding emotions. *It is knowing how you and others feel and managing those feelings in a rational manner that is good for both parties.* Consider Figure 9.2 (adapted from Snyder and Lopez, 2007).

We all have emotions and feelings that influence our thoughts and actions significantly. Emotions can manifest themselves in a wide range, from happiness to sadness, serenity to anger, and apathy to passion. You need to be able to recognize each of these emotions and employ appropriate skills for dealing with them. For example, let's say that you are discussing a political or religious issue with a friend of yours. You begin to sense that your friend is getting emotional and combative. You notice this in his or her voice and nonverbal behavior. An emotionally intelligent person would be able to sense what is going on, understand this situation and the consequences, and redirect the conversation to something more appropriate.

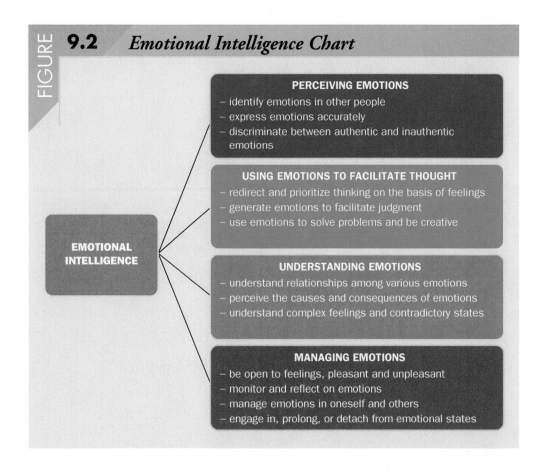

FIGURE 9.2 *Emotional Intelligence Chart*

EMOTIONAL INTELLIGENCE

PERCEIVING EMOTIONS
– identify emotions in other people
– express emotions accurately
– discriminate between authentic and inauthentic emotions

USING EMOTIONS TO FACILITATE THOUGHT
– redirect and prioritize thinking on the basis of feelings
– generate emotions to facilitate judgment
– use emotions to solve problems and be creative

UNDERSTANDING EMOTIONS
– understand relationships among various emotions
– perceive the causes and consequences of emotions
– understand complex feelings and contradictory states

MANAGING EMOTIONS
– be open to feelings, pleasant and unpleasant
– monitor and reflect on emotions
– manage emotions in oneself and others
– engage in, prolong, or detach from emotional states

Our emotions originate in the brain. If you have EI skills, your ***thinking mind*** and ***emotional mind*** should function together, making it more likely that you will craft sound, rational decisions. In other words, you will **think** before you **act**. When these two minds do not operate in harmony, you might make highly emotional decisions that can be viewed as irrational.

To become a successful, happy person, interpersonal relationships are important and learning to manage the entire spectrum of your personal emotions from the extreme **negative side** to the extreme **positive side** will be vitally important. This spectrum ranges from the darker side of your emotions (extreme negative pole) to the optimistic side (extreme positive pole).

FIGURE 9.3   *The Amygdala*

Don't let this word or concept frighten you. If you have never heard the word *"amygdala"* (pronounced ah-MIG-da-la), you're not alone. Most people have not. But this term and concept are important for you to be able to understand the overall aspects of EI. The amygdala, simply a part of the brain's emotional system, can cause us to go into default behavior based on what we remember from a similar experience. Do I use *fight* or *flight*? Basically, the amygdala is there to protect us when we become afraid or emotionally upset. When influenced by the amygdala, everything becomes *about us*. We become more judgmental. We don't stop to think about differences or the other person's feelings or the relationship. The amygdala can trigger an emotional response **before** the rest of the brain has had time to understand what is happening, and this situation causes us to have problems with others.

The amygdala remembers frustrations, fears, hurt feelings, and anger from our past. The tension from these past experiences causes the amygdala to go into default behavior—we *feel* before we *think*—and this can create a potentially explosive situation. If you had a bad experience several years ago and are placed in a similar situation, the amygdala will remember and trigger emotions that cause the body to respond. These feelings often cause people to bypass critical thinking (the logical brain) and to respond with angry words or actions (the emotional brain). For example:

▶ They get angry—you get angry.
▶ They curse you—you curse them.
▶ They use physical violence—you use physical violence.

However, if you remain calm and level-headed, you will begin to see that the other person usually begins to calm down, too. He or she will follow your emotional lead, positive or negative, and if you're calm and rational, anger and violence become out of place for most people.

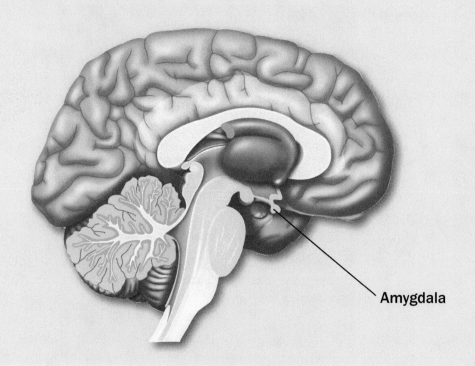

Amygdala

Study the spectrum of emotions illustrated in Figure 9.4. Think about which of these emotions you experience frequently and where you are located most of the time on this emotional continuum.

As you can see, the restraint and management of your personal emotional spectrum can impact you and your thinking skills greatly at home, at school, and at work. Today, this relatively new concept is being given a great deal of attention on college campuses and in the workplace. Not only will you find it helpful and necessary to manage your emotions at school, you will also need to be able to apply emotional management techniques at home and with family, friends, and work associates.

Think about one experience you've had in the past where your negative emotions "took over." Perhaps it was anger, fear, sorrow, hatred, or rage.

What was the situation and where were you when it happened? Be specific. _____
_____
_____

What triggered these emotions? _____
_____
_____

What were the negative consequences to you (or someone else) because of your emotions?
_____
_____

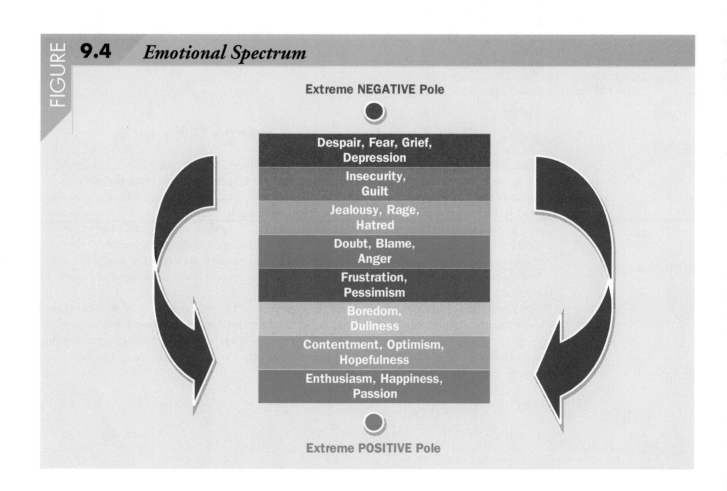

FIGURE **9.4** *Emotional Spectrum*

Extreme NEGATIVE Pole

Despair, Fear, Grief, Depression

Insecurity, Guilt

Jealousy, Rage, Hatred

Doubt, Blame, Anger

Frustration, Pessimism

Boredom, Dullness

Contentment, Optimism, Hopefulness

Enthusiasm, Happiness, Passion

Extreme POSITIVE Pole

FIGURE

9.5 *Guidelines for Emotional Management at School, Work, and Beyond*

▶ Face each day with an "I feel great, nothing is going to ruin my day" attitude.

▶ Hear all sides of an argument before you say anything, make a decision, or take an action.

▶ Practice a win-win philosophy at all times and work tirelessly to make it happen.

▶ Avoid letting your personal feelings about a person dictate your decisions.

▶ Never, never, never lose control!

▶ Avoid negative stereotyping and typecasting people into negative categories.

▶ Never look at or judge someone through someone else's eyes or experiences.

▶ Learn to keep a tight rein on any emotional "hotspots" such as anger, rage, and jealousy.

▶ Strive to treat people so well that you can always put your head on your pillow and sleep well, knowing that you have not been underhanded, rude, or unfair.

How did these emotions affect your ability to think clearly and critically? _____

_____

_____

_____

Because EI skills and knowledge are so important to your success in all areas of your life, you are encouraged to read extensively about this subject and to design your own personal plan for dealing with emotional concerns. Consider the tips in Figure 9.5 for managing your emotions on a daily basis.

 ## Step Two: Looking at Things Differently

Critical thinking involves looking at something you may have seen many times and examining it from many different angles and perspectives. It involves going beyond the obvious or beyond "easy" to seek new understanding and rare solutions. It encourages you to dig deeper than you have before, to get below the surface, to struggle, experiment, and expand. It asks you to look at something from an entirely different view so that you might develop new insights and understand more about the problem, situation, question, or solution. Critical thinking involves looking at *common issues* with uncommon eyes, *known problems* with new skepticism, *everyday conflicts* with probing curiosity, and *daily challenges* with greater attention to detail.

Review the following "brain teasers" in Figures 9.6–9.8 and take the time to solve them even though you may not "get" them quickly. You may need to break down a few barriers in your thought process and look at the puzzles from a new angle. Remember, these exercises do not measure intelligence. They are included to prod your thought process along and help you look at things differently.

FIGURE **9.6** *Brain Teaser #1:*
Looking at Common Terms Backward

Consider the following clues. Two examples are given to help you get started. Answer the following 10 teasers based on the clues.

Examples		
	4 W on a C	Four Wheels on a Car
	13 O C	Thirteen Original Colonies

1. SW and the 7D _____

2. I H a D by MLK _____

3. 2 Ps in a P _____

4. HDD (TMRUTC) _____

5. 3 S to a T _____

6. 100 P in a D _____

7. T no PLH _____

8. 4 Q in a G _____

9. I a SWAA _____

10. 50 S in t U _____

How did you do? Was it hard to look at the situation backward or have to look for clues within a series of letters and numbers? Most of us are not used to that. But part of critical thinking is trying to find **clues or patterns**. Perhaps the easiest teaser above was number two in Figure 9.6. Most people know MLK as Martin Luther King, Jr. When you figure that part out, the name of his most popular speech, *I Have a Dream*, becomes easy to figure out. Often, when trying to solve problems or dealing with unknowns, things become easier when you can find a clue or a pattern and build from WHAT you already know.

Examine the brain teaser in Figure 9.7. This teaser is included to help you look at an issue beyond what is actually given to you and considering what is not given.

Once again, you are given a basic clue, but you must go beyond what is given. You must look at the nine dots, but you must NOT let them confine you. You can't let the nine dots control your thoughts—you must move beyond what is given, beyond what you actually see. When you do this, the answer will come to you.

FIGURE **9.7** *Brain Teaser #2:*
Seeing What Is Not Given

Look at the design below. You will find nine dots. Your mission is to connect all nine dots with four straight lines without removing your pencil or pen from the paper. Do not retrace your lines.

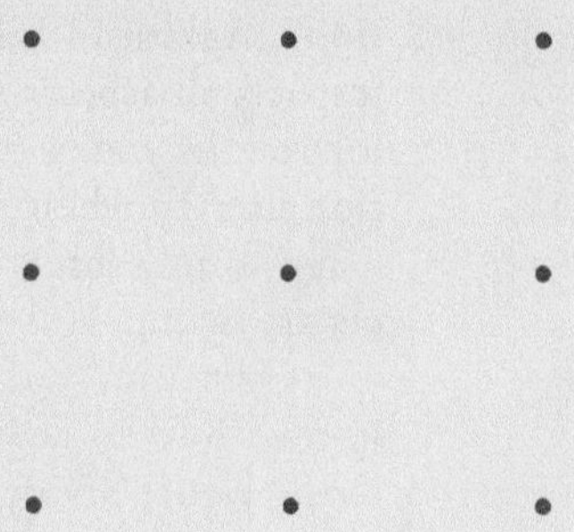

9.8 *Brain Teaser #3: The Penny*

Pretend that all life on earth has ended and all traces of civilization are gone–there are no buildings, no people, no animals, no plants–nothing is left but dirt and one penny. Someone from another planet, who knows our language, comes to earth and finds the penny. List all of the things that could be inferred about our civilization based on this one small penny. You should find at least 10 for each side.

1. _____
2. _____
3. _____
4. _____
5. _____
6. _____
7. _____
8. _____
9. _____
10. _____

As you continue to look at common things differently and think beyond the obvious, examine the penny in Figure 9.8

Drawing inferences often takes the ability to look at things differently and take something very common and examine it like you have never examined it before. Just as you looked at the penny, you learned new things about it by studying it with different eyes. Think about how you might solve a common problem that you face every day simply by looking at that problem with different eyes, too.

While these activities may seem somewhat trivial, they are provided to help you begin to think about and consider information from different angles. This is a major step in becoming a critical thinker: looking beyond the obvious, thinking outside the box, examining details, and exploring possibilities—basically, looking BEYOND what is given to you.

Step Three: Managing Information and Becoming Information Literate

Critical thinking involves knowing how to deal with all types of information, and *information literacy* refers to the skills a person needs to "recognize when information is needed and the ability to locate, evaluate, and effectively use the needed information" (American Library Association, 1989). *Information literacy* impacts all aspects of your college career and will later play a major role in your success in the workplace. You will use information literacy when you write a paper, read and evaluate an article, listen to presenters and determine if you believe what the speakers are saying, and prepare and make your own presentation.

Quite simply, if you are an information literate person, you have learned how to acquire and use information accurately and effectively. Figure 9.9 demonstrates a system for understanding and applying the concepts of information literacy.

"The sheer abundance of information will not in itself create a more informed citizenry without a complementary cluster of abilities necessary to use information correctly."
—ACRL

FIGURE **9.9**

The Essential Five: Major Steps in the Information Literacy Process

© Robert Sherfield and Patricia Moody

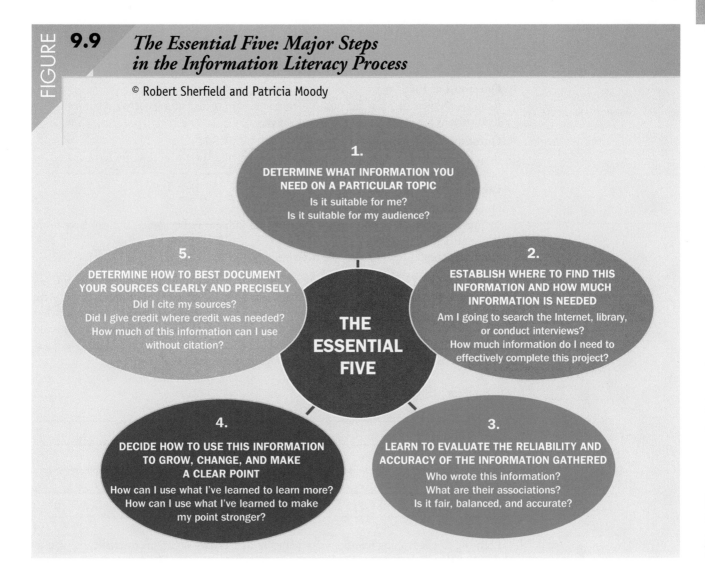

THE ESSENTIAL FIVE

1.
DETERMINE WHAT INFORMATION YOU NEED ON A PARTICULAR TOPIC
Is it suitable for me?
Is it suitable for my audience?

2.
ESTABLISH WHERE TO FIND THIS INFORMATION AND HOW MUCH INFORMATION IS NEEDED
Am I going to search the Internet, library, or conduct interviews?
How much information do I need to effectively complete this project?

3.
LEARN TO EVALUATE THE RELIABILITY AND ACCURACY OF THE INFORMATION GATHERED
Who wrote this information?
What are their associations?
Is it fair, balanced, and accurate?

4.
DECIDE HOW TO USE THIS INFORMATION TO GROW, CHANGE, AND MAKE A CLEAR POINT
How can I use what I've learned to learn more?
How can I use what I've learned to make my point stronger?

5.
DETERMINE HOW TO BEST DOCUMENT YOUR SOURCES CLEARLY AND PRECISELY
Did I cite my sources?
Did I give credit where credit was needed?
How much of this information can I use without citation?

Step Four: Asking Questions and Learning to Tolerate Uncertainty

You've asked questions all your life. As a child, you asked your parents, "What's that?" a million times. You probably asked them, "Why do I have to do this?" In later years, you've asked questions of your friends, teachers, strangers, store clerks, and significant others.

Questioning is not new to you, but it may be a new technique to you for exploring, developing, and honing your critical thinking skills. Curiosity may have killed the cat, but it was a smart cat when it died! Your curiosity is one of the most important traits you possess. It helps you grow and learn, and sometimes it may cause you to be uncomfortable. That's OK. This section is provided to assist you in learning how to ask questions to promote knowledge, solve problems, foster strong relationships, and critically analyze difficult situations. It is also included to help you understand the value of knowing how to tolerate uncertainty and avoid jumping to faulty conclusions because uncertainty "got the better of you." It is important to know that sometimes, ***the question is more important than the answer***—especially a faulty answer.

"It is not possible to become a good thinker and be a poor questioner. Thinking is not driven by answers, but, rather, by questions."
—Paul and Elder

Types of Questions

Basically, there are three types of questions, according to Paul and Elder (2006):

▶ **Questions of Fact**
Requires answers based in fact and evidence and have correct and incorrect reponses
Example: What is the freezing point of water?

▶ **Questions of Preference**
Requires answers that state a subjective preference and do not necessarily have correct or incorrect responses
Example: What is your favorite color?

▶ **Questions of Judgment**
Requires answers based on your judgment based in logic and evidence and can have more than one defensible answer
Example: Should Roe vs. Wade be overturned?

Asking questions helps us gain insight where we may have limited knowledge. Answering properly posed questions can also help us expand our knowledge base. For example, if you were assigned to write a paper or give a speech on the topic of ***creationism versus evolution***, what five questions would you definitely want that paper or speech to answer when you are finished writing/delivering it? Take some time to think about this issue. Write down at least five questions that you consider essential to the topic of creationism versus evolution.

My five questions are:

1. _____
2. _____
3. _____
4. _____
5. _____

Learning to ask probing questions can help you in everyday situations by challenging you to look beyond the obvious and critically examine everyday situations. **Examine the car advertisement in Figure 9.10.** The car dealership has provided some information, but it is not enough to make a smart, rational decision. What other questions would you ask the dealer to make sure that you are getting a good deal?

What additional questions would you need to ask the dealer to ensure that you are getting a "good" deal?

1. _____
2. _____
3. _____
4. _____
5. _____

I Am 100% Sure That I Am Not Sure

CAN YOU TOLERATE UNCERTAINTY?

Asking questions that can be answered is vitally important to critical thinking, but so is learning to tolerate uncertainty and learning to ask questions that may not have an **immediate answer**. Uncertainty causes you to keep going—to not get lazy or give up. If we thought we knew the

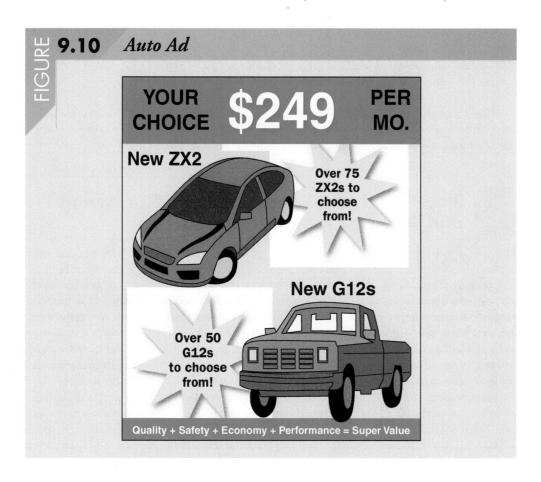

answers to everything, we would still be beating rocks together to make fire and we would still be walking everywhere instead of driving or flying. Uncertainty causes humanity to move forward and create new knowledge, to try new things, to consider the impossible. Uncertainty also breeds creative thinking.

Think about all of the uncertainty that can arise in your daily life:

"Can I be certain that my spouse/partner will not leave me?" No.
"Can I be certain that I will remain healthy?" No.
"Can I be certain that my children will turn out to be good, caring, loving adults?" No.
"Can I be certain what happens to me after I die?" No.
"Can I be certain that the plane won't crash or that someone won't crash into my car?" No.
"Can I be certain that this will not embarrass me or someone else?" No.
"Can I be certain that my investments will grow and I can retire comfortably?" No.

The inability to tolerate uncertainty can cause stress and anxiety. Sometimes, we just have to "let go" and accept that we do not know the answers. We can work hard to try to find the answers and/or direct our actions so that the answers will be favorable to us, but ultimately, many things in this universe require our tolerance of uncertainty. Sometimes, the best we can hope for is to keep asking questions and seeking the truth.

Think of the good things that initially unanswered questions and uncertainty brought to humanity in many fields of study.

"Can we send someone to the moon and have them return safely?"
"Can we transplant a human heart and have that person live and prosper afterward?"
"Can we establish a new country with a new constitution and have it work?"

*"Can we design and build a skyscraper that is over 140 stories high and have
     it remain safe?"*
"Can we create an automobile that will get over 50 miles per gallon of fuel?"
"Can we help reduce global warming and its effects on the polar ice caps?"

All of these uncertainties have contributed to the development of new knowledge, new skills, new jobs, new outlooks, and new ways of living. Therefore, it is important to remember that in your quest for answers, sometimes uncertainty can be the most important thing you discover.

Step Five: Identifying, Defining, Narrowing, and Solving Problems

What would your life be like if you had no problems? Most people do not like to face or deal with problems, but the critical thinker knows that problems exist every day and that they must be faced and hopefully solved. Some of our problems are larger and more difficult than others, but we all face problems from time to time. You may have transportation problems. You may have financial problems. You may have child care problems. You may have academic problems or interpersonal problems. Many people don't know how to solve problems at school, home, or work. They simply let the problem go unaddressed until it is too late to reach an amiable solution. But there are many ways to address and solve problems. In this section, we will discuss how to **identify and narrow** the problem, **research and develop** alternatives, **evaluate** the alternatives, and **solve** the problem.

Every problem may not have a solution. That can be a hard pill for many people to swallow, but it is a raw truth and a part of the uncertainty we just discussed. Many problems have solutions, but the solution may not be the one you wanted. It is imperative to remember the words of Mary Hatwood Futrell, President of the National Education Agency. She states that *"finding the right answer is important, of course. But more important is developing the ability to see that many problems have multiple solutions, that getting from X to Y demands basic skills and mental agility, imagination, persistence, patience."* Consider the problem-solving model in Figure 9.11.

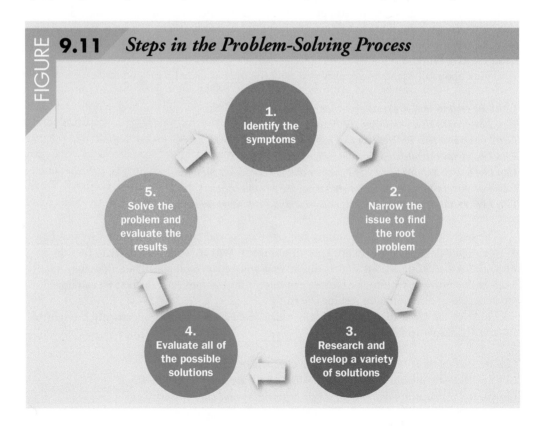

FIGURE **9.11** *Steps in the Problem-Solving Process*

1. Identify the symptoms
2. Narrow the issue to find the root problem
3. Research and develop a variety of solutions
4. Evaluate all of the possible solutions
5. Solve the problem and evaluate the results

9.12 *Solutions in Bloom Diagram*

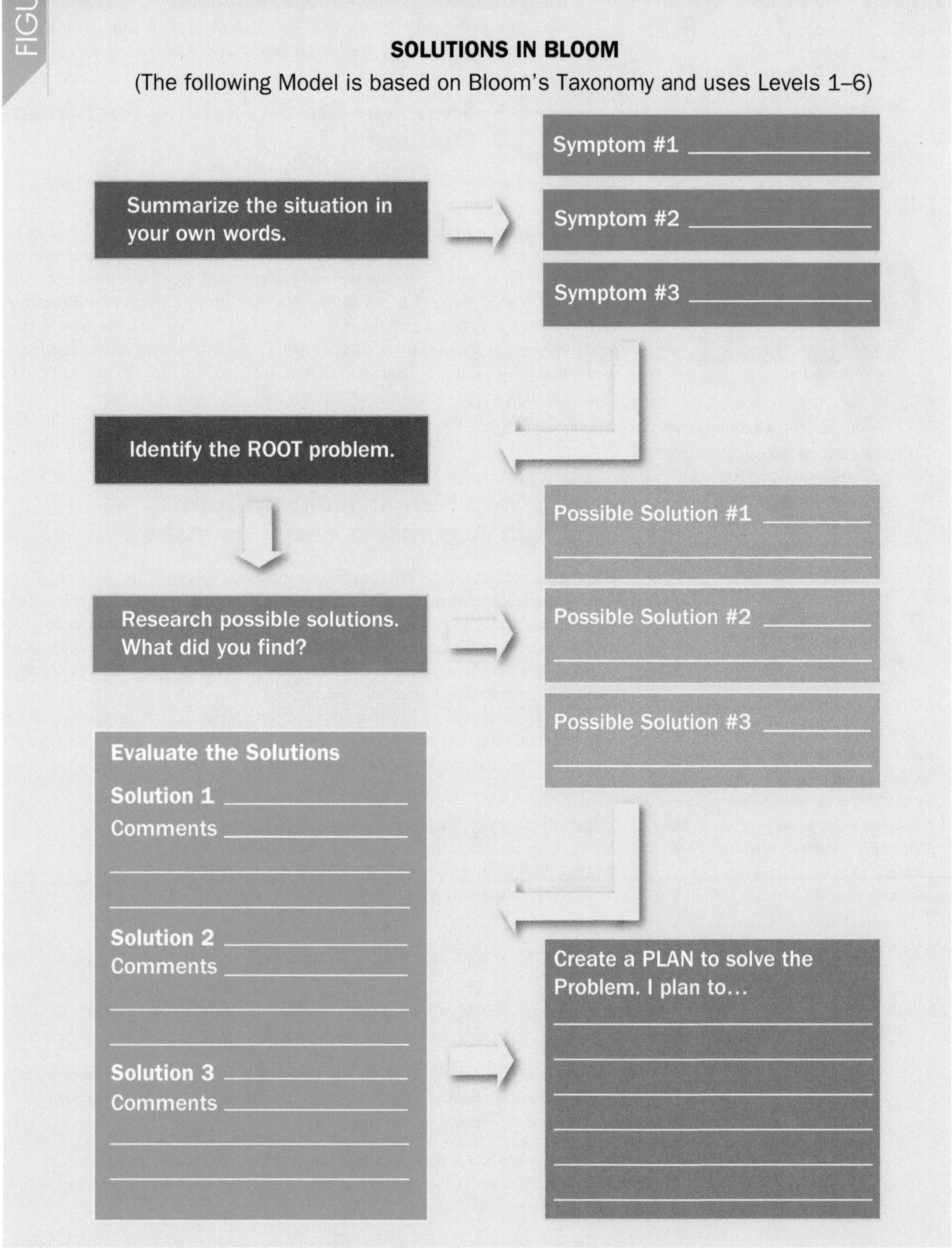

SOLUTIONS IN BLOOM

(The following Model is based on Bloom's Taxonomy and uses Levels 1–6)

Symptom #1 _____

Summarize the situation in your own words.

Symptom #2 _____

Symptom #3 _____

Identify the ROOT problem.

Possible Solution #1 _____

_____

Research possible solutions. What did you find?

Possible Solution #2 _____

Possible Solution #3 _____

Evaluate the Solutions

Solution 1 _____
Comments _____
_____
_____

Solution 2 _____
Comments _____
_____
_____

Solution 3 _____
Comments _____
_____
_____

Create a PLAN to solve the Problem. I plan to...
_____
_____
_____
_____
_____
_____
_____

> *"Everyone is entitled to their own opinion, but not their own facts."*
> —Senator Daniel Patrick Moynihan

not do well in high school. They have threatened to take away his car and kick him out of the house if he does not find a full-time job. Nathan is doing well and does not want to leave college. He has a goal of becoming an architect and knows that he has talent in this area. He is making A's and B's in all of his classes. This does not matter to his parents. They do not value education and see it as a luxury.

Step Six: Distinguishing Fact from Opinion

An important aspect of critical thinking is the ability to distinguish fact from opinion. *In most media—TV, radio, newspapers, magazines, and the Internet—opinions surface more often than facts. Reread the previous sentence.* This is an example of an opinion cloaked as a fact. There is no research supporting this opinion. It sounds as if it could be true, but without evidence and proof, it is just an opinion.

A fact is something that can be ***proven***, something that can be ***objectively verified***. An opinion is a statement that is held to be true, but has no objective proof. *Statements that cannot be proven should always be treated as opinion.* Statements that offer valid proof and verification from credible, reliable sources can be treated as factual.

Learning to distinguish fact from opinion can be a paramount step in building your critical thinking skills at work, with family, and especially when analyzing media.

Step Seven: Seeking Truth in Arguments and Persuasion

Whether or not you realize it, arguments and persuasive efforts are around you daily—hourly, for that matter. They are in newspaper and TV ads, editorials, news commentaries, talk shows, TV magazine shows, political statements, and religious services. It seems at times that almost everyone is trying to persuade us through arguments or advice. This section is included to assist you in recognizing faulty arguments and implausible or deceptive persuasion.

First, let's start with a list of terms used to describe faulty arguments and deceptive persuasion. As you read through the list on the next page, try to identify situations in which you have heard arguments that fit these descriptions.

Identifying Fallacious Arguments

Below, you will find statements intended to persuade you or argue for a cause. Beside each statement, identify which type of faulty persuasion is used.

AB	Ad baculum	**SA**	Straw argument	**AH**	Ad hominem
AT	Appeal to tradition	**AP**	Ad populum	**PF**	Plain folks
AV	Ad verecundiam	**PM**	Patriotism	**BW**	Bandwagon
ST	Scare tactic	**GG**	Glittering generalities		

_____ 1. *This country has never faltered in the face of adversity. Our strong, united military has seen us through many troubled times, and it will see us through our current situation. This is your country; support your military.*

_____ 2. *If I am elected to office, I will personally lobby for lower taxes, a new comprehensive crime bill, a $2,500 tax cut on every new home, and better education, and I will personally work to lower the unemployment rate.*

_____ 3. *This is the best college in the region. All of your friends will be attending this fall. You don't want to be left out; you should join us, too.*

_____ 4. *If you really listen to Governor Wise's proposal on health care, you will see that there is no way that we can have a national system. You will not be able to select your doctor, you will not be able to go to the hospital of your choice, and you will not be able to get immediate attention. His proposal is not as comprehensive as our proposal.*

_____ 5. *My father went to Honors College, I went to Honors College, and you will go to Honors College. It is the way things have been for the people in this family. There is no need to break with tradition now.*

_____ 6. *The witness's testimony is useless. He is an alcoholic; he is dishonest and corrupt. To make matters worse, he was a member of the Leftist Party.*

_____ 7. *The gentleman on the witness stand is your neighbor, he is your friend, he is just like you. Sure, he may have more money and drive a Mercedes, but his heart never left the Elm Community.*

_____ 8. *John F. Kennedy once said, "Ask not what your country can do for you; ask what you can do for your country." This is the time to act, my fellow citizens. You can give $200 to our cause and you will be fulfilling the wish of President Kennedy.*

_____ 9. *Out of the 7,000 people polled, 72% believe that there is life beyond our planet. Therefore, there must be life beyond earth.*

_____ 10. *Without this new medication, you will die.*

_____ 11. *I don't care what anyone says. If you don't come around to our way of thinking, you'd better start watching your back.*

> Why is it important to read and research possible solutions before you make decisions?

As you develop your critical thinking skills, you will begin to recognize the illogical nature of many thoughts, the falsehoods of many statements, the deception in some advertisements, and the irrational

Terminology for Fallacious Arguments

Ad baculum	Ad baculum is an argument that tries to persuade based on force. Threats of alienation, disapproval, or even violence may accompany this type of argument.
Ad hominem	Ad hominem is when someone initiates a personal attack on someone else rather than listening to and rationally debating the person's ideas. This is also referred to as "slander."
Ad populum	An ad populum argument is based on the opinions of the majority of people. It assumes that because the majority says X is right, then Y is not. It uses little logic.
Ad verecundiam	This argument uses quotes and phrases from people in authority or popular people to support one's own views.
Appeal to tradition	This argument looks only at the past and suggests that because we have always done it "this way," we should continue to do it "this way."
Bandwagon	The bandwagon approach tries to convince you to do something just because everyone else is doing it. It is also referred to as "peer pressure."
Glittering Generalities	This type of persuasion or argumentation is an appeal to generalities (Bosak, 1976). It suggests that a person, candidate, or professional is for all the "right" things: justice, low taxes, no inflation, rebates, full employment, low crime, free tuition, progress, privacy, and truth.
Patriotism	This form of persuasion asks you to ignore reason and logic and support what is right for state A or city B or nation C.
Plain folks	This type of persuasion is used to make you feel that the people making the argument are just like you. Usually, they are not; they are only using this appeal to connect with your sense of space and time.
Scare tactic	A scare tactic is used as a desperate measure to put fear in your life. If you don't do X, then Y is going to happen to you.
Straw argument	The straw argument attacks the opponent's argument to make one's own argument stronger. It does not necessarily make argument A stronger; it simply discounts argument B.

> *"There is nothing so powerful as truth, and often, nothing so strange."*
> —Daniel Webster

fears used to persuade. You will also begin to understand the depths to which you should delve to achieve objectivity, the thought and care that you should give to your own decisions and statements, and the methods by which you can build logical, truthful arguments.

Step Eight: Thinking Creatively and Being Resourceful

Creative thinking is a major and important aspect of critical thinking, in that you are producing something that is uniquely yours—introducing something to the world that is new, innovative, and useful. Creative thinking does not mean that you have to be an artist, a musician, or a writer. Creative thinking instead means that you have examined a situation and developed a new way of explaining information, delivering a product, or using an item. It can be as simple as discovering that you can use a small rolling suitcase to carry your books around campus instead of the traditional backpack. Creative thinking means that you have opened your mind to possibilities!

Creative thinking is really about being resourceful—and in today's times, resourcefulness is a powerful tool. Resourcefulness is an *internal* quality, not an *external* gift. If you have ever seen the TV series *Survivorman* or *Man vs. Wild*, you know that it takes a strong person to eat a slug just carved out of a tree trunk. It takes internal will to drink water with so many bacteria that flies die when they drink it. Yes, both shows are somewhat staged, but they show the basics of creativity, intelligence, imagination, and *resourcefulness*.

To truly understand resourcefulness, you need look no further than a child playing in the backyard. *"What does a worthless, old stick become?"* Because of a child's inability to see limitations, the stick becomes a medieval sword, Luke Skywalker's laser beam, an old man's cane, a crutch, a magic wand, a baseball bat, a witch's stirring stick, or a marshmallow roaster. An old stick now has limitless possibilities because the child refused to see it only as a stick. His refusal to be boxed into the confines of our adult reality created possibilities. Sometimes, we have to become that child and use every stick we have just to survive.

Think of internal resourcefulness as **renewable energy**. When you have to draw on your wits, creativity, and determination, these qualities multiply. The more you are required by circumstances to use these qualities, the stronger and more plentiful they become. Conversely, if you've always been able to buy anything you want or if all that you need is provided to you by an external force, your internal resourcefulness begins to wither and die like uneaten fruit on the winter vine. You are not forced to use the whole of yourself. Your energy fades. Your harvest dies.

Your inner resourcefulness and creativity also make you more secure and offer more protection from outside forces. When you know how to make ends meet, you can always do it. When you know how to pay the rent on limited income, you can always do it. When you know how to cut firewood to heat your home, you can always do it. When you know how to navigate the public transportation system in your town, you can always do it; even when the time comes that you don't have to "do it" anymore, you could if you had to. The more you know and the more inner strength and resourcefulness you have, the safer you are against the unknown. The more confidence you possess, the greater the likelihood that you can survive anything at any time. The more resourceful you are, the more you understand that this one quality will help you rebuild all that may have been lost. When the world *HAS* been handed to you on a silver platter, you cannot be ready for what the world *CAN* hand you.

To begin the creative process, consider the items in Figure 9.13. These are some of the characteristics creative thinkers have in common. Using your imaginative and innovative juices, think about how you would *creatively* solve the following problem. Write down at least five possibilities. Come on, make it count!

If you had to use your creativity to "survive" in the wild, could you do it?

Jennifer is a first-year student who does not have enough money to pay her tuition, buy her books, and purchase a few new outfits and shoes to wear to class and her work-study job on campus.

What should she do? Should she pay her tuition and purchase her books, or pay her tuition and buy new clothes and shoes to wear to class and work? What creative, resourceful ideas (solutions) can you give Jennifer?

MY CREATIVE SOLUTIONS:

1. _____

2. _____

3. _____

4. _____

5. _____

FIGURE **9.13** *Characteristics of Creative Thinking*

COMPASSION	Creative thinkers have a zest for life and genuinely care for the spirit of others.	**Example:** More than 40 years ago, community members who wanted to feed the elderly created Meals on Wheels, now a national organization feeding the elderly.
COURAGE	Creative thinkers are unafraid to try new things, to implement new thoughts and actions.	**Example:** An NBC executive moves the *Today Show* out of a closed studio onto the streets of New York, creating the number one morning news show in the United States.
TRUTH	Creative thinkers search for the true meaning of things.	**Example:** The astronomer and scientist Copernicus sought to prove that earth was *not* the center of the universe—an unpopular view at the time.
DREAMS	Creative thinkers allow themselves time to dream and ponder the unknown. They can see what is possible, not just what is actual.	**Example:** John F. Kennedy dreamed that space exploration was possible. His dream became reality.
RISK TAKING	Creative thinkers take positive risks every day. They are not afraid to go against popular opinion.	**Example:** Barack Obama took a risk and ran for President of the United States. He became one of only a few African Americans to ever run for the office and the only African American to be nominated by his party. In November of 2008, he became the first African-American President of the United States.
INNOVATION	Creative thinkers find new ways to do old things.	**Example:** Instead of continuing to fill the earth with waste such as aluminum, plastic, metal, and old cars, means were developed to recycle these materials for future productive use.
COMPETITION	Creative thinkers strive to be better, to think bolder thoughts, to do what is good and to be the best at any task.	**Example:** Tiger Woods had a several-season slump in golf. Most people thought he was a "has-been" especially after his knee surgery. He came back to win tournament after tournament because he knew that he could and he never gave up. He challenged himself.
INDIVIDUALITY	Creative thinkers are not carbon copies of other people. They strive to be true to themselves.	**Example:** A young man decides to take tap dancing instead of playing baseball. He excels and wins a fine arts dancing scholarship to college.
CURIOSITY	Creative thinkers are interested in all things; they want to know much about many things.	**Example:** A 65-year-old retired college professor goes back to college to learn more about music appreciation and computer programming to expand her possibilities.
PERSEVERANCE	Creative thinkers do not give up. They stick to a project to its logical and reasonable end.	**Example:** Dr. Martin Luther King, Jr., did not give up on his dream in the face of adversity, danger, and death threats.

From Ordinary to Extraordinary

REAL PEOPLE | REAL LIVES | REAL CHANGE

DR. WAYNE A. JONES
Assistant Professor and Thurgood Marshall Pathways Fellow
Department of Political Science and Public Administration
Virginia State University, Petersburg, VA

I come from a fine family. My mother is a retired social worker, college professor and community activist and my father, a retired Presbyterian minister and college professor. They provided a safe, structured environment and always have encouraged me to do well. Clearly, I had the foundation to do well in school. However I have not always followed my parents' advice. This was especially true for my senior year in high school. The outcome was that I did not graduate. So at 18, I was working, had my own apartment and things were OK. At least, so I thought.

I had always been interested in anything that had wheels on it. If it has wheels, I could drive it —or wanted to! I drove a bus for a few years and then I drove an ambulance. One day, however, I saw our local bookmobile and I wanted to drive it. I applied to do so, but found out that I had to have a high school diploma to be able to drive the bookmobile. At 19, this was my reason for going back to get my GED. Now, I could master driving yet another "thing" with wheels. It was not, however, as exciting as I thought it would be.

My parents begged me to begin my college studies. Reluctantly, at age 21, I enrolled at Virginia Commonwealth University. After only one year, I knew that college was not for me. I dropped out. In 1975, I began working for the Police Department in Chesterfield, VA. I was only the second African American police officer on the force. I held this position for five years.

My desire for wheels was still with me. I left the police department and began working for the Virginia Overland Transportation Company as a safety supervisor. I worked my way up to become supervisor of transportation. With this experience under my belt, I went to work for a transit company in Richmond, VA driving a city transit bus. I left the second bus company after a year to drive for a local construction company. This work, however, turned out to be very "seasonal" and I found myself frequently without income. I asked to be allowed to drive one of their trash trucks so that I could have a steady income and overtime, too. So, there I was in my late twenties, without a college degree,

driving a trash truck. There was not a lot to look forward to.

My late grandmother called me one day and asked me why I didn't go back to college. "You are far from dumb," I remember her telling me. I tried to explain to her that I was making decent money and I could not quit my job. I told her that it would take me at least eight years to get my degree. "I'll be too old by then," I told her. She then said the words that woke me up and changed my life. "Son," she said, "unless you die, you're going to be eight years older in eight years anyway, why not be eight years older with a college degree?"

That was my wake-up call. I found another job with more flexible hours and enrolled at John Tyler Community College with no idea of what I wanted to become. Shortly after I re-enrolled in college, my grandmother died. Her final gift to me was her wonderful words of wisdom.

So, there I was, working full-time, going to college full-time, and barely having enough time to even visit my family who lived nearby. One night, I received another phone call that

From Ordinary to Extraordinary

REAL PEOPLE | REAL LIVES | REAL CHANGE

changed my life again. My parents called me and told me that they wanted to talk with me about money. I visited them and to my surprise, they asked me to quit work and concentrate on my studies. "Grandmother had a vision," my mother told me. "She knew that you were going to do great things." They told me that if I quit, they would pay my bills until I finished college. I agreed to take their help.

I transferred from John Tyler Community College and enrolled again at Virginia Commonwealth University. My GPA was not great upon graduation. I took the Graduate Record Exam (GRE) and scored very badly. I was turned down for the graduate program in Public Administration. I was now 35. I met with the director of admissions and said to him, "Just give me a chance, I know I can do this."

In just a few short years, I managed to go from driving a trash truck to being a university professor.

After some conversation, he agreed to give me a chance. I completed my Masters of Public Administration in only 18 months. I applied to the doctoral program in public administration at VCU. The chairman of the doctoral program reviewed my GRE scores and basically told me that based on them, I should not have been able to obtain a master's degree. Then, I applied to George Washington University for their PhD program.

Once again, the admissions office looked at my scores and basically told me that my master's degree was "just a fluke." I was accepted provisionally and only five years later, I graduated with a 3.85. My dissertation won the Outstanding Dissertation of the Year Award in 2000 from the George Washington University chapter of Phi Delta Kappa. I was not a fluke anymore.

I began working as Director of Adult Day Care for a United Way Agency and loved it. It was then that the thought of becoming a college professor came to mind. I saw an ad in the paper for a part-time teaching position working with advanced-placement students. I found the love of my life — teaching. I later applied to become a full-time faculty member at Virginia State University and today, I teach freshman studies and public administration.

EXTRAORDINARY REFLECTION

Read the following statement and respond in your online journal or class notebook.

Dr. Jones was brave enough to take an enormous risk, quit his full-time job, accept help, and reach his goals. Whom do you have in your life that you can depend upon for support (maybe not monetary support, but crucial support of your goals, dreams, and educational plans)? Why?

CHANGING IDEAS TO *Reality*

REFLECTIONS ON CRITICAL AND CREATIVE THINKING

Critical thinking, emotional intelligence, and information literacy require a great deal of commitment on your part. They may not be easy for everyone at first, but with practice, dedication, and an understanding of the immense need of all three, everyone can think more critically and logically, evaluate information sources, and use emotional intelligence to best advantage.

Critical thinking and emotional intelligence can affect the way you live your life, from strengthening relationships to purchasing a new car, from solving family problems to investing money, from taking the appropriate classes for graduation to getting a promotion at work. Both are vitally important to your growth and education.

As you continue on in the semester and work toward personal and professional motivation and change, consider the following ideas:

> *"The significant problems we face cannot be solved at the same level of thinking we were at when we created them."*
> —Albert Einstein

- ▶ Use only *credible* and *reliable* sources.
- ▶ Learn to distinguish *fact* from *opinion*.
- ▶ Be *flexible* in your thinking and *avoid* generalizations.
- ▶ Use emotional intelligence and *restraint*.
- ▶ Avoid *stereotyping* and prejudging and strive for *objectivity* in your thinking.
- ▶ *Reserve* judgment until you have looked at every side.
- ▶ Do *not* assume—do the research and *ask* questions.
- ▶ Work hard to distinguish *symptoms from problems*.

Critical thinking is truly the hallmark of an educated person. It is a hallmark of character and integrity, and a hallmark of successful students. Let it be yours.

KNOWLEDGE *in* BLOOM

Developing a Rational, Logical Argument

Each chapter-end assessment is based on *Bloom's Taxonomy of Learning.* See the inside front cover for a quick review.

UTILIZES LEVEL 3 OF THE TAXONOMY

EXPLANATION: Thousands of articles are written every day for magazines, newspapers, online journals, and other print media. Depending on the article or where it is published, it can have a slant. You may have heard this called bias (as in "liberal" or "conservative" bias). One of journalism's objectives should be to present the FACTS of what has happened in an incident or the facts of what is being discussed. Bias should not enter the argument unless it is an editorial.

PROCESS: For this activity, you are to find an article (not an editorial) in a mainstream newspaper or magazine (*USA Today, Newsweek, Time, The New York Times, The Washington Post, The National Review*, etc.), read the article, and determine if the article has bias, unsubstantiated opinions, or research that is weak.

The list of questions below will help you evaluate and assess your article.

Name of the article:

_____

Author of the article: _____

His or her affiliation: _____

Publication in which the article was found: _____

Date of publication: _____

Before you read this article, based on the title and subject matter, what five questions do you want to be able to answer once you have read the article?

1. _____
2. _____
3. _____
4. _____
5. _____

After reading the article, what is the author's main reason for writing it?

What is/are the most important fact(s) or information in the article? _____
_____

By writing this article, what is the author implying? _____
_____
_____

By writing this article, what is the author proving? _____
_____
_____

In writing this article, what assumptions were made? _____
_____
_____

What sources does the writer cite to prove his or her point?_____
_____
_____

Is the article fairly presented? In other words, does the author examine both sides of the issue or just one side? Justify your answer. _____
_____
_____

Do you believe and trust the article? Why or why not? Justify your answer. _____
_____
_____

If this article is accurate (or inaccurate, depending on your judgment), what are the implications for society? _____
_____
_____

Answer the five questions you wrote previously in this exercise._____

1. _____
2. _____
3. _____
4. _____
5. _____

List one way that you can use the information in this article to enhance your creativity and/or resourcefulness. _____
_____
_____

(This project is adapted, in part, from the work of Richard Paul and Linda Elder, 2006.)

SQ3R *Mastery* STUDY SHEET

EXAMPLE QUESTION: *(from page 237)* Why is emotional intelligence important to critical thinking?		ANSWER:
EXAMPLE QUESTION: *(from page 244)* What is information literacy?		ANSWER:
AUTHOR QUESTION: *(from page 239)* Why is emotional intelligence important?		ANSWER:
AUTHOR QUESTION: *(from page 236)* Why is asking questions so important in critical thinking?		ANSWER:
AUTHOR QUESTION: *(from page 245)* Discuss the steps in information literacy.		ANSWER:
AUTHOR QUESTION: *(from page 252)* Define fact and opinion and give an example of each.		ANSWER:
AUTHOR QUESTION: *(from page 253)* Define ad hominem and find an example of this in a recent newspaper or magazine article.		ANSWER:
YOUR QUESTION: *(from page ___)*		ANSWER:
YOUR QUESTION: *(from page ___)*		ANSWER:
YOUR QUESTION: *(from page ___)*		ANSWER:
YOUR QUESTION: *(from page ___)*		ANSWER:
YOUR QUESTION: *(from page ___)*		ANSWER:

Finally, after answering these questions, recite this chapter's major points in your mind. Consider the following general questions to help you master this material.

▶ What was it about?
▶ What does it mean?
▶ What was the most important thing I learned? Why?
▶ What were the key points to remember?

ANSWERS TO TEASERS pp. 241–242

Brain Teaser #1, Looking at Common Terms Backwards

1. Snow White and the Seven Dwarfs

2. I Have a Dream by Martin Luther King, Jr.

3. Two peas in a pod

4. Hickory dickory dock, the mouse ran up the clock

5. Three sides to a triangle

6. One hundred pennies in a dollar

7. There's no place like home

8. Four quarts in a gallon

9. *It's A Small World After All*

10. Fifty states in the Union

Brain Teaser #2, Seeing What Is Not Given

(Hint: You have to think "outside the box." Look beyond what is given to you.)

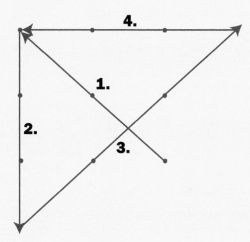

Brain Teaser #3, The Penny

Your answers might include things such as:

▶ We had more than one language.

▶ We knew geometry.

▶ We had a calendar system.

▶ We honored people.

▶ We knew metallurgy.

▶ We knew math.

▶ We knew architecture.

▶ We were united.

▶ We valued liberty.

TEAM BUILDING: Collaborative Solutions

SOLVE A PROBLEM

On a 3-by-5 card or a plain sheet of paper, each student in the class writes an academic problem; this could be specific to one class or general to all classes. Problems might involve a fear, a challenge, or a roadblock. Students hand these in without names. The instructor writes the list on the board.

Divide into groups of two to four. Each group chooses a different problem to work on. Use the empty problem-solving flowchart (Key 9.1 on the next page) to fill in your work.

1. Define the problem. Start by stating your specific problem. Together, explore what is causing the problem and what negative effects come from it.

2. Examine the problem. Pick it apart to see what's happening. Gather information from all group members, verify facts, and go beyond assumptions.

3. Generate possible solutions. From the most likely causes, derive possible solutions. Record all the ideas that group members offer. After 10 minutes or so, each group member should choose one possible solution to evaluate.

4. Evaluate each solution. Independently, each group member should take a couple of minutes to weigh potential positive and negative effects of this solution and think about how the solution addresses the causes of the problem. Is it a good one? Will it work?

5. Choose a solution. Group members then come together, share observations and recommendations, and take a vote: Which solution is the best? Try to find the solution that most people agree on, or consider combining elements of different solutions to create a new one. Then, together, come up with a plan for putting your solution to work.

6. Evaluate your solution. As a group, discuss whether you think the chosen solution can be successful. List the positive and negative effects you think it may have.

KEY 9.1 *Work through a Problem using this Flowchart*

DEFINE PROBLEM HERE: ANALYZE THE PROBLEM

Use boxes below to list possible solutions:

POTENTIAL POSITIVE EFFECTS	SOLUTION #1	POTENTIAL NEGATIVE EFFECTS
List for each solution:		*List for each solution:*

SOLUTION #2

SOLUTION #3

Now choose the solution you think is best—circle it and make it happen.

ACTUAL POSITIVE EFFECTS	ACTION TAKEN	ACTUAL NEGATIVE EFFECTS
List for chosen solution:		*List for chosen solution:*

FINAL EVALUATION: Was it a good or bad solution?

Source: Based on heuristic created by Frank T. Lyman Jr. and George Eley, 1985.

Test Prep: START IT NOW

USE YOUR ANALYTICAL THINKING SKILLS TO BROADEN YOUR KNOWLEDGE

Many essay tests require you to take your thinking beyond recall and into the realm of critical thinking. Name a course you are currently taking that will have at least one essay test:

_____

Now, name an important topic in the course that you need to know inside out.

_____

On a separate sheet of paper or on a computer file, use what you learned to prepare yourself for the test. Create notes on:

▶ Themes and patterns that define the topic
▶ Facts and opinions about this topic and evidence that supports them
▶ How parts of this topic are similar to or different from one another as well as other topics
▶ Causes and effects that are part of this topic
▶ Arguments you might make to support your point of view
▶ Assumptions that people tend to make about this topic

When you are done, you should be ready to handle an essay question on your chosen topic.

NOTES

Chapter 3

1. R. A. Clark and J. G. Delia, "*Topoi* and Rhetorical Competence." *The Quarterly Journal of Speech,* 65, (1979): 197–206.
2. W. R. Cupach and S. Metts, *Facework* (Thousand Oaks, Calif.: Sage, 1994).
3. Ibid.
4. Ibid.
5. M. L. McLauglin. W. J. Cody, and H. D. O'Hair, "The Management of Failure Events: Some Contextual Determinants of Accounting Behavior," *Human Communication Research,* 9 (1983): 208–224.
6. Cupach and Metts, *Facework.*
7. McLauglin, Cody, O'Hair, "The Management of Failure Events."
8. Ibid.
9. Ibid.
10. Ibid.
11. S. Petronio, "The Use of Communication Boundary Perspective to Contextualize Embarrassment Research," *Communication Yearbook/13,* ed. J. Anderson (Newbury Park, Calif.: Sage, 1990), pp. 365–373.
12. S. Metts, and W. R. Cupach, "Situational Influence on the Use of Remedial Strategies in Embarrassing Situations," *Communication Monographs,* 56 (1989): 151–162. See also W. R. Cupach and S. Metts, "The Effects of Type of Predicament and Embarrassability on Remedial Responses to Embarrassing Situations," *Communication Quarterly,* 40 (1992): 149–161.
13. D. B. Buller and J. K. Burgoon, "Deception: Strategic and Nonstrategic Communication," in *Strategic Interpersonal Communication,* ed. J. A. Daly and J. M. Wiemann, (Hillsdale, N. J.: Lawrence Erlbaum, 1994), pp. 191–223. See also H. D. O'Hair and M. J. Cody, "Deception," in *The Dark Side of Interpersonal Communication,* ed. W. R. Cupach and B. H. Spitzberg (Hillsdale, N.J.: Lawrence Erlbaum, 1994), pp. 181–213.
14. Ibid.
15. J. W. Neuliep and M. Mattson, "The Use of Deception as a Compliance-Gaining Strategy," *Human Communication Research,* 16 (1990): 409–421.
16. J. K. Burgoon, et al. "Interpersonal Deception: V. Accuracy in Deception Detection," *Communication Monographs,* 61 (1994): 303–325. Also see S. A. McCornack and T. R. Levine, "When Lovers Become Leery: The Relationship Between Suspicion and Accuracy in Detecting Deception," *Communication Monographs,* 57 (1990): 219–230.
17. D. B. Buller, K. D. Strzyzewski, and F. G. Hunsaker, "Interpersonal Deception: II. The Inferiority of Conversational Participants as Deception Detectors," *Communication Monographs,* 58 (1991): 25–40.
18. McCornack and Levine, "When Lovers Become Leery."
19. Burgoon et al., "Interpersonal Deception."
20. M. A. deTurk and G. R. Miller, "Training Observers to Detect Deception: Effects of Self-Monitoring and Rehearsal," *Human Communication Research,* 16 (1990): 603–620.
21. M. A. deTurk and G. R. Miller, "Deception and Arousal: Isolating the Behavior Correlates of Deception," *Human Communication Research,* 12 (1985): 181–202.
22. D. B. Buller, K. D. Strzyzewski and J. Comstock, "Interpersonal Deception: I. Deceiver's Reactions to Receiver's Suspicions and Probing," *Communication Monographs,* 58 (1991): 1–24.
23. D. A. Infante and C. J. Wigley. III, "Verbal Aggressiveness: An Interpersonal Model and Measure," *Communication Monographs,* 53 (1986): 61–69.
24. Ibid.
25. J. L. Hocker and W. W. Wilmot, *Interpersonal Conflict,* 3rd ed. (Dubuque, Iowa: Brown, 1991).
26. Discussion of the advantages and disadvantages draws from J. L. Hocker and W. W. Wilmot, *Interpersonal Conflict,* 2nd ed. (Dubuque, Iowa: Brown, 1985).
27. J. Gibb, "Defensive Communication," *Journal of Communication,* 11 (1961): 141–148.

Chapter 3: p. 52, A Ramey/PhotoEdit; p. 59, Lemont Brown. Copyright 1998 Darrin Bell. www.lemontbrown.com and www.editorialcartoons.com; p. 64, Tony Savino/The Image Works.